Learning
Windows® 95

Margaret Brown

DDC Publishing

TO MY FAMILY Larry, Sheldon, Sheila, and Miles

Thank you for your love, patience, and caring.

Acknowledgments

Managing Editor
Kathy Berkemeyer
DDC Publishing
Chicago, IL

English Editor
Rebecca Fiala
Cambridge, MA

Technical Editor
Kathy Berkemeyer
DDC Publishing
Chicago, IL

Design Consultation
Karl Schwartz
Staten Island, NY

Desktop Publishers
Karl and Joanne Schwartz
Staten Island, NY

About This Book

Learning Windows 95 introduces you to the Windows 95 user interface in 8 lessons with 23 topics, 114 exercises, and 17 worksheets. The book guides you, step by step, through 100 useful Windows 95 tasks. The tutorial style of this book is designed to let you work at your own pace. Time estimates for completing the book range from 20 to 40 hours; since everyone works at a different rate, your time frame may be different.

Page layout

Most pages have a side column on the outside that includes the exercise number and name (easy to spot) and various support information, while the main part of the page contains exercise instructions. Facing pages are illustrated below:

left page		*right page*	
side column	*main page*	*main page*	*side column*

Topics

Topics teach basic Windows 95 concepts through easy-to-understand explanations and illustrations. Topics are found at the beginning of every lesson except Lesson Eight.

Lessons

- Lessons consist of short, task-oriented, step-by-step **exercises**.
- **Practice exercises** at the end of each lesson review and repeat the concepts covered in the lesson.
- Reinforcing **worksheets** for each lesson are found in Appendix D.

Exercises

- Exercises are easy to locate; the exercise number is in the top outside corner of the page.
- The name of each exercise reflects the windows 95 task to be performed.
- Each task is defined.
- Exercise instructions appear in the main page.
- Exercise steps are clearly numbered.
- Results of exercise steps are explained and/or illustrated where appropriate.
- Occasional notes explain concepts within the exercise steps.
- Tasks that are reviewed often refer to specific pages for more information.
- New terms are defined in the side column.
- Warnings, important comments, and notes appear in the side column when needed.
- (KEYBOARD) STEPS in the side column list the *keyboard* steps to perform the exercise task.

Exercise Results

The results of exercise steps are explained and/or illustrated immediately after a procedure so you have instant feedback. To conserve space when illustrating the results, unimportant portions are sometimes omitted.

Worksheets

Worksheets covering the terms for each lesson are provided in Appendix D.

Worksheet Solutions

Worksheet solutions are in Appendix E. They may be removed without losing other appendix information if the book is being used in a training setting.

Check-Off List

A check-off list with a place to check off every exercise, printout, and worksheet is provided in Appendix C.

The end-user information in this book is based on information on
Windows 95 made public by Microsoft as of July 24, 1995.

Read Me First!

Assumptions

- It is assumed that you can provide two blank floppy disks that fit your disk drive A:
- It is assumed that Windows 95 has been properly installed on your computer.
- It is assumed that your printer has been properly installed.

Tips

- Be aware that line endings in certain exercises may vary because of differences in printers.
- Directions usually refer to drive A: without reference to size since drive A: may be either 3½" or 5¼". (Illustrations in the book show drive A: as 3½".)
- As you work through the exercises up to Lesson Six in this book, you will develop a data disk. This disk should be accurate enough to insure that the exercises in Lesson Six can be performed correctly.
- The practice exercises should be done so that the data disk needed in Lesson Six has all the correct files.
- Appendix F has a condensed set of directions to prepare the necessary data disk for Lesson Six.
- If you prefer, you can purchase the **Learning Windows 95 data disk** that has the necessary files and folders to do the exercises in Lesson Six from DDC Publishing at (800) 528-3897.

Conventions

- Every action in the exercises starts with a bullet (●) and a **bold** action word.
- ⏎ refers to the **Enter** key.
- Keys that should be pressed together have a plus (+) between them. For example, Ctrl + →
- Keys that should be pressed in succession are separated by commas. For example, Alt, F, X

Tour: Ten minutes to using Windows 95

If this Windows 95 program is installed, be sure to run through it. In order to save disk space, the Tour is not installed if using the *typical* installation option. If the Tour is not installed, and if you have Windows 95 on a CD-ROM, you can run the Tour from the CD-ROM. Make sure the CD-ROM is inserted, then click the Start button, click Help, and finally, click Tour: Ten minutes to using Windows 95.

Keyboard Shortcuts and Procedures

Appendix I contains many useful keyboard shortcuts and certain common procedures.

Upgrading to Windows 95?

If you are already familiar with Windows 3.1, Appendix A shows you where to find familiar Windows features and briefly describes what's new in Windows 95.

Reference material

Learning Windows 95 can be used as a reference when you complete it. You can look up the task you want to perform, review it if needed, and then apply the steps to perform Windows 95 tasks to your specific situation. A sequential and alphabetical list of Windows 95 tasks are provided on pages ix and x, and a list of topics is provided on page viii. A glossary defines terms used in this book.

Quick Reference Guide for Windows 95. DDC Publishing publishes a "Quick Reference Guide for Windows 95" by Karl and Joanne Schwartz. This reference guide is designed to help you master Windows 95 without searching through lengthy manuals. Step-by-step directions show you how to perform Windows 95 procedures. The *Quick Reference Guide* is a good companion book for **Learning Windows 95** book. Look for DDC Quick Reference Guides in bookstores or call DDC at (800)528-3897.

Table of Contents—At a Glance

Table of Contents—Lessons

List of Topics

Sequential List of 100 Tasks
(Exercises)

Alphabetical List of 100 Tasks
(Exercises)

Lesson One
Windows Basics

Table of Contents

TOPIC 1

Computer System, Hardware

— Terms and Notes —

hardware
The group of parts that make up the computer system. Hardware can be seen and touched.

computer
An electronic device that performs complex tasks at high speed and with great accuracy. There are two main parts of a computer—the *processor* and the *memory*.

processor (CPU)
The part of the computer that processes the instructions in the memory.

memory (RAM)
The area of the computer that holds the instructions (programs) and information you give it. When you turn the computer off, everything in RAM disappears.

read only memory (ROM)
A chip that holds information that cannot be changed.

disk drive
A mechanical device that you use to transfer information back and forth between the computer's memory and a disk.

floppy disk
A magnetically coated disk on which information can be stored and retrieved.

hard disk
A large capacity storage area that offers fast access to store and retrieve information.

monitor
A screen that displays the information in the computer.

keyboard
A device used to enter data and issue commands to the computer.

printer
A device that makes a hard copy of data in the computer.

mouse
A small, hand-held device used to control the pointer on the screen.

The computer system is your assistant. It has its own:
- brain (**processor** or *central processing unit—CPU*),
- workspace (**memory** or *random access memory—RAM*),
- built-in instructions (**read only memory chips—ROM**),
- file cabinets (**disk drives**), and
- storage medium (**hard disk** and **floppy diskettes**).

Your computer comes with a:
- **monitor** (for showing you what is going on),
- **printer** (for making printed copies of documents),
- **keyboard** (so you can enter commands and data), and a
- **mouse** (so you can control a pointer on the screen).

Other hardware becoming common with today's computer systems includes:
- **modem or fax/modem**
- **CD-ROM**
- **speakers**
- **scanner**
- **network interface card**

Basic Computer System, Hardware

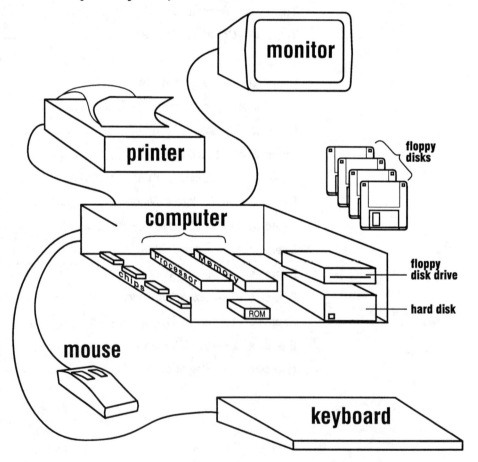

However, your assistant is missing something. Its memory is empty. The computer can do nothing until it is given instructions—software. **Software** is a *set of instructions* that tells the computer what to do. There are two main kinds of software:

- **application software** (programs) and
- **system software** (firmware and Windows).

Software is an essential part of your computer system, and an operating system is the *most important* software. An **operating system** controls all the parts of the computer system.

Basic Computer System, Software

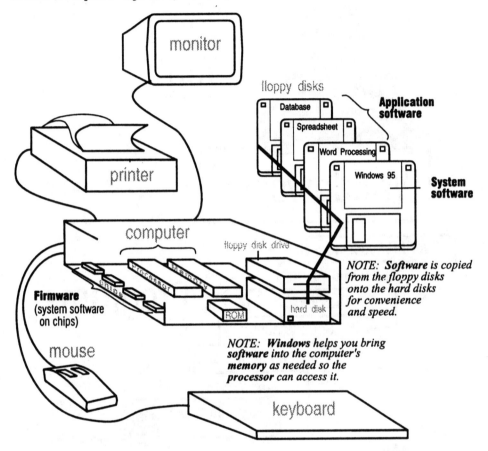

NOTE: *Software is copied from the floppy disks onto the hard disks for convenience and speed.*

NOTE: *Windows helps you bring software into the computer's memory as needed so the processor can access it.*

— Terms and Notes —

software
Instructions that tell your computer how to perform a task. Software is stored on disks in program files *(see topics 11 and 12)*. Software cannot be seen or touched. There are two main kinds of software:
- application software and
- system software.

application software (program)
Software that does a specific task, such as word processing.

system software
Software that runs the computer system.

firmware
A kind of *system software*—instructions that are built into the computer system on ROM chips.

operating system
Software that acts as a link between you, application software (programs), and hardware.

TOPIC 3
What is Windows?

— Terms and Notes —

Microsoft Windows 95
An operating system that uses a graphics environment to connect you to the computer system's hardware and software in an easy-to-understand, intuitive way. Microsoft Windows also offers many useful programs.

operating system
Software that acts as a link between you, application software (programs), and hardware.

you
The operator (or user) of the computer system (its hardware and software).

graphical user interface (GUI)
A phrase that is commonly used to describe Microsoft Windows and other similar programs that use *pictures* to help you *communicate* with the computer.

program (application)
A set of instructions that your computer carries out to perform a specific task, such as word processing.

Windows is an Operating System

Windows is an operating system. An **operating system** links you to your programs (also called applications or software) and then links your programs to the computer system's hardware. The Windows 95 operating system is called a **graphical user interface** (GUI) because it has *pictures* that *you use* to *communicate* with the computer.

Windows has been redesigned to provide you with an easier, more manageable operating system.

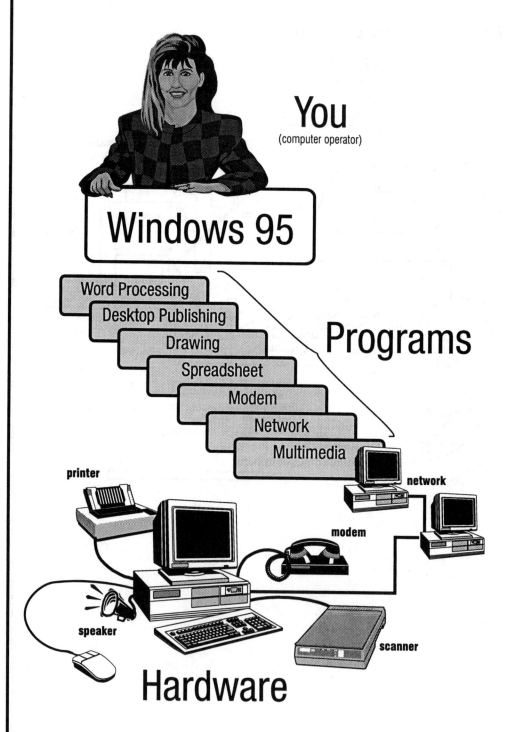

What Does Windows 95 Do?

Microsoft Windows 95:

- **Provides an easy way to start programs.**
  (the Start button does this)

- **Runs more than one program at a time.**
  (called multitasking)

- **Provides an easy way switch between open programs.**
  (the taskbar does this)

- **Lets you view more than one program at a time.**
  (it uses windows to do this)

- **Makes it easy to work with files, folders and objects.**
  (the Explorer program does this)

- **Transfers information between programs in a powerful way.**
  (called Object Linking and Embedding (OLE))

- **Provides networking support.**
  (use Network Neighborhood for easy access)
  NOTE: You must be connected to a network to use network features.

- **Provides communications programs.**
  (programs such as Remote Access, Microsoft Exchange, At Work Fax, Chat, Phone Dialer, and Briefcase)
  NOTE: You must have a modem and/or fax to use communications programs.

- **Provides multimedia programs.**
  (programs such as CD Player to play compact disks; Media Player to run multimedia files; and Sound Recorder to record, edit, and play recorded sounds)
  NOTE: You must have special hardware to use most of the multimedia features.

- **Provides other general use programs.**
  (programs that are called accessories, for example, WordPad, Paint, Calculator, and several games)

The newly designed Windows 95 program is improved from its predecessor Windows 3.1 in two main areas:

1. The operating system has been updated to provide an easier, more intuitive user interface while offering more sophisticated features.

2. There is improved support for the latest technologies available—those which many users are eager to use—networking, telecommunications, and multimedia.

   NOTE: The latest technologies require hardware (and sometimes software) that is beyond the basic computer system. Because of the large variety of and differences in this hardware (and software), this book covers mainly the basics of learning to use the Windows operating system and its primary general-use programs.

TOPIC 4

What Does Windows 95 Do?

— Terms and Notes —

multimedia
The combination of many various communication methods, including text, graphics, sound, animation, and video.

telecommunication
Remote access through a modem or fax/modem which allows you to:
- Communicate with bulletin board services.
- Transfer files.
- Send and receive faxes.

networking
Two or more computers that are linked together to share programs, data, and certain hardware components, for example, a printer.

multitasking
The ability of an operating system to run more than one program at one time.

object
One of the many *things* that you use when working with the computer system—items such as: files, Control Panel tools, programs, My Computer, folders, Network Neighborhood, shortcuts, The Recycle Bin, disk drives, and My Briefcase.

TOPIC 5
The Desktop

— Terms and Notes —

desktop 🖱️
The simple opening screen in Windows 95 that contains a few objects, the Start button, and a taskbar.

object
One of the many *things* that you use when working with the computer system—items such as: files, Control Panel tools, programs, My Computer, folders, Network Neighborhood, shortcuts, the Recycle Bin, disk drives, and My Briefcase.

NOTE: As used here, object is really just another catch-all term for an item, element, thing, whatcha-ma-call-it, or thing-a-ma-jig. The terms object and object-oriented have a more formal computer-related meaning that is not used in this book.

Start button
The button located at the left end of the taskbar that is labeled *Start*. You click the Start button to open the Start menu from which you can open other menus and launch programs.

taskbar
The bar on the desktop that lets you quickly start programs and easily switch between tasks.

shortcut
An icon containing a direct route to a specific object and displaying a small jump-arrow in the lower-left corner. Double-click a shortcut to quickly open the file or program it represents. You can customize your desktop by creating shortcuts for the programs you use most often.

The Windows Desktop

The redesigned Windows desktop is clean and straightforward. There is one obvious starting point—the Start button.

Windows 95 Desktop

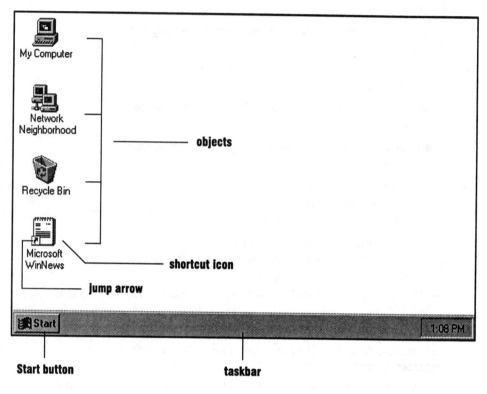

Windows 95 Desktop with Popup Menus Displayed

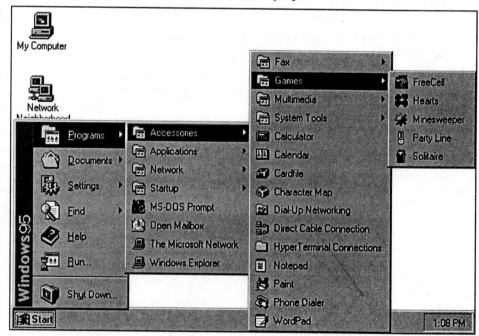

Window Elements

Window elements are parts of a window, many of which you use to activate a command.

Minimize button
Click to remove a window from the desktop, but not close it.

Control menu button
Click to open the Control menu.
Double-click to close the window.

NOTE: The Control button icon is a copy of the program's icon.

Maximize button
Click to enlarge a window to its maximum size.

Close button
Click to close a window.

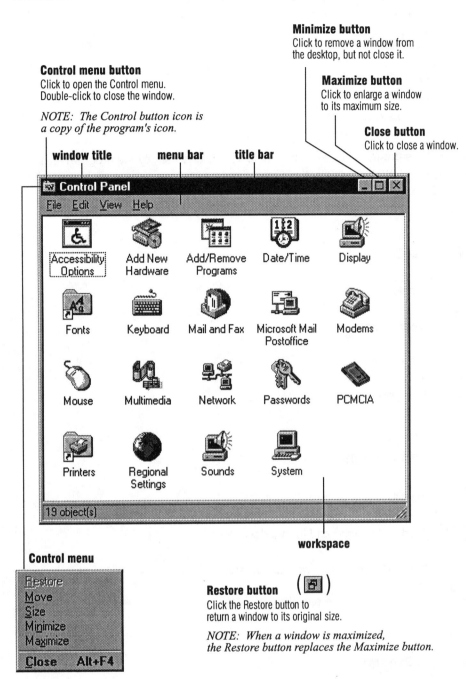

window title   menu bar   title bar

workspace

Control menu

Restore button (🔲)
Click the Restore button to return a window to its original size.

NOTE: When a window is maximized, the Restore button replaces the Maximize button.

— Terms and Notes —

window
The rectangular work area for a task, folder, program, or document.

Control menu button
An icon at the left side of the title bar that opens the Control menu. The Control button icon matches the icon for the document type that is open.

Control menu
A menu with items that you use to manipulate a program window (Restore, Move, Size, Minimize, Maximize, and Close). It is opened by clicking the Control button or by right-clicking the task button for the program.

Minimize button 🔲
A button located at the right side of the title bar that you can click to reduce a window to a task button on the taskbar.

Maximize button 🔲
The button in the middle of the three buttons located at the right end of the title bar; it enlarges a window to its greatest possible size. When you maximize a window, the Maximize button is replaced by the Restore button.

Restore button 🔲
The button in the middle of three buttons located at the right end of the title bar on a maximized window; it returns a maximized window to its previous size. When you restore a maximized window, the Restore button is replaced by the Maximize button.

Close button ☒
A button located at the right end of the title bar that you click to close a window.

window title
The name of a window, located just to the right of the Control menu button. The document name, if any, is listed first followed by the program name.

title bar
The horizontal bar at the top of a window that holds the window's name.

menu bar
The bar located under the title bar that lists the available menus.

workspace
The inner part of the window where the work in a program or document is carried out.

TOPIC 7
Windows Accessories

— Terms and Notes —

accessories
Different kinds of programs (applications) that come with Windows.

NOTE: Depending on your hardware (i.e. modem or network capabilities) some accessories may not be displayed in Windows or, if displayed, you may not be able to use them. Certain other programs are not installed if you choose the "typical" installation.

Windows Accessories

In addition to being an operating system, Windows 95 offers many kinds of useful programs called **accessories**. There are programs for:

- games
- general use
- multimedia
- telecommunications
- networking
- system tools

Each Windows program has an icon to help you quickly identify the program. Many accessory icons are shown below.

Games

 **FreeCell**

 Hearts

Minesweeper

 Party Line

Solitaire

General Use Programs

Paint to create pictures.

WordPad to write and format documents.

Notepad to write and view documents.

Calculator to make calculations.

Multimedia Programs

 **CD Player** to play compact disks.

Media Player to play multimedia files.

Sound Recorder to record, edit, and play sound files.

 Volume Control to adjust the sound level.

Topic 7 continued...

Communications Programs

Hyperterminal to connect to other computers

Microsoft Network to use the Microsoft online service

Compose New Fax to send and receive FAX messages

Retrieve Fax to exchange typed messages

Cover Page Editor to edit FAX cover pages.

Phone Dialer to place calls from your computer

Programs for More than One Computer

Network Neighborhood to access computers on networks.

Dial-Up Networking to connect to a computer
(and its network) using a modem.

Direct Cable Connection to connect to a computer using a cable.

Briefcase to synchronize files used on more than one computer.

System Tools

Disk Defragmenter to speed up your hard disk.

DriveSpace to increase drive space.

Net Watcher to monitor shared resource use.

Scan Disk to detect and repair disk errors.

System Monitor to monitor your computer's network or disk access.

TOPIC 8
Controlling Windows

— Terms and Notes —

commands
Instructions that cause an action to be carried out.

mouse
A small, hand-held device used to control the pointer on the screen.

pointer (mouse pointer)
The arrow-shaped cursor on the screen that moves with the mouse as you slide it over a flat surface. The pointer's shape changes depending on the job it is doing.

Common Pointer Shapes

SHAPE	NAME
	arrow (the standard shape)
	sizing (sizes windows)
	move (moves windows)
	busy (signals for you to wait)
	hand (jumps between Help topics)
	I-beam (text select)
	unavailable (cannot perform action)

Controlling Windows

Windows is controlled using **commands**, which are instructions that cause an action to be carried out.

The Windows **graphics environment** is designed to take advantage of the mouse to issue commands though they can also be issued from the keyboard; there are usually several different ways to issue commands. While this can lead to confusion for beginners, it offers enough flexibility to meet the needs of many different Windows users.

The Mouse

The **mouse** is a small, hand-held device that is used to control the pointer on the screen. The **pointer** (or **mouse pointer**) is the arrow on the screen that moves with the mouse as you slide it over a flat surface. The pointer's shape changes depending on the job it is doing.

A mouse usually has at least two buttons; the **primary mouse button** (usually the left button) and the **secondary mouse button** (usually the right button).

There are six main mouse actions:

Move	Move the pointer on an item.
Click	Quickly press and release the *left* mouse button.
Right-click	Quickly press and release the *right* mouse button.
Double-click	Quickly press and release the *left* mouse button *twice*.
Drag	Move the pointer to an item, hold down the *left* button, slide the pointer to a new location, and release the button.
Right-drag	Move the pointer to an item, hold down the *right* button, slide the pointer to a new location, and release the button.

Topic 8 continued...

The Keyboard

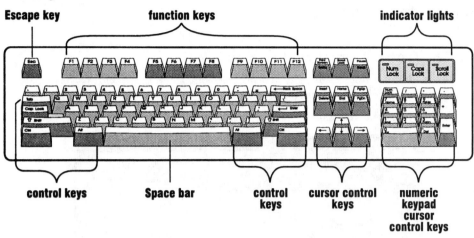

Escape key

function keys

indicator lights

control keys   Space bar   control keys   cursor control keys   numeric keypad cursor control keys

The **keyboard** is used to enter data into the computer and to issue commands to the computer.

The twelve keys located across the top (or ten keys located on the left side) of the keyboard that are labeled F1, F2, etc. are called **function keys**. They are used to issue commands.

Control keys (Shift, Ctrl, and Alt) are used in combination with other keys to issue commands.

Keyboard shortcuts are key combinations that can be used to activate certain commands instead of using the mouse *(see right)*. A menu item that has a keyboard shortcut will display the key combination to the right of the menu item.

Using Keys Together

When two keys are used together to issue a command, a plus sign (+) is shown between the keys. For example: Alt+Tab

To issue this command, you should press and hold down Alt, tap Tab, and then release Alt

Using Keys in Succession

Keys are used in succession when two or more keys are pressed one after the other to issue a command. Keys used in succession are illustrated with a comma separating them. For example: F4, M, E. Press each key in succession.

Two Special Keys

Esc (Escape) is used to back out of situations. Occasionally you find yourself in a place you don't want to be; Esc will often get you out of the situation without doing any damage.

F1 is used to get Help *(see page 84)*.

— Terms and Notes —

keyboard
A device used to enter data and issue commands to the computer.

keyboard shortcuts
Key combinations that are used to activate certain commands instead of using the mouse.

Keyboard Shortcuts

COMMAND	SHORTCUTS
New	Ctrl+N
Open	Ctrl+O
Save	Ctrl+S
Print	Ctrl+P
Undo	Ctrl+Z
Cut	Ctrl+X
Copy	Ctrl+C
Paste	Ctrl+V
Clear	Del
Select All	Ctrl+A
Find	Ctrl+F
Replace	Ctrl+H
Bold	Ctrl+B
Italic	Ctrl+I
Underline	Ctrl+U
Center Justify	Ctrl+E
Left Justify	Ctrl+L
Right Justify	Ctrl+R
Switch to	Alt+Esc or
	Alt+Tab
Start menu	Ctrl+Esc
Start button	Ctrl+Esc, Esc
Taskbar	Ctrl+Esc, Esc, Esc
Control menu (application window)	Alt+Space
Control menu (document window)	Alt+↓ or
	Alt+- (hyphen)

NOTE: Many of these keyboard shortcuts are available only in applications (programs).

EXERCISE 1
Start Windows

To turn the computer on and enter a password so you can access the Windows desktop.

— Terms and Notes —

user name
A name given to a Windows user. By using different user names and passwords for different people, each user's work can be kept secure.

password
A combination of characters that you type, when prompted, in order to access Windows (or some Windows feature). The characters appear as small x's when you type them. The password feature is a security feature that prevents access to a Windows network (or other feature) without the correct combination of characters.

dialog box
A special kind of window that offers different controls for you to manipulate.

---

*IMPORTANT   When instructed to **click** or **double-click**, <u>always use the left mouse</u> unless otherwise instructed.*

Begin with the computer turned off.

❶ •   **Turn on** the monitor and computer.

NOTE: On some computer systems, the monitor is plugged into the computer so you only need to turn on the computer.

A Welcome to Windows dialog box asks for your password.

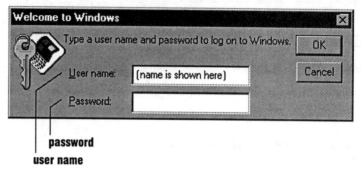

   password
  user name

IF your system is networked, the opening window will be different; it will ask for a password to log on to the network.

IF someone previously disabled the Password feature, it is possible that NO Welcome to Windows dialog box appears asking for a password.

IF the Windows desktop appears (see Topic 5), skip step 2 and go on to Exercise 2.

❷ Enter the password:

NOTES: If Windows is being started for the first time since it was installed, you will be asked to enter a User name and create a Password of your choice. Be sure to remember the password for future reference when starting Windows.

*To add other Windows users, you can enter a **new** User name and then create a new Password at the **Welcome to Windows** dialog box. (See Appendix B.)*

•   **Type** the password in the Password text box.
The letters you type appear as small x's.

•   **Click** OK
NOTE: If you typed an incorrect password, the box will reappear so you can try again.
The Windows desktop appears.

or

Cancel the opening dialog box:

•   **Click** Cancel or **Press** Esc
The Windows desktop appears.

① Open the Start menu:

- **Click** 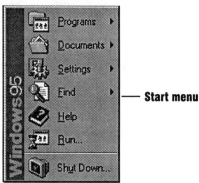 (the Start button).
  The Start menu pops open.

—— **Start menu**

② Open cascading menus:

NOTE: A cascading menu is opened whenever the mouse pointer rests on a menu item that is followed by a right-pointing arrow (▶).

- **Move** the mouse pointer on Find ▶ until the Find menu opens.

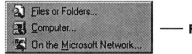

—— **Find menu**

- **Move** the mouse pointer on Settings ▶ until the Settings menu opens.

—— **Settings menu**

- **Move** the mouse pointer on Documents ▶ until the Documents menu opens.
  A menu appears displaying up to 15 of the last documents used.

- **Move** the mouse pointer on Programs ▶ until the Programs menu opens.

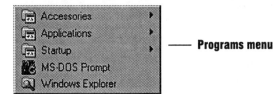

—— **Programs menu**

NOTE: Your Programs menu may not match the illustration.

- With the Programs menu open, **Move** the mouse pointer on Accessories ▶ until the Accessories menu opens.

- **Move** the mouse pointer off of the menus.
  The menus remain open.

③ Close the menus:

- **Click** a clear area on the desktop (do not click a menu item or other object on the desktop).
  The menus close.

④

- **Repeat** steps 1-3.

EXERCISE 2
Open and Close Menus

To cause a menu (or cascading menu) to open and display the menu items within it.

— Terms and Notes —

menu
A list of items from which you may choose one.

menu item
One of the choices on a menu.

cascading menu
A menu that opens when you choose a menu item that is followed by a right-pointing triangle (➤).

 **STEPS to**

Open the Start menu

- Press Ctrl + Esc
  or
  Press Alt + S (Start)

Choose a menu item

- **Type** the underlined letter of the desired menu item.
  or
  Type the first letter of the desired menu item.
  IF more than one item starts with the same letter, press the letter until the desired menu item is highlighted, then...
  Press

Close an open menu

- Press Esc

EXERCISE 3

Start a Program

(Launch an Application)
To use Windows to run a program.

— Terms and Notes —

application (program)
Means the same thing as *program*. While the term *application* is used a lot in Windows, this book uses the term *program* more often.

program (application)
A set of instructions that your computer carries out to perform a specific task, such as word processing.

launch (start a program)
A term that is sometimes used to mean start a program (*or application*).

NOTE: Remember that program means the same thing as **application**.

 **STEPS to**

Start a program

—USING THE START MENU—

1   Press `Ctrl` + `Esc`
    or
    Press `Alt` + `S` (Start)
2   **Type** the underlined letter of the desired menu item.
    or
    Type the first letter of the desired menu item.
    IF more than one item starts with the same letter, press the letter until the desired menu item is highlighted, then...
    Press `↵`
3   Repeat step 2 until you reach and open the desired program.

Start a Program

There are other phrases that are used to mean *start a program*:
*   **launch a program** (or application)
*   **open a program** (or application)
*   **run a program** (or application)

In this exercise, you will start a program by working your way through the Start menu, the Programs menu, and finally the Accessories menu to find and then start two accessory programs that come with Windows.

Below are other ways to start programs that will be covered later:
*   Create shortcuts to programs and put them on your desktop or in a folder.
*   Use the Run command.
*   Double-click a program in a list of files.
*   Use the Startup folder to specify programs that you want to start automatically when Windows starts.

① Start Calculator:
*   **Click** ▦**Start** (the Start button).
*   **Open** Programs.
*   **Open** Accessories.
*   **Click** 🖩 (Calculator).
    The Calculator program opens. Notice that its name and icon appear on the taskbar:

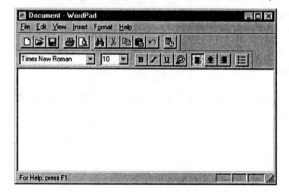

② Start WordPad:
*   **Click** ▦**Start** (the Start button).
*   **Open** Programs.
*   **Open** Accessories.
*   **Click** 📝 (WordPad).
    A warning message is displayed for a short time, then WordPad opens.

③ *   **Go on** to Exercise 4 without stopping.

You can Exit programs several different ways; you can use the:
- Close button
- Control menu button
- File menu

Control menu button   **Close button**

| untitled - WordPad   _ □ X |
| File Edit View Insert Format Help |

File menu

WARNING: If you make any kind of change in a program (for example, draw a line in Paint or type in WordPad), when you exit, a dialog box appears asking: Do you want to save the current changes. If this happens, click No (to exit without saving the changes).

❶ Use the Exit button to exit a program:

With WordPad still open:
- **Click** 🅧 (the WordPad Exit button, located on the right side of the title bar).
  WordPad closes; Calculator remains open.

❷ Use the Control menu button to exit a program:

- **Click** (the Control menu button on the calculator).
  The Control menu for Calculator drops down.

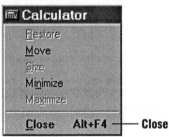
| 🖩 Calculator |
| Restore |
| Move |
| Size |
| Minimize |
| Maximize |
| Close   Alt+F4 ——— **Close** |

- **Click** Close.
  Calculator closes.

❸ Double-click the Control menu button to exit a program:

- **Start** Calculator (review, Exercise 3).
- **Double-click** (the Control menu button).
  Calculator closes.

❹ Use the File menu to exit a program:

- **Start** WordPad (review, Exercise 3).
- **Click** File, Exit.
  WordPad closes.

❺ Use any method to exit a program:

- **Start** Paint (review, Exercise 3).
- **Exit** Paint.
- **Start** Character Map.
- **Exit** Character Map.
- **Start** Notepad.
- **Exit** Notepad.

Exit a Program

To use Windows to close a program, removing it from the computer's memory.

— Terms and Notes —

Control menu button
An icon at the left side of the title bar that opens the Control menu. The Control button icon matches the icon for the document type that is open.

Control menu
A menu with items that you use to manipulate a program window (Restore, Move, Size, Minimize, Maximize, and Close). It is opened by clicking the Control button or by right-clicking the task button for the program.

Close button 🅧
A button located at the right end of the title bar that you click to close a window.

Exit
A command that lets you leave a Windows program (application). It is usually found on the File menu.

Close
A command that lets you leave a Windows program (application). It is usually found on the Control menu.

NOTE: The Exit command is found on the File menu while the Close command is found on the Control menu; both commands remove programs from the computer's memory.

 **STEPS to**

Exit a program
- Press [Alt] + [F4]

— *WITH THE PROGRAM'S TITLE BAR HIGHLIGHTED*—

1 Press [Alt] + [Space]
2 Type [C] (Close)

or

1 Press [Alt] + [F] (File)
2 Type [X] (Exit)

EXERCISE 5

Maximize a Window

To enlarge a window to its greatest possible size.

— Terms and Notes —

Maximize button 🔲
The button in the middle of the three buttons located at the right end of the title bar; it enlarges a window to its greatest possible size. When you maximize a window, the Maximize button is replaced by the Restore button.

Restore button 🔲
The button in the middle of three buttons located at the right end of the title bar on a maximized window; it returns a maximized window to its previous size. When you restore a maximized window, the Restore button is replaced by the Maximize button.

desktop 🖥
The simple opening screen in Windows 95 that contains a few objects, the Start menu, and a taskbar.

taskbar
The bar on the desktop that lets you quickly start programs and easily switch between tasks.

 **STEPS to**

Maximize a window

1 Press **Alt** + **Space**

2 Type **X** (Ma**x**imize)

16   Lesson One — Windows Basics

---

❶ Start WordPad:

- **Start** WordPad (review, Exercise 3).

- **IF** the restore button (🔲) is displayed in the middle of the series of buttons in the top right corner of WordPad,

  Click 🔲 (the restore button) so WordPad will not be maximized.
  WordPad is an unmaximized window.

Unmaximized window

Maximize button — 🔲

❷ Maximize a window (WordPad):

- **Click** 🔲 (the maximize button).

  or Double-click the title bar.

  or Click the Control menu button, then Ma**x**imize.

  WordPad enlarges to its greatest size, leaving only the taskbar displayed at the bottom of the desktop; the Maximize button (🔲) changes to a Restore button (🔲).

Maximized window

Restore button — 🔲

❸

- **Go on** to Exercise 6 without stopping.

❶ Restore a window:

- **Click** 🗗 (the Restore button).

  or Double-click the title bar.

  or Click the Control menu button, then **R**estore.

  WordPad returns to its previous size; the Restore button is replaced by the Maximize button.

Restored window

Maximize button

![Restored WordPad window screenshot]

❷
- **Maximize** the WordPad window again (review, Exercise 5).
- **Restore** the WordPad window again (review, step 1).
- **Exit** WordPad (review, Exercise 4).

❸
- **Start** Paint (review, Exercise 3).
- **Maximize** Paint.
- **Restore** Paint.
- **Exit** Paint.

❹ Open a window that has a dimmed Maximize button:

- **Start** Calculator.

  Notice that the Maximize button in Calculator is **dimmed**. A dimmed command cannot be used in the current situation.

- **Exit** Calculator.

EXERCISE 6

Restore a Window

To return a maximized window to its previous size.

— Terms and Notes —

Restore button 🗗
The button in the middle of three buttons located at the right end of the title bar on a maximized window; it returns a maximized window to its previous size. When you restore a maximized window, the Restore button is replaced by the Maximize button.

dimmed command
A command that cannot be used in the current situation; it is displayed in gray instead of black.

 **STEPS to**

Restore a window

1 Press `Alt` + `Space`
2 Press `↵`
  or
  Type `R` (Restore)

EXERCISE 7

Minimize a Window

To shrink a window to a task button on the taskbar.

— Terms and Notes —

Minimize button 🔲
A button located at the right side of the title bar that you can click to reduce a window to a task button on the taskbar.

task
An open (but not necessarily active) program.

task button
A button located on the taskbar that represents an open program; each task button displays the program's icon and its name.

pressed
A 3-D effect in which a button (or other item) appears sunken, indicating it is selected (or active).

unpressed
A 3-D effect in which a button (or other item) appears raised, indicating it is deselected (or inactive).

active task button
A task button located on the taskbar that appears to be pressed, thus indicating that the task it represents is active.

inactive task button
A task button located on the taskbar that is unpressed, thus indicating the task it represents is open, but not active.

---

① Start a program:

- **Start** WordPad (review, Exercise 3).
  WordPad opens; a button for WordPad appears on the taskbar.

  Notice that the WordPad task button on the taskbar appears **pressed**.

  active task button

- **Notice** the minimize button on the right end of the title bar.

  Minimize button

  📄 Document - WordPad   ▁ ☐ ✕
  File   Edit   View   Insert   Format   Help

② Minimize a window:

- **Click** 🔲 (the minimize button).

  or

  Click the Control menu button, then Mi<u>n</u>imize.
  WordPad shrinks into its task button on the taskbar.

  Notice that the WordPad task button on the taskbar appears **unpressed**.

  inactive task button

③ Activate a minimized window:

- **Click** 📄 Document - WordPad (the WordPad button on the taskbar)
  The WordPad program opens into a window.

  Notice that the WordPad button on the taskbar appears to be pressed again.

④ - **Exit** WordPad (review, Exercise 4).
  WordPad closes; the WordPad task button disappears from the taskbar.

⑤ - **Start** Calculator.
- **Minimize** Calculator *(see step 2).*
- **Activate** the minimized Calculator *(see step 3).*
- **Exit** Calculator.

 **STEPS to**

Minimize a window

1 Press <kbd>Alt</kbd> + <kbd>Space</kbd>

2 Type <kbd>N</kbd> (Mi<u>n</u>imize)

Begin with the desktop displayed and with no tasks on the taskbar.

NOTE: If there are task buttons on the taskbar, click each task button and exit the program.

❶ Open three programs:

- **Start** WordPad (review, Exercise 3).
- **Start** Notepad.
- **Start** Calculator.
  As each program opens, its task button appears on the taskbar. The Calculator task button is active (pressed).

❷ Switch between tasks using the "click on window" method:

- **Click** the Notepad or WordPad window.
  The clicked window moves to the front, hiding part of all of Calculator.

❸ Switch between tasks using the "taskbar" method:

- **Click** the Calculator task button.
  Calculator moves to the front.
- **Click** the WordPad task button.
  WordPad moves to the front.
- **Click** the Notepad task button.
  Notepad moves to the front.

❹ Maximize Notepad and WordPad:

- **Maximize** Notepad (review, Exercise 5).
  Notepad now hides Calculator and WordPad.
- **Click** the WordPad task button.
  WordPad moves to the front.
- **Maximize** WordPad.
  WordPad now hides Calculator and Notepad.

❺ Switch between tasks using the "cycle through icons" method:

- **Press** and **Hold** [Alt] while tapping [Tab] and watch the screen as icons of the open tasks are displayed. Each press of [Tab] causes the next icon to become outlined while its name appears below the set of icons.
- **Release** both keys when Calculator is selected.

- **Switch** to Notepad using the *cycle through icons* method.
- **Switch** to WordPad using the *cycle through icons* method.

❻
- **Exit** WordPad (review, Exercise 4).
  Notepad will probably become active.
- **Exit** Notepad.
  Calculator should become active.
- **Exit** Calculator.

EXERCISE 8
Switch Tasks

To move between open programs.

— Terms and Notes —

active window
The window whose title bar is highlighted, indicating that it is currently being used.

Four ways to switch tasks:
- Click the task button on the taskbar.
- Click the window itself (if it is visible).
- Press [Alt] + [Tab] to cycle through icons of open windows.
- Press [Alt] + [Esc] to cycle through open windows.

 **STEPS to**

Switch tasks
To cycle through windows:
- **Press** [Alt] + [Esc] until the program you want moves to the top.

To cycle through *icons* of windows:
- **Press** [Alt] + [Tab] until the icon of the program you want is outlined and its name is displayed below the icons.

EXERCISE 9

Move a Window

To change the location of a window.

— Terms and Notes —

title bar
The horizontal bar at the top of a window that holds the window's name.

drag (mouse action)
Move the pointer on an item.
Hold down the left button.
Slide the pointer to a new location.
Release the button.

move pointer ✛
The shape the pointer takes when the Move command is used to move a window.

Begin with the desktop displayed and no tasks on the taskbar.

1 • **Start** Calculator (review, Exercise 3).

2 **Use the drag action to move a window:**
- **Move** the pointer onto the Calculator's title bar.
- **Press** and **Hold** the left mouse button.
- **Drag** the window to the bottom right corner of the desktop.
- **Release** the mouse button.

3 • **Move** the Calculator window to the top right corner of the desktop.
- **Move** the Calculator window to the center of the desktop.

4 **Use the keyboard to move a window:**
With the Calculator window active (its title bar highlighted):
- **Press** Alt + Space to open the Calculator's Control menu.
- **Press** M (Move)
- **Press** → until the window reaches the right side of the desktop.
- **Press** ↓ until the window reaches the bottom of the desktop.
- **Press** ↵

5 Follow the directions in step 4 to:
- **Move** the Calculator window back to the center of the desktop.
- **Exit** Calculator.

6 • **Start** WordPad.
  NOTE: If WordPad is maximized, click the Restore button to return it to its previous size.
- **Move** WordPad to the bottom left corner of the desktop.
- **Move** WordPad to the top right corner with none of it off the desktop.
- **Exit** WordPad.
- **Start** WordPad. (Did it remember its last position?)
- **Move** WordPad to the bottom left corner with part of it off the desktop.
- **Exit** WordPad.
- **Start** WordPad. (Did it remember its last position?)
- **Exit** WordPad.

 **STEPS to**

Move a window
1 **Select** the desired window.
2 Press Alt + Space
3 Press M (Move)
4 Press ↑, ←, → or ↓ to move window as desired.
5 Press ↵

Begin with the desktop displayed and with no tasks on the taskbar.

Illustration of the Notepad window sized small

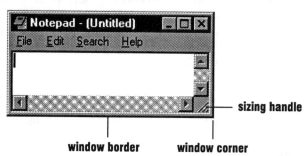

sizing handle

window border   window corner

1 • **Start** Notepad (review, Exercise 3).

2 ## Size a window using a window border:

• **Move** the pointer to the right border of the Notepad window so that a horizontal **double-headed arrow** (⟷) appears.

• Use the drag mouse action (described on the previous page) to drag the double-headed arrow (and the window's right border) about an inch to the right.

3 ## Size a window using a sizing handle:

• **Move** the pointer to the sizing handle in the bottom right corner of the Notepad window so that a diagonal **double-headed arrow** (↖) appears.

• **Drag** the double-headed arrow up and left about an inch.

4 • **Size** the Notepad as small as you can.
The Notepad can be sized so that only its Control menu, partial name, and buttons appear.

• **Size** the Notepad to about its original size.

• **Exit** Notepad.

5 ## Try to size a window that cannot be sized:

• **Start** Calculator.

• **Move** the pointer on the window border and notice that no double-headed arrow appears.
Calculator cannot be sized. Note that its borders are narrower than the borders of windows that can be sized.

• **Exit** Calculator.

6 ## Size Paint:

• **Start** Paint.

• **Restore** Paint if it is maximized (review, Exercise 6).

• Use the sizing handle to enlarge the Paint window.

• Use the sizing handle to make the Paint window as small as possible.
Paint keeps a size that is large enough to display its tools and color palette.

• **Exit** Paint.

• **IF** asked to save, **click** | No |

EXERCISE 10

Size a Window

To change the area of a window.

— Terms and Notes —

double-headed arrow
The shape the pointer takes when it is used to size a window or the taskbar.

Double-headed arrows appear as:

↕   Vertical
(appears on the top or bottom window border)

⟷   Horizontal
(appears on the right or left window border)

↖   Diagonal
(appears on the top left and bottom right corner of window)

↗   Diagonal
(appears on the bottom left and top right corner of window)

sizing handle
An area in the bottom right corner of windows that can be sized; it is used to size windows.
(You can size a window using any of its corners. However, because the bottom right corner's sizing handle is a large sizing area, the pointer changes to a diagonal arrow easier than it does in the other window corners.)

⌨ STEPS to

Size a Window
1 **Select** the desired window.
2 **Press** [Alt] + [Space]
3 **Press** [S] (Size)
4 **Press** [↑], [↓], [→], or [←] once in the direction of the border to be sized.
5 **Press** [↑], [←], [→], or [↓] until the desired size is obtained.
6 **Press** [↵]

EXERCISE 11

Scroll Through a Window

To use the scroll bars to move through data in a window that is beyond the window's borders.

— Terms and Notes —

scroll bar
A bar that appears at the right and/or bottom edge of a window whose contents are not completely visible. Each scroll bar contains two scroll arrows and a proportional scroll box (when data is present).

scroll arrows
The arrows at each end of a scroll bar, used to scroll through the contents of a window.

scroll box
The box in a scroll bar; it shows two things:
1 The *position* of the information <u>displayed</u> in relation to the <u>entire document.</u>
   For example, if the scroll box is in the center of the scroll bar, you are looking at the center of the document.
2 The *size* of the entire document in relation to the screen size.
   For example, if the scroll box takes up a large part of the scroll bar, you can see most of the entire document; but, if the scroll box takes up just a little part of the scroll bar, you can see only a small portion of the entire document.

 **STEPS to**

Scroll through a window
• Use the key(s) below to move as desired:

line up	↑
line down	↓
character right	→
character left	←
screen up	Page Up
screen down	Page Down
to beginning of document	Ctrl + Home
to end of document	Ctrl + End

Look at Scroll Bars

Below are illustrations showing **scroll bars**, **scroll arrows**, and **scroll boxes**. In Windows 95, scroll boxes are called *proportional*, which means that their size is related to the amount of information in the document. The larger the scroll box, the smaller the document (in relation to the window); the smaller the scroll box, the larger the document (in relation to the window).

The size of the bottom scroll box (*see the illustration below*) is over half the length of the scroll bar. The scroll box is telling you that the window is displaying over half of the width of the text in the document.

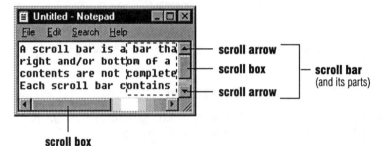

scroll box

In the illustration below, the bottom scroll box has been moved as far right as possible. Notice that the text inside the dashed box is some of the same text that appears in the illustration above. You can see that the small Notepad window displays a little over half of the text in the program.

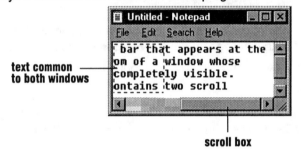

scroll box

Begin with the desktop displayed and with no tasks on the taskbar.

❶ • **Start** Help (**click** Start, then <u>H</u>elp).
   • **Click** the Index tab.
     The Index page of Help moves to the front.
     Notice the size of the scroll box in the scroll bar. (Is there a lot more of the document than what you can see in the display?)
     The very small scroll box tells you there are many more screenfuls of information.

❷ Scroll up and down one *line* at a time:
   • **Click** the *bottom* scroll arrow once.
     The list scrolls up one line.
   • **Click** the *bottom* scroll arrow about ten times and watch as the items in the list move up one line at a time.
   • **Click** the *top* scroll arrow several times and watch as the items on the list move down one line at a time.

Exercise 11 continued...

③ Scroll data up and down one *screenful* at a time:

- **Notice** what the bottom line of the display says.
- **Click** the scroll bar *above* the bottom arrow.
  The list scrolls up almost one full screen—the line that was previously at the bottom of the display is now at the top.

  This helps you be certain that you did not miss any data as you move through data one screenful at a time.
- **Click** the scroll bar *above* the bottom arrow five more times and watch as the list scrolls up one screenful at a time.
- **Click** the scroll bar *below* the top arrow and watch as the list moves down one screen.

  NOTE: To scroll up one screenful at a time, you can click anywhere above the bottom arrow and the scroll box. To scroll down one screenful at a time, you can click anywhere below the top arrow and the scroll box.

④ Scroll to a general location:

- **Drag** the scroll box to about the middle of the scroll bar.
  The Index displays about the middle of the list.
- **Drag** the scroll box to the bottom of the scroll bar.
  The Index displays the end of the list.
- **Drag** the scroll box to the top of the scroll bar.
  The Index displays the beginning of the list.
- **Exit** Help (review, Exercise 4).

⑤
- **Start** Control Panel (**click** Start, S̲ettings, C̲ontrol Panel).
- **Size** Control Panel to about a 4" by 4" square.
- **Click** the *right* scroll arrow (bottom of window) until the scroll box moves to the right side of the scroll bar.
- **Click** the scroll bar *above* the bottom scroll arrow (right side of window).
- **Drag** the *bottom* scroll box slowly to the left side of the scroll bar and watch the contents of the window scroll right.
- **Drag** the *right* scroll box slowly to the top of the scroll bar and watch the contents of the window scroll down.
- **Drag** the scroll boxes slowly back and forth (and up and down) a few times and watch what happens.
- **Exit** Control Panel.

— Terms and Notes —

Scroll actions

Scroll up or down one line at a time:
- Click the *top* arrow to scroll up one line at a time.
- Click the *bottom* arrow to scroll down one line at a time.

Scroll up or down screenful at a time:
- Click *below* the top arrow to scroll up one screenful at a time.
- Click *above* the bottom arrow to scroll down one screenful at a time.

Scroll to a general location:
- Drag the scroll box to the location on the scroll bar that represents the part of the document to which you want to scroll.

EXERCISE 12
Exit Windows

To use the Shut Down Windows dialog box to leave Windows and shut down your computer.

— Terms and Notes —

warm boot
The process of restarting the computer by simultaneously pressing `Ctrl` + `Alt` + `Del` instead of using the on/off switch.

IMPORTANT: ALWAYS exit Windows before you turn off your computer.

Begin with the desktop displayed and with no tasks on the taskbar.

❶ Exit Windows:

- **Click** Start.

- **Click** 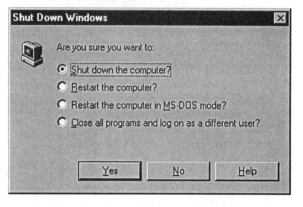 (The Shut Down button).

  The Shut Down Windows dialog box appears.

  Shut Down Windows

  Are you sure you want to:
  - ○ Shut down the computer?
  - ○ Restart the computer?
  - ○ Restart the computer in MS-DOS mode?
  - ○ Close all programs and log on as a different user?

  [Yes]   [No]   [Help]

- **Click** [Yes] to accept the default option in the Shut Down Windows dialog box.

  The Shut Down Windows window appears.

It's now safe to turn off your computer.

❷ - **Turn off** the computer.

  or restart Windows:
  - **Press** `Ctrl`+`Alt`+`Del` (warm boot) to restart the computer.

 **STEPS to**

Exit Windows

1   Press `Alt` + `Esc`
2   Type `U` (Shut Down)
3   Press `↵`
4   **Turn off** the computer.

Begin with the computer off...
or skip step one and begin with the desktop displayed and with no tasks on the taskbar.

1 **Start** Windows.

2 **Click** Start.

3 **Open** Settings.

4 **Start** Control Panel.

5 **Maximize** Control Panel.

6 **Restore** Control Panel.

7 **Minimize** Control Panel.

8 **Click** the Control Panel task button to activate the Control Panel.

9 **Exit** Control Panel.

10 **Start** WordPad.

11 **Start** Paint.

12 **Start** Calculator.

13 **Switch** to Paint.

14 **Maximize** Paint.

15 **Switch** to WordPad.

16 **Maximize** WordPad.

17 **Switch** to Paint using the cycle through method (Alt + Tab).

18 **Switch** to Calculator using the task button method.

19 **Switch** to WordPad using the method you prefer.

20 **Minimize** WordPad.

EXERCISE 13
Practice
**Lesson One
Beginning Windows Tasks**

Tasks Reviewed:
- Start Windows
- Open and Close Menus
- Start a Program
- Exit a Program
- Maximize a Window
- Restore a Window
- Minimize a Window
- Switch Tasks
- Exit Windows

Exercise 13 continued...

Exercise 13 (continued)
PRACTICE

WARNING: Remember that when you <u>exit</u> a program, if you made <u>any</u> kind of change in that program (for example, draw in Paint or type in WordPad), a dialog box will appear asking:

Do you want to save the current changes?

Click No to exit without saving the changes.

Exercise 13 (continued)

21 **Switch** to Paint.

22 **Minimize** Paint.

23 **Activate** WordPad.

24 **Restore** WordPad.

25 **Exit** WordPad.

26 **Activate** Paint.

27 **Switch** to Calculator.

28 **Exit** Calculator.

29 **Exit** Paint.

30 **Exit** (shut down) Windows.

Lesson One Worksheets (1–6) are in Appendix D

Lesson Two
Beyond Basics

Table of Contents

TOPIC 9
Dialog Boxes

— Terms and Notes —

dialog box
A special kind of window that offers different controls for you to manipulate.

controls
Different kinds of elements in dialog boxes that allow you to manipulate a program's appearance and function.

common dialog boxes
Dialog boxes, such as Open, Save, and Print, that are basically the same in different programs. Common dialog boxes make it easier for you to learn new programs.

WARNINGS: If you accidently open a dialog box that you do not want to be in, the safest thing to do is **click** Cancel *or press* Esc *to allow you to back out of the dialog without making changes.*

Pressing ⏎ *while in a dialog box will usually activate the settings and close the dialog box since the command button* OK *is usually selected.*

What are Dialog Boxes?

Dialog boxes are windows that contain one or more different kinds of *controls* that you use to:

- Change the function of a program (such as save a file).
- Change the appearance of a program (such as changing the font).

You can make one or several changes in a dialog box, then you can usually click OK to leave the dialog box and activate the new settings.

Open dialog box

drop-down list box

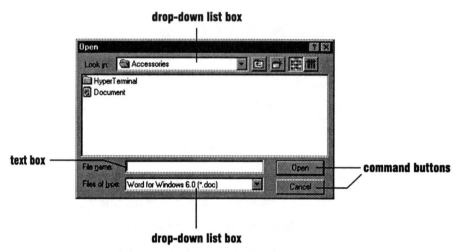

text box

command buttons

drop-down list box

Dialog Box Controls

command buttons

Carry out an action, such as:

OK **or** Cancel

option buttons

A group of circles (each circle by an option) from which you may select *only one* of a related group. A dot in the circle ⦿ means an option button is selected.

NOTE: ***Option buttons*** *can also be diamond shaped.*

Measurement units
- ⦿ Inches
- ○ Centimeters
- ○ Points
- ○ Picas

check boxes

Squares, each by an option, that you may select as desired. Selected boxes contain a check mark ☑.

Toolbars
- ☑ Toolbar
- ☑ Format bar
- ☐ Ruler
- ☑ Status bar

Topic 9 continued...

text box

A box that provides space for typing information needed to carry out a command.

File name:

list box

A box that displays a list of options from which you can choose one.

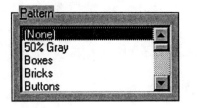

drop-down list box

Similar to a list box, but it must be opened by clicking it or by clicking its arrow. Drop-down list boxes are usually found in small or crowded dialog boxes.

Files of type: Word for Windows 6.0 (*.doc) — **closed**

Files of type: Word for Windows 6.0 (*.doc)
Word for Windows 6.0 (*.doc)
Windows Write(*.wri)
Rich Text Format(*.rtf) — **opened**
Text Only Files (*.txt)
All Files(*.*)

spin box

A box that is used to set a value by clicking an up or down arrow to change the original value. (A new value can also be typed in.)

during the previous 1 month(s)

slider

Lets you set a value within a continuous range.

Pointer speed
Slow ———————— Fast

tabs

Lets you switch between pages of information.

TOPIC 10
Property Sheets

— Terms and Notes —

property sheet
A special kind of dialog box that groups the settings for an object's properties.

object
One of the many *things* that you use when working with the computer system—tems such as:

- files
- programs
- folders
- shortcuts
- disk drives
- Control Panel tools
- My Computer
- Network Neighborhood
- The Recycle Bin
- My Briefcase

NOTE: As used here **object** *is really just another catch all term for an item, element, thing, whatcha-ma-call-it, or thing-a-ma-jig. The terms* **object** *and* **object-oriented** *have a more formal computer-related meaning that is not used in this book.*

property
A characteristic of an object. Many properties can be changed by using a control in a dialog box.

What are Property Sheets?

Property sheets are a special kind of dialog box that let you set the properties associated with an *object*. Since an object often has a lot more property settings than would fit in a simple dialog box, Property sheet dialog boxes use **page tab controls** to conveniently arrange the many property settings. Each page name is always visible. To switch between pages, simply click the tab you want.

Mouse Properties dialog box

page tabs —

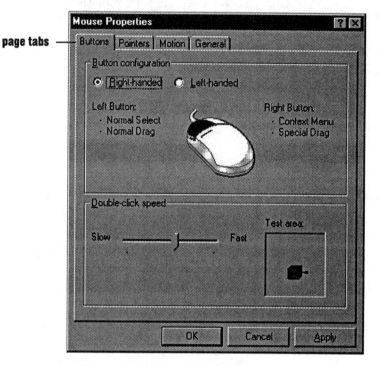

Properties for Various Objects and Their Tab Names

Notice the variety of properties associated with different objects.

THESE OBJECTS	CONTAIN THESE PAGE TABS
Taskbar	Taskbar Options, Start Menu Programs
Display	Background, Screen Saver, Appearance, Settings
Add/Remove programs	Install/Uninstall, Windows Setup, Startup Disk
Passwords	Change Passwords, Remote Administration, User Profiles
Date/Time	Date & Time, Time Zone
Network	Configuration, Identification, Access Control
System	General, Device Manager, Hardware Profiles, Performance
Multimedia	Audio, Video, MIDI, CD Music, Advanced
Modems	General, Diagnostics
Regional Settings	Regional Settings, Number, Currency, Time, Date
Keyboard	Speed, Language, General
My Briefcase	General, Sharing
Recycle Bin	Global, [C:]
Windows 95 Release Notes	General, Shortcut
DOS programs	Program, Font, Memory, Screen, Misc

Begin with the desktop displayed and with no tasks on the taskbar.

1 **Open Notepad and type a sentence:**

- **Start** Notepad (**click** Start, Programs, Accessories, Notepad).
  Notepad opens.
- **Type:** Now is the time for all good computer users to learn Windows 95.
- **Press** `Home` to move the cursor to the beginning of the sentence.

2 **Open the Find dialog box:**

- **Click** Search, then Find.
  The Find dialog box opens with the blinking cursor in the Find what text box.

Find what text box

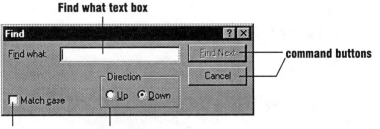

command buttons

check box   option buttons

3 **Use a dialog box:**

- **Type:** good in the text box.
- **Click** the **Match case** check box.
  A check mark appears in the box.
- **Click** the **Match case** check box again.
  The check mark disappears.
- **Click** the **Up** option button.
  A dot appears in the circle by Up and the dot disappears in the circle by Down.
- **Click** the **Down** option button.
  The dot disappears in the Up option button and appears in the Down option button.
- **Click** `Find Next`
  The word good is highlighted where it occurs in the sentence.
- **Click** `Find Next` again.
  A small dialog box appears saying: Cannot find "good".
- **Click** `OK`
  The small dialog disappears.
- **Click** `Cancel` (in the Find dialog box).

4 **Exit Notepad:**

- **Exit** Notepad (review, Exercise 4).
  A dialog box appears with a warning. It says: The text in the (Untitled) file has changed. Do you want to save the changes?

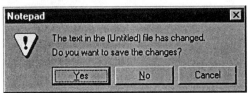

- **Click** `No` (you do *not* want to save the changes).
  Notepad closes.

EXERCISE 14

Use a Dialog Box

Open a dialog box, make changes in it, and activate it.

 **STEPS to**

Open a dialog box

1 **Press** `Alt`
2 **Type** the highlighted letter in the menu name you want.
3 **Type** the highlighted letter in the command (with an ellipsis (...)) you want.

Cancel a dialog box

(and any changes you made in it)

- **Press** `Esc`

Move within a dialog box

- **Press** `Tab` to move forward.
  or
  Press `Shift` + `Tab` to move backward.

Type information in a text box

1 **Press** `Tab` until you move to the text box you want.
2 **Type** the information you want.

Select an item in a list box

1 **Press** `Tab` until you move to the list box.
2 **Press** `↓` or `↑` until the item you want is highlighted.

Select/deselect a check box

1 **Press** `Tab` until the cursor moves to the check box by the item you want.
2 **Press** `Space` to select or deselect the item.

Select an option button

1 **Press** `Tab` until the cursor is in the option button area.
2 **Press** `↓` or `↑` until the dot moves to the item you want.

Choose a command button

1 **Press** `Tab` until the cursor moves to the command button you want.
2 **Press** `↵`

Complete original command

1 **Press** `Tab` until the cursor moves to the OK command button.
2 **Press** `↵`

EXERCISE 15

Use a Property Sheet

To open a property sheet, make changes in it and activate it.

— Terms and Notes —

right-click
Quickly press and release the *right* mouse button.

NOTES: A Property Sheet dialog box is like having many dialog boxes in one, since each page that a tab opens is a separate dialog box.

Right-clicking an object brings up a menu with a properties option if properties are available for that object.

 **STEPS to**

Use property sheets

Move forward through the pages:
* Press `Ctrl` + `Tab`

Move backward through the pages:
* Press `Ctrl` + `Shift` + `Tab`

Begin with the desktop displayed and with no tasks on the taskbar.

① Right-click an object (the desktop) to get a menu:

* **Right-click** a blank space anywhere on the desktop.
  A small menu appears that has an option for Desktop properties.

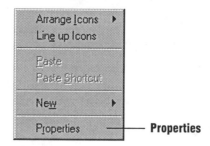
Properties

② Open a Property Sheet dialog box:

* **Click** P*r*operties.
  The Display Properties dialog box opens.

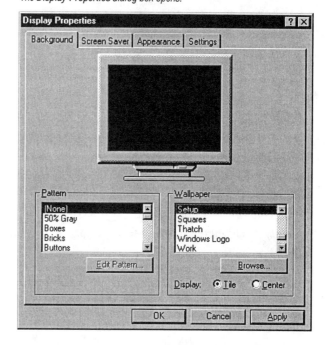

③ Move from page to page in a Property Sheet dialog box:

WARNING: Do not make any changes on any of the pages.

* **Click** the Screen Saver tab.
  The Screen Saver page moves forward.
* **Click** the Appearance tab.
  The Appearance page moves forward.
* **Click** the Settings tab.
  The Settings page moves forward.
* **Click** the Background tab.
  The Background page moves forward.

Exercise 15 continued...

❹ Change the wallpaper:

IMPORTANT: NOTICE THE CURRENT WALLPAPER SO YOU CAN RETURN TO YOUR ORIGINAL SETTING! Look in the Wallpaper list box and write down the highlighted option.

- **Click** the Background tab (if it is not in front).
- **Scroll** through the Wallpaper list box and look at the names of the wallpapers that are available.
- **Click** on Red Bricks to select (highlight) it.
  The screen display (on the Background page) shows small red bricks.
  NOTE: If you cannot find Red Bricks, use a different wallpaper.
- **Click** the Tile option button.
- **Click** [Apply]
  The desktop changes to red bricks.
- **Click** the Background wallpaper name that you wrote down at the beginning of step 4 (if you don't know what it was, select (None) at the top of the list).
- **Click** [Apply]
  The desktop changes back to its original wallpaper (or none).

❺ Change the screen saver:

IMPORTANT: NOTICE THE CURRENT SCREEN SAVER SETTING SO YOU CAN RETURN TO YOUR ORIGINAL SETTING! Look in the Screen Saver drop-down list box and write down the option that is showing.

- **Click** the Screen Saver tab.
- **Click** the Screen Saver drop-down list box (or its arrow).
  The list box drops down.
- **Click** (None), and then **click** (None) again (unless it is already highlighted).
- **Click** the Screen Saver drop-down list box again.
- **Press** [↓] (the down arrow key) twice so it is on Curves and Colors.
  The screen display (on the Screen Saver page) shows the screen saver.
- **Press** [↓] slowly (looking at the sample of the screen saver in the display) until you reach the bottom of the list box.
- **Click** on Curves and Colors.
  The drop-down list box closes with Curves and Colors displayed.
- **Click** Preview.
  The entire screen displays the Curves and Colors Screen Saver.
- **Click** anywhere to stop the display and return to the dialog box.
- **Click** the Screen Saver drop-down list box (or its arrow).
- **Click** the screen saver name that you wrote down at the beginning of step 5 (if you don't know what it was, select (None) at the top of the list).

❻ Cancel a Property Sheet dialog box:

- **Click** [Cancel]
  The Display Properties dialog box disappears.
  NOTES: Clicking Cancel will cancel any changes you made in the dialog box EXCEPT for instances in which you already clicked Apply.
  Clicking [OK] will activate any and all changes you made, even if you did not click Apply at the time you made the change.

EXERCISE 16

Use a Program

To start a program and use the workspace.

— Terms and Notes —

workspace
The inner part of the window where the work in a program or document is carried out.

 **STEPS to**

Move the cursor in Notepad

TO MOVE	PRESS
word right	`Ctrl` + `→`
word left	`Ctrl` + `→`
to beginning of line	`Home`
to end of line	`End`
to beginning of file	`Ctrl` + `Home`
to end of file	`Ctrl` + `End`
screen down	`Page Down`
screen up	`Page Up`
screen right	`Ctrl` + `Page Down`
screen left	`Ctrl` + `Page Up`

STEPS to

Activate/deactivate the menu bar

• Press `Alt`

Open a menu

1 Press `Alt`
2 **Type** the *underlined letter* of the menu you want.

> *NOTE: These steps can be performed either together (`Alt` + the letter) or one after the other (`Alt` , the letter).*

Choose a command

With a menu open:

• **Type** the *underlined letter* of the command you want.

Begin with the desktop displayed and with no tasks on the taskbar.

❶ Use a program's workspace:

• **Start** Notepad.
• **Maximize** Notepad.
• **Type** the following text, pressing 🔲 where indicated:

```
Notepad is a program (also called an application) that is used🔲
to create and edit unformatted text files.  An unformatted text🔲
file is a file that contains only ASCII text characters (letters, 🔲
numbers, and symbols) and a few codes such as a carriage return.🔲🔲
WordPad is a simple word processor.  WordPad has automatic🔲
word wrap, so you do not have to press Enter at the end of each🔲
line (as you do in Notepad).  You press Enter only at the end🔲
of short lines and paragraphs in WordPad. 🔲🔲
```

• **Press** `Ctrl`+`Home` to move to the beginning of the document.
• **Press** `End` to move to the end of the line.
• **Press** `Home` to move to the beginning of the line.
• **Press** `Ctrl`+`End` to move to the end of the document.
• **Press** `Ctrl`+`Home` to move to the beginning of the document.

❷ Open the menus:

• **Click** File.
  The File menu drops down:

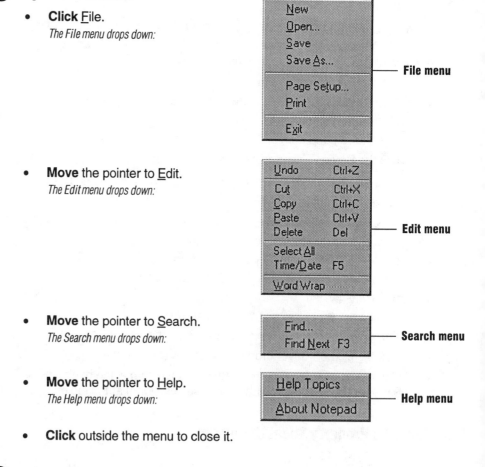

• **Move** the pointer to Edit.
  The Edit menu drops down:

• **Move** the pointer to Search.
  The Search menu drops down:

• **Move** the pointer to Help.
  The Help menu drops down:

• **Click** outside the menu to close it.

❸ • **Go on** to Exercise 17 without stopping.

Common Dialog Boxes

This exercise uses a dialog box that is common to other programs in Windows 95; the Save As dialog box. After you learn to use the Save As dialog box here, you will know how to save in other programs as well.

Saving on Drive A: (or B:)

This book instructs you to save your file on drive A: because there are many instances (especially in a training setting) in which it is better to *not* save files on the hard disk. While you are instructed to save on drive A:, if you prefer to save files on drive B:, substitute drive B: for drive A: throughout this book.

IMPORTANT: You need a blank, formatted floppy data disk for this exercise.

1 **Open the Save As dialog box:**

- **Click** File, then Save (or Save As).
  The Save As dialog box opens.

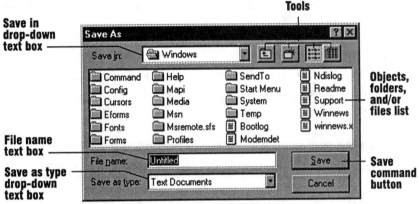

Save in drop-down text box — Tools

File name text box

Save as type drop-down text box

Objects, folders, and/or files list

Save command button

*NOTE: There is no **Save** dialog box; just a Save command. The Save command saves changes to a named document that you are working on. However, when you Save an unnamed (Untitled) document, Windows automatically opens the **Save As** dialog box so you can name your file.*

- **Click** the Save in drop-down list box.
  The list opens to reveal the available options. (Your list may be different.)

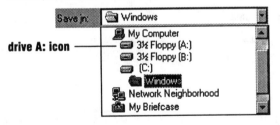

drive A: icon

2 **Save a document on drive A:**

- **Insert** your blank, formatted disk into drive A:.
- **Click** 3½ Floppy (A:)
  The drive A: icon appears in the Save in drop-down list box.
- **Click** the File name text box.
  The cursor appears in the text box.
- **Delete** any characters in the box.

Exercise 17 continued...

EXERCISE 17

Save a Document

To name and save a new file, to resave an already named file, or to rename and save an existing file on a disk (permanent storage media).

— Terms and Notes —

Three ways to save

1. **Click** File, then Save.
2. **Press** Ctrl + S (not in Notepad)
3. **Click** 🖫 on the toolbar (not available in Notepad)

NOTE: The Save command opens the Save As dialog box the first time you save a document; if a document is named, the Save command saves changes to the document (without asking any questions). If you want to save a document with a different name, you must use the Save As command.

Save
The command that saves changes to a previously named document on which you are working.

Save As
A command that opens a dialog box that lets you save a new document or rename a previously saved document.

file
A set of data or program instructions that is saved on a disk as a named unit.

program file
A file that holds a set of instructions that performs a task, such as word processing.

data file (document)
A file that consists of data that has been created in a program, such as a letter typed in WordPad or a picture drawn in Paint.

document (data file)
Any data you create with a program, for example, a report or a picture. A document and a data file are the same thing.

data disk
A floppy disk on which you can save data files.

 **STEPS to**

STEPS to are on the next page.

SAVE A DOCUMENT

— Terms and Notes —

default
An automatic setting in a program.

associated file
A file that has been identified as belonging to a certain program, such as .TXT with Notepad, .BMP with Paint, or .DOC with Word6. When you open an associated file, the program related to the file opens automatically.

IMPORTANT: If you use the Save As dialog box to save a file with a name that matches an existing filename, you get this message:

You DO NOT get this message when you save a previously named document using the Save command (even though the file's name matches an existing filename).

STEPS to

Save a previously named file Ctrl + S

NOTE: This option is not available in Notepad.

1 Press Alt + F (File)
2 Press S (Save)

Save a new file or rename a file

1 Press Alt + F (File)
2 Press A (Save As)
3 Type the filename.
   IF you want to change the location:
   • Press Alt + I (Save in)
   • Press ↓ (down arrow)
   • Press ↓ or ↑ (down or up arrow) to highlight the desired location.
   • Press ↵
4 Press ↵

• **Type:** `savefile` (do not put a period at the end; Notepad adds the extension .txt which associates the text file with Notepad).
   NOTE: Folders, files, and filenames are covered in Lesson Three.
• **Click** Save
   The dialog box closes, the file is saved on drive A:, and the filename appears on the title bar.

filename

> ▤ savefile - Notepad
> File Edit Search Help

❸ Resave (update) a previously named file:

• **Move** the cursor to the bottom of the document (Ctrl + End).
• **Type** the following text, pressing ↵ where indicated:
   ```
   The Save command either resaves a previously named document or↵
   opens the Save As dialog box so you can name and save a new↵
   document. ↵↵
   ```
   NOTE: Be sure to leave one blank line between the previous text and the new text.
• **Click** File, then Save.
   The drive A: light goes on as the revised document is saved, updating the file.
   NOTE: The program automatically remembers the filename and location that you set previously.

❹ Rename and save a previously named file:

• **Move** the cursor to the bottom of the document (Ctrl + End).
• **Type** the following text, pressing ↵ where indicated:
   ```
   The Save As... command opens a dialog box to let you either name↵
   and save a new document or rename and save a previously named↵
   document. ↵↵
   ```
   NOTE: Be sure to leave one blank line between the previous text and the new text.
• **Click** File, then Save As.
   The Save As dialog box opens with the previous filename highlighted in the File name text box and with the cursor blinking at the beginning of the filename and the drive A: icon in the Save in drop-down list box.

   previous filename

   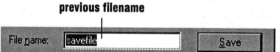

• **Type:** `saveas`
   The new filename replaces the existing one.
   NOTES: When text is highlighted in a text box, it is deleted when you start typing over it. If you press Home, End, or an arrow key, the highlighting disappears and the text remains so you can edit the text if you desire.
   The program remembers the location (drive name) that you set as long as you remain in the program. When you exit the program, the Save in text box defaults back to Windows the next time you start the program.
• **Click** Save
   The document is saved on drive A: with a new filename. The document with the original filename remains on the disk as well.

❺ • **Go on** to Exercise 18 without stopping.

Continue from Exercise 17 without stopping

The New Command

The New (clear the screen) command is common to all Windows 95 programs. If unsaved data exists in a program, the New command displays a dialog box asking if you want to save the changes. If you choose <u>Y</u>es, the Save As dialog box opens and you can enter the commands to save the file in the desired location with the desired filename. If you choose <u>N</u>o, the screen will be cleared without saving the changes.

❶ Clear the screen:

- **Click** <u>F</u>ile, then <u>N</u>ew.
  The screen clears.
  NOTE: Click No if you get a dialog box asking if you want to save changes.

❷ Clear a screen with unsaved data and save the data:

- **Type:** Windows is a user-friendly program.
- **Click** <u>F</u>ile, then <u>N</u>ew.
  A dialog box appears telling you that the file has changed and asking if you want to save the changes.

Notepad ⚠	✕

  ⚠ The text in the [Untitled] file has changed.
  Do you want to save the changes?

  [<u>Y</u>es]   [<u>N</u>o]   [Cancel]

- **Click** [<u>Y</u>es]
  The Save As dialog box appears with the cursor in the highlighted File name text box.
- **Type:** winfun
- **Notice** that the disk location, in the <u>S</u>ave in drop-down list box, still contains drive A: since you have not exited Notepad. When you select a drive, it remains selected until you change it again or exit.
- **Click** [<u>S</u>ave]
  The file is saved on drive A: and the screen clears.

❸ Clear a screen with unsaved data and do NOT save the data:

- **Type:** Windows has many features that are common to all Windows programs.
- **Click** <u>F</u>ile, then <u>N</u>ew.
  Again a dialog box appears telling you that changes were made and asking if you want to save the changes.
- **Click** [<u>N</u>o]
  The screen clears.

❹ Remove and label your floppy disk:

- **Remove** your data disk from drive A:.
- **Label** your data disk with your name and store it. YOU WILL NEED YOUR DATA DISK THROUGHOUT THIS BOOK.

❺ • **Exit** Notepad.

EXERCISE 18
Start a New Document

To clear the screen.

— Terms and Notes —

Three ways to start a new document
1 **Click** <u>F</u>ile, then <u>N</u>ew.
2 **Press** [Ctrl] + [N] (not in Notepad)
3 **Click** [🗋] on the toolbar
   (not available in Notepad)

common commands
Commands such as New and Save that work the same in most Windows programs.

⌨ STEPS to

Clear the screen without saving
1 **Press** [Alt] + [F] (<u>F</u>ile)
2 **Press** [N] (<u>N</u>ew)
3 **Press** [N] (<u>N</u>o)

Clear the screen and save
1 **Press** [Alt] + [F] (<u>F</u>ile)
2 **Press** [N] (<u>N</u>ew)
   A dialog box appears asking if you want to save.
3 **Press** [⏎] to save.
   The Save As dialog box appears.
4 **Type** a filename in the File <u>n</u>ame text box.
   IF you want to change the location:
   - **Press** [Alt] + [I] (Save <u>i</u>n)
   - **Press** [↓] (down arrow)
   - **Press** [↓] or [↑] (down or up arrow) to highlight the desired location.
   - **Press** [⏎]
5 **Press** [⏎]

EXERCISE 19

Open a Document

To retrieve a file from permanent storage (a disk) into a program's workspace.

— Terms and Notes —

Three ways to open

1 Click File, then Open.

2 Press Ctrl + O (not in Notepad)

3 Click 📂 on the toolbar
   (not available in Notepad)

NOTE: The Open dialog box is a common dialog box, as are the Save As and Print dialog boxes.

STEPS to

Open a document Ctrl+O

NOTE: This option is not available in Notepad.

1 Press Alt + F (File)

2 Press O (Open)
   The Open dialog box appears.
   IF the existing file has been changed, a small dialog box appears asking if you want to save the changes:
   - Press Y (Yes) to save changes.
   - Save the file.
   or
   - Press N (No) not to save changes.
   The Open dialog box appears.
   IF you want to change the location to Look in:
   - Press Alt + I (Look in)
   - Press ↓ (down arrow)
   - Press ↓ or ↑ (down or up arrow) to highlight the desired location.
   - Press ↵

STEPS to *Continued on next page.*

Begin with the desktop displayed and with no tasks on the taskbar.

① • **Start** and **maximize** Notepad.

② **Open the Open dialog box:**
   - **Click** File, then Open.
     The Open dialog box opens.
   - **Notice** the similarity to the Save As dialog box (in Exercise 17).

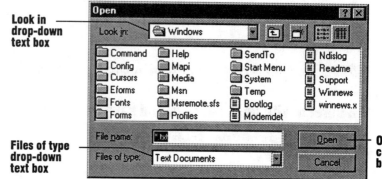

③ **Locate a file to open:**
   - **Insert** your data disk in drive A:.
   - **Click** the Look in drop-down list box.
     The list opens to display the available options.

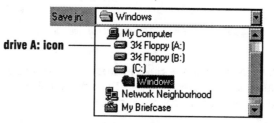

   - **Click** 💾 3½ Floppy (A:)
     The files on drive A: appear in the large list box.

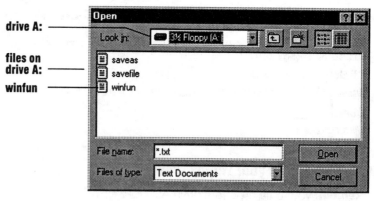

④ **Open a document:**
   - **Click** 📄 winfun, then [Open]
     or
   Double-click 📄 winfun
     The winfun.txt file opens in the Notepad workspace.

Exercise 19 continued...

5 • **Clear** the screen (review, Exercise 18).

6 ## Open the saveas file:
• **Click** File, then Open, then **saveas**, then [Open]

7 ## Open a new file when a program contains an unchanged file:
If the existing file in Notepad has not been changed, when you start a new file, the existing file just disappears and the new file opens into the program.

• **Open savefile** (File, Open, **savefile**, [Open]).

8 ## Open a new file when a program contains a changed file:
• **Move** the cursor to the end of the document (file).
• **Type:** I am changing this file by typing this text.
• **Open** the Open dialog box.
A dialog box appears saying that the file has changed and asking if you want to save the changes.
• **Click** [No] since you do not want to save the changes.
The Open dialog box appears.
• **Open winfun.**
• **Exit** Notepad.

9 ## Open a document in WordPad:
• **Start** WordPad (if the toolbar is not displayed, click View, then Toolbar).
A warning message appears briefly, then WordPad opens with the toolbar displayed.

Open   Print   Find Cut   Paste   Date/Time

WordPad toolbar

New   Save   Print Preview   Copy   Undo

• **Maximize** WordPad, if it is not already maximized.
• **Click**
The Open dialog box for WordPad matches the Open dialog box for Notepad.
• **Change** the Look in drop-down box to drive A:.
None of your files are displayed because WordPad is looking for DOCument files.

10 ## Change the file type in the Open dialog box:
Notice that the Files of type box defaults to Word for Windows 6.0 (*.doc). You want to open a document (file) created in Notepad; remember that the file type associated with Notepad is Text Files (*.txt).

• **Click** the Files of type drop-down list box.
The list opens up.

Files of type: Word for Windows 6.0 (*.doc)
Word for Windows 6.0 (*.doc)
Windows Write(*.wri)
Rich Text Format(*.rtf)
Text Documents (*.txt)
Text Documents - MS-DOS Format (*.txt)
All Documents (*.*)

• **Click** the Text Documents (*.txt) option.
Your files now appear in the display.
• **Open saveas.**
• **Exit** WordPad and **remove** your data disk from drive A:.

— Terms and Notes —

unchanged file
A file that has not been modified (edited) since it was last saved.

changed file
A file (or workspace) that has had some kind of modification—either the file is new or the file has been edited in some way since it was last saved.

associated file
A file that has been identified as belonging to a certain program, such as .TXT with Notepad, .BMP with Paint, or .DOC with Word6. When you open an associated file, the program related to the file opens automatically.

toolbar
A row of buttons that provide quick access to frequently used commands.

STEPS to continued

IF you want to change the type of file the program will display:
• **Press** Alt + T (Files of type)
• **Press** ↓ (down arrow)
• **Press** ↓ or ↑ (down or up arrow) to highlight the desired type.
• **Press** ↵
3 **Press** N (File name)
4 **Type** the filename.
5 **Press** ↵ to activate the Open command

EXERCISE 20

Print a Document

To use the printer to make a hard copy of the data in a program.

— Terms and Notes —

Three ways to print

1   Click 🖨 on the toolbar
    (not available in Notepad)
2   Click File, then Print.
3   Press Ctrl + P (not in Notepad)

ASSUMPTION: It is assumed that your printer has been properly installed.

Print dialog box
The Print dialog box has three sections: Printer, Print range, and Copies. The Print range and Copies are used mainly for multiple page documents. The commands in each section are summarized below:

Printer section
• Name	Lists the printers that are set up on your computer.
• Status	May show data about printer.
• Type	May show data about printer.
• Where	May show data about printer.
• Comment	May show data about printer.
Properties...	Opens a Property Sheet dialog box in which you may set options for the selected printer; options vary with different printers.

Print range section
• All	Prints the entire document.
• Pages	Prints the indicated range of pages.
• Selection	Prints the highlighted data.

Copies section
• Number of copies	Prints the number of copies you set.
• Collate	Specifies if you want the copies collated (only if more than one copy is set).

 **STEPS to**

Print a document Ctrl + P

1   Press Alt + F (File)
2   Press P (Print)
3   Press ↵ to accept OK.

---

*NOTE: Notepad does not use a Print dialog box to print because it is a **text editor** (not a word processor) and uses no special printing codes. All other programs in Windows use a Print dialog box when you print. Since the purpose of this exercise is to use a Print dialog box, you are instructed to print using WordPad instead of Notepad.*

Begin with the desktop displayed and with no tasks on the taskbar.

❶
- **Start** and **maximize** WordPad.
- **Insert** your data disk in drive A:.
- **Open** the Open dialog box (review, Exercise 19, step 2).
- **Change** Files of type to Text Documents (*.txt) (review, Exercise 19).
- **Change** to drive A: (review Exercise 19, step 3) and **open saveas**.

❷ Print a document:
- **Click** File, then Print.
  The Print dialog box opens.

Printer section →

Print range section →

Print range section → ← **your printer name**

← **Copies section**

```
Print                                                    ? ✕
┌ Printer ──────────────────────────────────────────────┐
│ Name:    [HP LaserJet 4/4M          ▼]   [ Properties... ]│
│ Status:  Default printer; Ready                         │
│ Type:    HP LaserJet 4 on LPT1:                         │
│ Where:                                                  │
│ Comment:                                                │
└────────────────────────────────────────────────────────┘
┌ Print range ──────────────┐  ┌ Copies ─────────────────┐
│ ⦿ All                      │  │ Number of copies: [1  ▲▼]│
│ ○ Pages  from:[1] to:[  ]  │  │ [1][1] [2][2] [3][3] ☐ Collate│
│ ○ Selection                │  │                          │
└───────────────────────────┘  └─────────────────────────┘
                              [  OK  ]   [ Cancel ]
```

- **Notice** that the default setting for the Print range section is All and the default setting for the Copies section is for a single copy. These are the settings used most often.
- **Make sure** that your printer is turned on and ready to receive data.
- **Click** [OK]
  *The **saveas** file is printed.*

```
    Notepad is a program (also called an application) that is used
    to create and edit unformatted text files.  An unformatted text
    file is a file that contains only ASCII text characters (letters,
    numbers, and symbols) and a few codes such as a carriage return.

    WordPad is a simple word processor.  WordPad has automatic
    word wrap, so you do not have to press Enter at the end of each
    line (as you do in Notepad).  You press Enter only at the end
    of short lines and paragraphs in WordPad.

    The Save command either resaves a previously named document or
    opens the Save As dialog box so you can name and save a new
    document.

    The Save As... command opens a dialog box to let you either name
    and save a new document or rename and save a previously named
    document.
```

❸ Print the document using the toolbar:
  NOTE: If the toolbar is not displayed, click View, then Toolbar (see page 39.)
- **Click** 🖨 on the toolbar.
  *The **saveas** file is printed again, this time without opening the Print dialog box.*

❹
- **Exit** WordPad without saving (if asked) and **remove** your data disk.

Begin with the desktop displayed and with no tasks on the taskbar.

1 • **Start** WordPad.
   • **Maximize** WordPad (if it is not already maximized).

2 **Open the Page Setup dialog box:**
   • **Click** File, then Page Setup.
     The Page Setup dialog box opens.

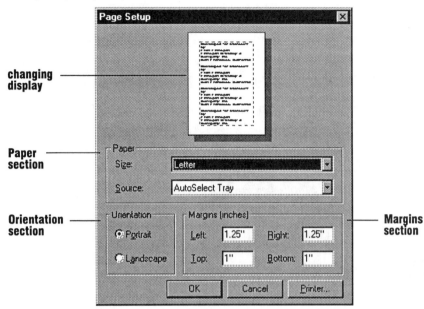

changing display

Paper section

Orientation section

Margins section

3 **Highlight options in the Size list box:**
   • **Click** the Size drop-down list box.
     The Size list box opens.
   • **Notice** the definition in the Size list box (probably Letter).
   • **Press** the up arrow (or down arrow) until you reach the opposite end.
     The page illustration changes with every different page size definition.
   • **Click** the original definition.

4 **Change the Orientation:**
   • **Click** the Landscape option button.
     The page illustration changes to a landscape orientation.
   • **Click** the Portrait option button.
     The page illustration returns to a portrait orientation.

5 **Change the Margins:**
   • **Click** the Left margin text box and **change** the margin to 2".
   • **Click** the Right margin text box and **change** the margin to .5".
   • **Click** the Bottom margin text box and **change** the margin to 3".
     The page illustration changes to reflect each margin change.

6 **Cancel the Page Setup dialog box:**
   • **Click** Cancel to close the dialog box without saving changes.

7 • **Exit** WordPad.

EXERCISE 21
Page Setup

To change settings and notice how the changing display reflects your changes.

— Terms and Notes —

NOTE: Page Setup is a wonderful example of a dialog box that uses a changing display to reflect the changes you make in the dialog box.

portrait
A paper orientation in which the paper is taller than it is wide, as are typical portraits.

landscape
A paper orientation in which the paper is wider than it is tall, as are typical landscapes.

 **STEPS to**

Change settings in Page Setup

1 Press `Alt` + `F` (File)
2 Press `U` (Page Setup)
3 Choose options below as desired:
   Change the paper size
   • Press `Alt` + `Z` (Size)
   • Press `Alt` + `↓` (down arrow)
   • Press `↓` or `↑` (down or up arrow) to highlight the desired paper definition.
   • Press `↵`
   Change the paper source
   • Press `Alt` + `S` (Source)
   • Press `Alt` + `↓` (down arrow)
   • Press `↓` or `↑` (down or up arrow) to highlight the desired paper source.
   • Press `↵`
   Change the paper orientation
   • Press `Alt` + `O` (Portrait)
     or Press `Alt` + `A` (Landscape)
   Change the paper margins
   • Press `Alt` + `L` (Left)
   • Type the desired setting.
     or Press `Alt` + `R` (Right)
   • Type the desired setting.
     or Press `Alt` + `T` (Top)
   • Type the desired setting.
     or Press `Alt` + `B` (Bottom)
   • Type the desired setting.
4 Press `↵` to accept OK.

EXERCISE 22

Arrange Windows

To use the taskbar menu commands to position the windows in the desktop so that they can all be seen.

— Terms and Notes —

taskbar
The bar on the desktop that lets you quickly start programs and easily switch between tasks.

cascade
To resize and layer windows on the desktop so that the title bar of each window is visible.

tile horizontally
To resize and arrange the windows on the desktop *one on top of the other* so that each window displays part of its workspace.

tile vertically
To resize and arrange the windows on the desktop *side by side* so that each window displays part of its workspace.

*NOTE: Certain windows do not adjust to the shapes that are best suited to the **Tile** commands. For example, Calculator keeps its size and Paint's minimum size does not always fit in with the other windows.*

 **STEPS to**

Steps to are on the next page.

42   Lesson Two — Beyond Basics

Begin with the desktop displayed and with no tasks on the taskbar.

① Open several programs:
- **Start** WordPad.
- **Start** Calculator.
- **Start** Notepad.
- **Start** Paint.

② Right-click the taskbar to open its menu:

Right-click taskbar on an empty spot.

- **Right-click** an *empty* spot on the taskbar (just before the clock).
  The taskbar menu opens. The commands in the menu may vary slightly depending upon conditions at any given time.

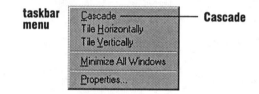

③ Cascade windows:
- **Click** Cascade.
  The windows on the desktop are cascaded.

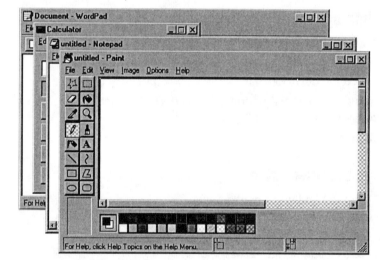

④ Undo the Cascade command:
- **Right-click** an empty spot on the taskbar.
  The taskbar menu opens.

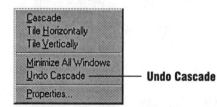

- **Click** Undo Cascade.
  The windows return to their previous size and position.

Exercise 22 continued...

⑤ Tile windows horizontally:

- **Right-click** an empty spot on the taskbar.
- **Click** Tile Horizontally.
  The windows tile with uneven windows.
- **Exit** Calculator.
- **Exit** Paint.
- **Right-click** an empty spot on the taskbar.
- **Click** Tile Horizontally.
  The windows positioned one on top of the other with even windows.

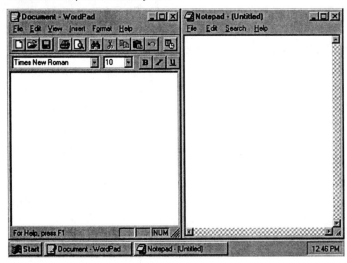

⑥ Undo the Tile command:

- **Right-click** an empty spot on the taskbar.
- **Click** Undo Tile.
  The windows return to their previous size and position.

⑦ Tile windows vertically:

- **Right-click** an empty spot on the taskbar.
- **Click** Tile Vertically.
  The windows are positioned side by side.

⑧ • **Exit** WordPad and Notepad

 **STEPS to**

Arrange Windows

—WITH MORE THAN ONE WINDOW OPEN—

1 **Press** `Ctrl` + `Esc`, `Esc`
   The Start button is selected.

2 **Press** `Tab`
   *The Start button is no longer selected, and although there is no indication of it, the **taskbar** is selected.*

3 **Press** `Shift` + `F10`
   The taskbar's right-click menu opens.

4 **Choose a way to arrange windows:**
   - **Press** `Alt` + `C` (Cascade)
     or
     Press `Alt` + `H` (Tile Horizontally)
     or
     Press `Alt` + `V` (Tile Vertically)
     or
     Press `Alt` + `U` (Undo Cascade or Tile)

EXERCISE 23
Move the Taskbar

To drag the taskbar to one of the four edges of the desktop.

① Move the taskbar to the right edge:

- **Move** the pointer on the taskbar.
- **Drag** the pointer up and right until a taskbar outline appears on the right edge of the desktop.

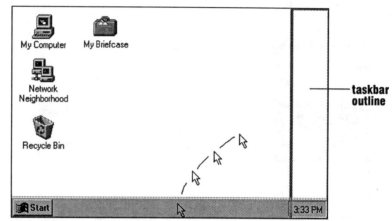

- **Release** the mouse button.

  The taskbar jumps to the right edge of the desktop.

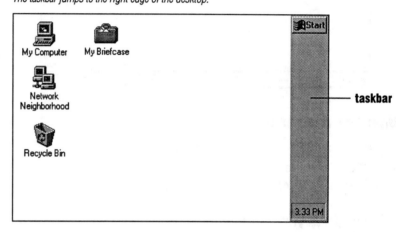

②
- **Follow** the procedure in step 1 to **move** the taskbar back to the bottom of the desktop.
- **Move** the taskbar to the *top edge* of the desktop.
- **Move** the taskbar to the *left edge* of the desktop.
- **Move** the taskbar to the *bottom edge* of the desktop.

 **STEPS to**

Move the taskbar

1 Press [Tab] until the Start button is selected.

2 Press [Alt] + [Space]
   A menu appears.

3 Press [M] (Move)
   A four-headed arrow appears.

4 **Use** arrow keys to move the arrow until the *taskbar outline* appears on the desired edge of the desktop.

5 Press [↵]

① Change the taskbar size:

- **Move** the pointer on the top edge of the taskbar until it becomes a double-headed arrow.

double-headed arrow

- **Drag** the double-headed arrow *up* until the taskbar doubles its size.

- **Release** the mouse button.
  The taskbar is sized to twice its original size.

②
- **Move** the taskbar to the *top* of the desktop (review, Exercise 23).
  The taskbar does not keep its larger size.

- **Move** the taskbar back to the *bottom* of the desktop.
  The taskbar returns to its larger size.

③ Return the taskbar to its original size:

- **Move** the pointer on the *top edge* of the taskbar until it changes to a double-headed arrow.

- **Drag** the double-headed arrow *down* until the taskbar returns to its original size.

- **Release** the mouse button (if you accidently move the taskbar until it disappears, see step 6 to recover it).

④ Change the size of the taskbar on the side of the desktop:

- **Move** the taskbar to the *right edge* of the desktop.

- **Move** the pointer on the *left edge* of the taskbar until it changes to a double-headed arrow.

- **Drag** the double-headed arrow *left* until the taskbar doubles its size.

- **Release** the mouse button.

- **Size** the taskbar to its original size.

- **Move** the taskbar back to the *bottom* of the desktop.

⑤ Size the taskbar until you cannot see it:

Since this procedure can happen accidently, it is useful to do it purposely now and use the steps below to recover the taskbar.
The taskbar should be in its default position and size, on the bottom of the desktop and one layer thick:

- **Move** the pointer on the *top edge* of the taskbar until it changes to a double-headed arrow.

- **Drag** the double-headed arrow *down* to the bottom of the desktop.

- **Release** the mouse button.
  The taskbar disappears.

⑥ Recover the taskbar:

- **Move** the pointer the *bottom* of the desktop until it changes to a double-headed arrow.

- **Drag** the double-headed arrow *up* until the taskbar outline appears.

- **Release** the mouse button.
  The taskbar reappears.

EXERCISE 24

Size the Taskbar

To change the dimensions of the taskbar.

— Terms and Notes —

NOTES: You may want to resize the taskbar when you have so many tasks on it that they become difficult to identify.

You can size taskbar to take up as much as half of the desktop.

 **STEPS to**

Size the taskbar

1 Press `Tab` until the Start button is selected.

2 Press `Alt` + `Space`
   A menu appears.

3 Press `S` (Size)
   A four-headed arrow appears.

4 Press `↑` (up arrow)
   A double-headed arrow appears.

5 Press `↑` to increase the taskbar to the desired size.
   or
   Press `↓` to decrease the taskbar to the desired size.

6 Press `↵`

EXERCISE 25

Hide the Taskbar

To reduce the taskbar to a thin line at the bottom of your screen.

— Terms and Notes —

NOTE: If you want the taskbar to be accessible when you run a maximized program, be sure that both Always on top and Auto hide are checked.

Begin with the desktop displayed and with no tasks on the taskbar.

❶ Access the Taskbar Properties dialog box:

- **Right-click** an empty spot on the taskbar.
  The taskbar menu opens.
- **Click** P**r**operties.
  The Taskbar Properties dialog box opens with the Taskbar Options tab in front.

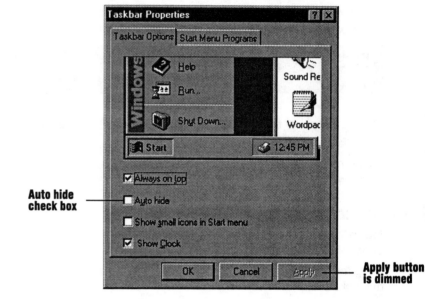

Auto hide check box

Apply button is dimmed

❷ Hide the taskbar:

- **Click** A**u**to hide.
  Both Auto hide and Always on top should be checked (by default, Show Clock is also checked) and the Apply button is no longer dimmed.
- **Click** [Apply]
  The taskbar disappears.

❸ Temporarily display the taskbar:

- **Move** the pointer to the bottom of the screen until the taskbar appears.
  When the pointer reaches the bottom of the screen, it turns into a double-headed arrow, and then the taskbar appears.

❹ Undo the temporary taskbar display:

- **Move** the pointer *up* the screen until the taskbar disappears.

❺ Change Auto hide so the taskbar is always visible:

- **Click** A**u**to hide (to deselect the check box).
  The check mark disappears from the Auto hide check box.
- **Click** [OK]
  The taskbar reappears and the Taskbar Properties dialog box closes.

 **STEPS to**

Hide the taskbar

1 **Press** `Ctrl` + `Esc`
  The Start menu opens.

2 **Press** `S` (**S**ettings)
  The Settings menu opens.

3 **Press** `T` (**T**askbar)
  The Taskbar Properties opens.

4 **Press** `Alt` + `U` (A**u**to Hide)
  Toggles between selecting and deselecting Auto Hide.

5 **Press** `↵`

46   Lesson Two — Beyond Basics

Accessing the desktop

IT IS VERY IMPORTANT TO UNDERSTAND THIS PROCEDURE.

It is important to be able to easily access the desktop since the desktop is home to special programs and customized shortcuts that you may create.

Begin with the desktop displayed and with no tasks on the taskbar.

1
- **Start** Calculator.
- **Start** and **maximize** Notepad.
- **Start** WordPad.
- **Start** WordPad again.
- **Start** and **maximize** Paint.

2 **Quickly access the desktop:**
- **Right-click** an empty spot on the taskbar.

  NOTE: Empty spots on the taskbar can get very small; you can always click just before the clock.

  The taskbar menu opens.

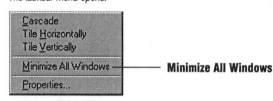 **Minimize All Windows**

- **Click** <u>M</u>inimize All Windows.

  All the programs are minimized, and the desktop appears.

3 **Return the windows to their previous state:**
- **Right-click** an empty spot on the taskbar.

  The taskbar menu opens.

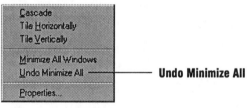 **Undo Minimize All**

- **Click** <u>U</u>ndo Minimize All.

  The programs return to their previous condition.

4 **Use the Minimize All feature when a dialog box is open:**
- **Right-click** an empty spot on the taskbar.
- **Click** <u>P</u>roperties.

  The Taskbar Properties dialog box opens.
- **Right-click** an empty spot on the taskbar.
- **Click** <u>M</u>inimize All Windows.

  The Taskbar Properties dialog box remains opens.
- **Notice** that the taskbar dialog box does not have a minimize button on its title bar. It cannot be minimized.
- **Exit** the Taskbar Properties dialog box.

5
- **Go on** to Exercise 27 without stopping.

Access the Desktop

To use the taskbar right-click menu to minimize all the open programs and display the desktop.

— Terms and Notes —

shortcut
An icon containing a direct route to a specific object and displaying a small jump-arrow in the lower-left corner. Double-click a shortcut to quickly open the file or program it represents. You can customize your desktop by creating shortcuts for the programs you use most often.

 **STEPS to**

Access the desktop

—WITH ONE OR MORE WINDOWS OPEN—

1 Press `Ctrl` + `Esc`, `Esc`
   The Start button is selected.

2 Press `Tab`
   *The Start button is no longer selected, and although you see no indication of it, the **taskbar** is selected.*

3 Press `Shift` + `F10`
   The taskbar's right-click menu opens.

4 Press `M` (Minimize All Windows)

EXERCISE 27

Control Programs from the Taskbar

To access and use the Control menu for programs from the taskbar.

— Terms and Notes —

Control menu
A menu with items that you use to manipulate a program window (Restore, Move, Size, Minimize, Maximize, and Close). It is opened by clicking the Control button or by right-clicking the task button for the program.

active window
The window whose title bar is highlighted, indicating that it is currently being used.

 **STEPS to**

Control programs from the taskbar

—WITH ONE OR MORE WINDOWS OPEN—

1 Press `Ctrl` + `Esc`, `Esc`
   The Start button is selected.

2 Press `Tab`
   *The Start button is no longer selected, and although there is no indication of it, the **taskbar** is selected.*

3 Press `→` and `←` until the task button for the program you want to control is selected.

4 Press `Shift` + `F10`
   The Control menu for the program opens.

5 Choose a way to control the program:
   • Press `R` (Restore)
     or
     Press `M` (Move)
     or
     Press `S` (Size)
     or
     Press `N` (Minimize)
     or
     Press `X` (Maximize)
     or
     Press `C` (Close)

Continue from Exercise 26 without stopping

❶ Use the Control Menu for Paint:

• **Right-click** the Paint task button (identify it by its icon 🖌️).
  The Control menu for Paint opens.

> **Restore**
> Move
> Size
> Minimize
> Maximize
> ―――――――――――
> Close   Alt+F4

• **Click** Restore.
  Paint is displayed on the desktop and it is active.
  NOTE: You can use either the left or right mouse button on the Control menu when it is accessed from the taskbar.

• **Right-click** the Paint task button again.

• **Click** Minimize.
  Paint is reduced to the Paint task button (minimized) again.

❷ Use the Control menu to close minimized windows:

• **Right-click** the Paint task button.

• **Click** Close.
  The Paint task button disappears and Paint is exited.

❸ Use the Control menu to close active windows:

• **Click** the Calculator task button.
  Calculator is displayed on the desktop and it is active.

• **Click** the Notepad task button.
  Notepad is displayed on the desktop and it is now active.

• **Right-click** the Calculator task button.

• **Click** Close.
  Calculator is closed.

• **Right-click** the Notepad task button.

• **Click** Close.
  Notepad is closed.

❹
• **Click** one of the WordPad task buttons.

• **Type:** I am going to close this program from the taskbar.

• **Right-click** the pressed WordPad task button.

• **Click** Close.
  A dialog box asks if you want to save changes to the document.

• **Click** [No]
  WordPad closes.

❺
• **Close** WordPad from the taskbar.

Document Types Used by WordPad

While some programs work with only one type of document, WordPad can work with several different types of documents:

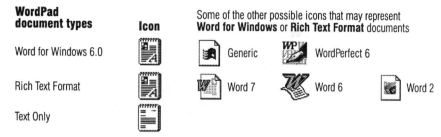

WordPad document types	Icon	Some of the other possible icons that may represent Word for Windows or Rich Text Format documents			
Word for Windows 6.0			Generic		WordPerfect 6
Rich Text Format			Word 7		Word 6
Text Only					Word 2

WordPad defaults to using the *Word 6* document type (which ends with the .DOC extension). However, if you have Word 6 on your computer, Windows will associate Word 6 documents with Word 6 rather than WordPad (even though they are created in WordPad), and it will create a Word 6 icon. This book instructs you to use *Rich Text Format* instead of Word 6 in an attempt to get a consistent icon regardless of whether or not you have Word 6. However, Rich Text Format is also associated with Word 6 (if it is on your system), and although the Rich Text Format icon (shown above) was displayed in most of our tests, your system may use a different icon. If so, your WordPad icons will not match the illustrations in this book—only the file names will match.

Begin with the desktop displayed and with no tasks on the taskbar.

1 • **Start** and **maximize** WordPad.

• **Type** the following, **pressing** ⏎ *only* where indicated:

```
WordPad can work with documents in three different formats:  Word for
Windows 6.0, Rich Text Format, and Text Document.  This book instructs
you to use Rich Text Format most of the time, Text Document once, and
Word for Windows 6.0 twice.⏎ ⏎  The icons associated with Word for
Windows documents is different depending on whether or not you have
Word for Windows on your system.  Word for Windows is a word processor
made by Microsoft.
```

2 **Change the Save in location to drive A:**

• **Click** File, then Save As.
The Save As dialog box opens.

• **Click** the Save in drop-down list box.
The list opens to reveal the available options.

• **Click** Floppy A:.

3 **Change to the Rich Text Format:**

• **Click** the Save as type drop-down list box.
The list opens to reveal the four possible formats that WordPad can use.

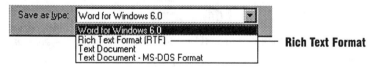

Rich Text Format

• **Click** Rich Text Format (RTF).

4 **Name and save the document:**

• **Click** the File name text box.

• **Delete** the existing text and **type:** richtext

• **Click** Save

Exercise 28 continued...

Use Rich Text Format with WordPad

To change the type of document created in WordPad to Rich Text Format.

— Terms and Notes —

Rich Text Format
A file format that is commonly used by programmers. Windows 95 Help files use Rich Text Format.

Word for Windows
A sophisticated and commonly used word processing program made by Microsoft but not shipped with the Windows 95 program.

file type icon
The icon that is connected with a particular file type, such as Word 6 documents or text documents. File type icons for a particular file type may differ depending upon:
• the program the file type is associated with (not the program they are created in) and
• the icon that is designated for its association.

NOTE: You can view (and change) file type associations from the File Type tab of the Options dialog box (opened from the View menu in either a folder window or the Explorer). When you select the desired file type, the file extension icon and program it is associated with appear under the list.

document type
Different kinds of documents that are defined by the programs that create them. While some programs create only one type of document, WordPad can create three different types of document:
Word for Windows 6.0 (file extension is .DOC)
Rich Text Format (file extension is .RTF)
Text Only (file extension is .TXT)

NOTE: Windows 95 recognizes file types by their filename extensions (which are usually hidden), but you can distinguish file types by their icons as well.

 **STEPS to**

STEPS to are on the next page.

USE RICH TEXT FORMAT WITH WORDPAD

— Terms and Notes —

associated file
A file type that has been identified as belonging to a certain program, such as .TXT with Notepad, .BMP with Paint, or .DOC with Word 6. When you open an associated file, the program related to the file opens automatically.

NOTES: You can view (and change) file type associations from the File Type tab of the Options dialog box (opened from the View menu in either a folder window or the Explorer). From the File Type tab, when you select the desired file type, the file extension icon and program it is associated with appear under the list of file types.

Every file type must be associated with one, and only one, program (that is, the program which starts when you open a document); but not every program must have a file type formally associated with it. For example, WordPad can use Word 6, Rich Text, and Text file types, and those file types can all be associated with different programs (Text documents with Notepad, and Word 6 documents and Rich Text documents with Word 6.

 **STEPS to**

—WITH WORDPAD OPEN—

Start a new Rich Text document
1 Press **Alt** + **F** (File)
2 Press **N** (New)
3 Press **↓** to select Rich Text Document
4 Press **↵**

Change to Rich Text Format when saving
1 Press **Alt** + **F** (File)
2 Press **A** (Save As)
3 Press **Alt** + **T** (Save as type)
4 Press **↓** or **↑** until Rich Text Format (RTF) is selected.
5 Press **↵**
6 **Name** and **Save** document as usual.

Change Word wrap to Wrap to ruler
1 Press **Alt** + **V** (View)
2 Press **O** (Options)
3 Press **Ctrl** + **Tab** until the Rich Text tab is selected.
4 Press **A** (Wrap to ruler)
5 Press **↵**

---

⑤ Start a new Rich Text Format document:

- **Click** <u>F</u>ile, then <u>N</u>ew.
  The New dialog box opens.

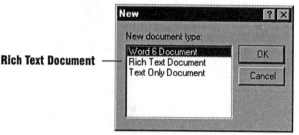

Rich Text Document

- **Click** Rich Text Document, then [OK]
- **IF** a box appears asking you to save changes to document, **click** [No]
  The WordPad workspace is cleared.

⑥ Open a Rich Text Format document:

- **Click** <u>F</u>ile, then <u>O</u>pen.
  - The Open dialog box appears,
  - the Look in box is displaying Floppy (A:),
  - ***richtext*** is displayed, and
  - Files of type is displaying Rich Text Format (*.rtf).
- **Click** the Files of <u>t</u>ype drop-down list box, then All Documents (*.*).
  Four files now appear in the dialog box: ***richtext, saveas, savefile,*** *and* ***winfun.***

   richtext —— **Rich Text Format file created in WordPad**
   saveas ⌉
   savefile ├— **Text Only files created in Notepad**
   winfun ⌋

- **Notice** the difference between the Notepad and WordPad icons.
- **Double-click richtext.**

⑦ Make text wrap to ruler (rather than window):

- **Click** <u>V</u>iew, then <u>O</u>ptions.
  The Options dialog box opens with the Rich Text tab in front.
- **Click** W<u>r</u>ap to ruler, then [OK]
  The text adjusts to the margins rather than the window (as it may have been).

⑧ Print a Rich Text Format document:

- **Make sure** that your printer is turned on and ready to receive data.
- **Click** <u>F</u>ile, then <u>P</u>rint, then [OK]

> WordPad can work with documents in three different formats: Word for Windows 6.0, Rich Text Format, and Text Document. This book instructs you to use Rich Text Format most of the time, Text Document once, and Word for Windows 6.0 twice.
>
> The icons associated with Word for Windows documents is different depending on whether or not you have Word for Windows on your system. Word for Windows is a word processor made by Microsoft.

- **Exit** WordPad (without saving, if asked).

Begin with the desktop displayed and with no tasks on the taskbar.

❶
- **Start** and **maximize** WordPad.
- **Type:** The Find dialog box is opened differently in WordPad than it is in Notepad.
- **Move** the cursor to the beginning of the document.
- **Click** Edit, Find (to open the Find dialog box).
- **Use** the dialog box controls to find all instances of the word in.
- **Cancel** the Find dialog box.
- **Exit** WordPad without saving.

❷
- **Right-click** the desktop then **click** Properties to open the Display Properties dialog box.
- **Access** the different pages, ending with the Background page in front.
- **Change** the wallpaper to Autumn Leaves, select the Tile display, and Apply the wallpaper.
  NOTE: If you cannot find Autumn Leaves, use a different wallpaper.
- **Change** the wallpaper to other designs of your choice, and Apply them.
- **Change** the wallpaper to None (top of list), and Apply it.
- **Cancel** the Display Properties dialog box.

❸
- **Start** and **maximize** WordPad.
- **Open** each of the menus on the menu bar.
- **Type** the following, **pressing** 🔲 *only* where indicated:

  When WordPad is started, the cursor (a blinking vertical line) is displayed in the top left corner of the workspace. The cursor is called an "insertion point" because it shows where the next character you type will be "inserted." 🔲 🔲 You create a

  document by typing. Press the ENTER key only at the end of short lines and paragraphs or to insert blank lines. WordPad will automatically move a word to the next line when the word is too long to fit on the present line. 🔲 🔲

- **Insert** your data disk in drive A:.
- **Save** the document on drive A: using the Rich Text Format.
- **Name** the document **Create1**.

❹
- **Type** the following text at the bottom of the document:

  You can move the "insertion point" by using the arrow keys or the mouse. The mouse pointer shape appears as an "I-Beam" in the WordPad workspace. To move the cursor with the mouse, you can move the "I-Beam" to the desired location AND CLICK THE MOUSE BUTTON. 🔲 🔲

- **Save** the changed document, and then...
- **Save** the file with a different name, **Create2**.
- **Clear** the screen (start a new document), and **click** Rich Text Document, then [OK] to change to Rich Text Format.

Tasks Reviewed:
- Use a Dialog Box
- Use a Property Sheet
- Save a File
- Start a New Document
- Open a File
- Print a File
- Page Setup
- Use Rich Text Format with WorPad
- Arrange Windows
- Move the Taskbar
- Size the Taskbar
- Hide the Taskbar
- Access the Desktop
- Use Control Menus from the Taskbar

Exercise 29 continued...

PRACTICE

— Terms and Notes —

WARNING: REMEMBER THAT WHEN YOU EXIT A PROGRAM, IF you made <u>any</u> kind of change in that program (for example, draw in Paint or type in WordPad), a dialog box will appear asking: Do you want to save the current changes? Click No (to exit without saving the changes).

5 • **Open** Create2.
   • **Print** Create2.

> When WordPad is started, the cursor (a blinking vertical line) is displayed in the top left corner of the workspace. The cursor is called an "insertion point" because it shows where the next character you type will be "inserted."
>
> You create a document by typing, Press the ENTER key only at the end of short lines and paragraphs or to insert blank lines. WordPad will automatically move a word to the next line when the word is too long to fit on the present line.
>
> You can move the "insertion point" by using the arrow keys or the mouse. The mouse pointer shape appears as an "I-Beam" in the WordPad workspace. To move the cursor with the mouse, you can move the "I-Beam" to the desired location AND CLICK THE MOUSE BUTTON.

6 • **Open** the Open dialog box.
   • **Change** Files of <u>type</u> to All Documents (*.*).
   • **Open** savefile (a Text Only file).
     Savefile opens as a text file (the font is Courier, a fixed-pitch font—the same font used in Notepad).
   • **Print savefile.**

```
Notepad is a program (also called an application) that is used
to create and edit unformatted text files.  An unformatted text
file is a file that contains only ASCII text characters (letters,
numbers, and symbols) and a few codes such as a carriage return.

WordPad is a simple word processor.  WordPad has automatic
word wrap, so you do not have to press Enter at the end of each
line (as you do in Notepad).  You press Enter only at the end
of short lines and paragraphs in WordPad.

The Save command either resaves a previously named document or
opens the Save As dialog box so you can name and save a new
document.
```

7 • **Open** the Page Setup dialog box.
   • **Change** the orientation to landscape
   • **Change** all the margins to 2".
   • **Notice** the page illustration in the dialog box.
   • **Change** the left and right margins to 1.25".
   • **Change** the top and bottom margins to 1".
   • **Change** the orientation to portrait.
   • **Cancel** the Page Setup dialog box.
   • **Exit** WordPad.

8 • **Start** WordPad, Calculator, Notepad, and Paint.
   • **Arrange** the windows in a cascade order.
   • **Undo** the cascade arrangement.
   • **Exit** Calculator and Paint.
   • **Arrange** the windows in a vertical tile order.

Exercise 29 continued...

⑨
- **Undo** the tile arrangement.
- **Arrange** the windows in a horizontal tile order.
- **Arrange** the windows in a cascade order.
- **Exit** WordPad and Notepad.
  There should be no task buttons on the taskbar.

⑩
- **Move** the taskbar to the left side of the desktop.
- **Move** the taskbar to the top of the desktop.
- **Move** the taskbar to the bottom of the desktop.

⑪
- **Start** and **maximize** WordPad.
- **Hide** the taskbar (and keep the Always on top box checked).
  (Click the workspace once or twice if the taskbar does not disappear.)
- **Move** the pointer to the bottom of the screen to display the taskbar.
- **Move** the pointer up until the taskbar disappears.
- **Move** the pointer up and down a few more times.
- **Change** the Auto hide command so the taskbar is always visible.
- **Close** Taskbar Properties.

⑫
- **Start** Calculator, Notepad, WordPad (again), Paint, and Paint (two Paints).
- **Size** the taskbar so that it becomes a two-layer bar at the bottom of the screen. Notice that the task buttons enlarge to use the entire bar.
- **Size** the taskbar back to a one-layer bar.
- **Access** the desktop.
  HINT: Start by right-clicking the taskbar.
- **Undo** the Minimize All Windows command.

⑬
- **Use the Control menu from the taskbar to:**
- **Close** both WordPads.
- **Close** Calculator.
- **Maximize** Notepad.
- **Restore** Notepad.
- **Close** Notepad.
- **Close** one Paint.
- **Maximize** Paint.
- **Minimize** Paint.
- **Close** Paint.
  There should be no task buttons on the taskbar.

Lesson Two Worksheets (7 and 8) are in Appendix D

Lesson Three
My Computer

Table of Contents

TOPIC 11
Files

file
A set of data or program instructions that is saved on a disk as a named unit.

program file
A file that holds a set of instructions that perform a task, such as word processing.

data file (document)
A file that consists of data that has been created in a program, such as a letter typed in WordPad or a picture drawn in Paint.

filename
The name assigned to a collection of data that is stored on a disk.

filename extension
The optional *period and up to three characters* at the end of a filename.

short filename
A filename that is no longer that eight characters, can contain a filename extension, and *cannot* contain spaces and certain symbols.

long filename
A filename that is up to 255 characters long and *can* contain spaces and most symbols.

file types
Different kinds of files that are defined by the programs that create the files. Every file has a file type icon associated it.
Below are examples of file types and their icons:

WordPad Document
Document Find File
Briefcase
Help File
Font File
Bitmap Image
MS-DOS Application
TrueType Font file
MIDI Sequence

associated file
A file that that has been identified as belonging to a certain program, such as .TXT with Notepad, .BMP with Paint, or .DOC with Word 6. When you open an associated file, the program related to the file opens automatically.

Files

A **file** is a *collection of data* that is given a **filename** and stored on a disk. Some of the file managing jobs that Windows helps you do are:

name files	resave files	copy files	create shortcuts to files
organize files	open files	delete files	view files
save files	print files	rename files	browse files

Files are identified and categorized in several ways. Most files are either **program files** (instructions that perform a task) or **data files** (information created in a program file, such as a letter).

Conventional File Naming Rules

Files have traditionally been named using the following rules:

1. The filename can be no longer than eight characters.
2. You *cannot* use these characters: . " / \ [ ] < > + = ; , ?
3. You *cannot* use a space.
4. You *can* use an optional **filename extension** of a period and up to three characters.

Filename extensions

Filename extensions are usually used to identify groups of related files. There are certain standard extension that have special meanings, however:

.EXE (execution)	for program files.
.SYS (system)	files that work with your hardware.
.TXT (text)	for text files.
.BMP (bitmap)	associated with Paint.
.DOC (document)	associated with Word 6.

Windows 95 hides filename extensions by default.

Long Filenames

You are not confined to the conventional file naming rules when naming files created with Windows 95 programs (applications).

Below are rules for long filenames:

1. The filename can be up to 255 characters.
2. You *cannot* use these characters ."\<>?
3. You *can* use a space.
4. Windows creates a related, short filename for every long filename.

When you save a file with a long name, Windows 95 saves not only the long filename, but a short name that meets the conventional filename rules above. While Windows 95 displays the long filename, these same files are accessed using their short filenames by programs that do not read long filenames.

EXAMPLE: If you install Windows 95 over Windows 3.1, programs in Windows 3.1 that are carried over to Windows 95 will not support long filenames.

Where are Files Stored?

All files are stored on disks in **folders** *(see the next page for more information).*

Files

Folder

Disk Drives

Your computer system comes with at least two disk drives. One **floppy disk** drive, named drive A: and one **hard disk drive**, typically named drive C:. You may also have a second floppy disk drive, usually named drive B:. Many computers today also have a **CD-ROM drive**—they can hold much more information than a floppy disk.

Floppy disk drives hold floppy disks that are either 3½" or 5¼" in size depending on the disk drive's size. If your disk drive A: is 3½" then Windows 95 calls it *3½ Floppy (A:)*; if 5¼", *5¼ Floppy (A:)*. In this book, your disk drive A: is called *Floppy (A:)*—without the size since it varies for different users.

Folders

Disks are used to store files. **Folders** are created on disks (especially the hard disk) to efficiently organize the many files that are stored on disks. Folders may also hold other folders (sometimes referred to as **subfolders**), which, in turn, may hold still more files and folders. The resulting multi-level structure forms a **hierarchy**, that is, a system of folders ranked one above the other. In Windows 95, folders are always marked with a folder icon 📁 . Windows 95 uses the term folder to describe what used to be called *directories. See also, Topic 21—A Look at Structure (page 140).*

The illustration below shows a possible structure of folders on drive C:. Notice that all the folders below the Start Menu folder are group folders. **Group Folders** represent continuation menus that branch off of the Start menu.

Structure of Folders on the Hard Disk

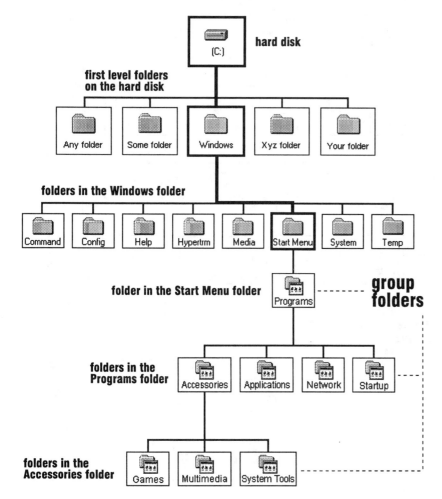

— Terms and Notes —

disk drive
A mechanical device that you use to transfer information back and forth between the computer's memory and a disk.

hard disk drive 🖴
A built-in storage device that has a nonremovable disk (a fixed disk) with a large capacity. Hard disks provide fast retrieval and storage of files.

floppy disk drive 🖴
A storage device that retrieves and stores files on a removable media called *floppy disks*.

CD-ROM drive 💿
(Compact Disk Read Only Memory drive) A read-only optical disk that can store large amounts of data when compared to regular disk drives.

disk
Media on which information is stored and retrieved in named units called *files*.

folder 📁
A structure that holds files and/or other folders that are stored on a disk. A folder can also hold other objects, such as printers and disk drives. (Folders have traditionally been called *directories*.)

subfolder 📁
A folder that is within another folder, or below another folder in the folder structure.

group folder 📁
A folder within the Start Menu folder that holds groups of program shortcuts and other folders; they represent menus within the Start Menu.

hierarchy
A system of things (or people) ranked one above the other. On computers, the term *hierarchy* describes the multilevel structure of folders and subfolders on a disk; or, in the case of Windows 95, it describes a multilevel structure of objects on the entire computer system. The structure is also referred to as a *tree*.

TOPIC 13
Windows' Structure

— Terms and Notes —

desktop 🖥️
The simple opening screen in Windows 95 that contains a few objects, the Start button, and a taskbar.

My Computer 💻
My Computer is the obvious, quick, easy-to-use route to the folders, files, and other objects on your computer system.

Network Neighborhood 🖧
An object that may appear on the desktop; it lets you browse through other computers on your network.

My Briefcase 💼
An object that may appear on the desktop; it lets you keep files on one computer up-to-date from a remote location by using a second computer and modems.

browse
To look at files, folders, printers, programs, documents, and other objects on your computer system.

*NOTE: The fact that the **desktop** is at the top of Windows' hierarchical structure is somewhat of an illusion. In fact, there is a **hidden directory** (folder) named **desktop** (a subdirectory of Windows) on drive C:. The illusion is that the desktop is the top of the structure when its folder is actually on **drive C:** (which is below the desktop on the structure). It is true, however, that the logical top of Windows' structure is the desktop.*

To make hidden directories and files visible:

1 *Open Explorer*
2 *Choose the View menu*
3 *Choose Options*
4 *Choose the View tab*
5 *Select Show all files*
6 *Choose OK*

See Topic 22—Explorer Options (page 142).

Windows' Structure Consists of More than Disks and Folders

Microsoft has designed Windows 95 with networking capabilities (using Network Neighborhood). So, if you have the required hardware, you will be able to access folders and files on computers *other* than your immediate computer. If you do *not* have a networked system the Network Neighborhood icon will not appear on your desktop.

The **desktop** is the heart of Windows. The illustration below shows the desktop at the top of the Windows structure. From the desktop you can choose to look at folders and files on My Computer or the Network Neighborhood.

In the illustration below, dashed lines surrounding the hard disk (C:) structure to distinguish it from the Windows structure above the hard disk. The heavy lines show the route from the desktop to the Start menu folder. The Start menu folder represents the Start menu on your desktop. The group folders below the Start menu represent continuation menus that branch off of the Start menu. Keep this structure in mind when you are browsing folders.

Windows' Structure

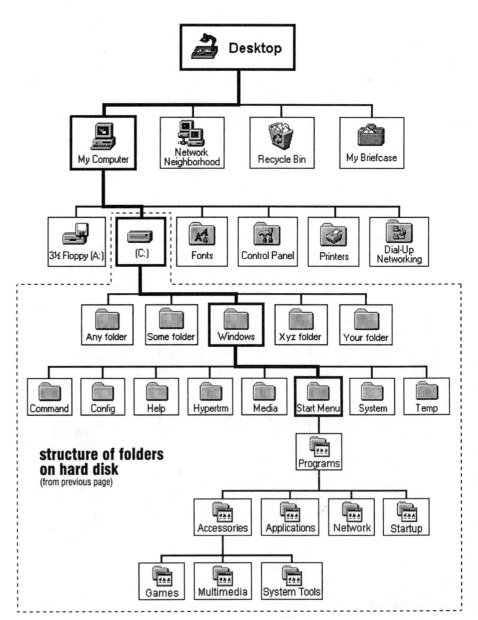

structure of folders on hard disk
(from previous page)

The My Computer Folder Window

My Computer is located in the top left corner of your desktop. Double-click the My Computer to open a window to the objects, folders, and files on your computer system.

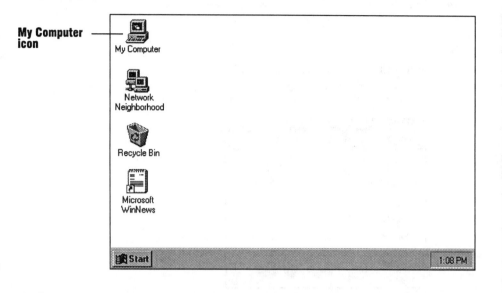

My Computer icon

My Computer
My Computer is the obvious, quick, easy-to-use route to the folders, files, and other objects on your computer system.

folder window
A window that displays the contents of a folder (or certain other objects, such as disk drives). Folder windows offer many of the same folder managing features as the Explorer. Double-click a folder to open its window and see what is in it.

My Computer is a smaller version of the Explorer, offering many of the same features as the Explorer (covered in a Lesson Six). Every object in My Computer opens a **folder window** that displays the contents of that object. Double-click an object's icon to open it. From My Computer, you can work your way to any resource on your computer.

NOTE: The contents of your My Computer may differ from those displayed below.

My Computer Folder without the Toolbar Displayed

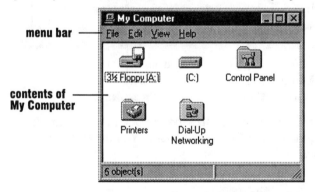

menu bar

contents of My Computer

My Computer Folder with the Toolbar Displayed

toolbar

EXERCISE 30

Use My Computer

To open My Computer, display the toolbar, and change the way the items are shown in the workspace.

— Terms and Notes —

toolbar
A row of buttons that provide quick access to frequently used commands.

workspace
The inner part of the window where the work in a program or document is carried out.

Items in the My Computer workspace can be displayed 4 different ways:

1 Large Icons
Displays items by using large icons.

2 Small Icons
Displays items by using small icons in a left-to-right order.

3 List
Displays items in a list in a top-to-bottom order.

4 Details
Displays information about each item in the window.

Begin with the desktop displayed and with no tasks on the taskbar.

1 Open My Computer:

- **Double-click** (the My Computer icon).

  or

  Right-click My Computer and **click** Open.
  The My Computer program opens with disk drives listed first, and then folders. The toolbar may or may not be displayed; the illustration below shows My Computer without the toolbar.

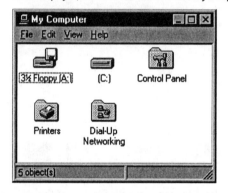

2 Display the toolbar in My Computer:

- **IF** the entire toolbar (illustrated below) is already displayed, go on to step 3.
- **IF** the toolbar is *not* displayed, **click** View, then Toolbar.
  The toolbar is displayed.

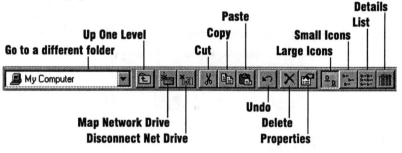

- **IF** the *entire* toolbar is *not* displayed, **size** the My Computer window to make it wide enough to display the entire toolbar. You may also have to **move** the window.

3 Hide the toolbar in My Computer:

- **Click** View.
  Because the toolbar is currently displayed, a checkmark appears by the toolbar option.

- **Click** Toolbar.
  The toolbar disappears from My Computer.

4 Display and hide the toolbar:

- **Display** the toolbar (review, step 2).

  | ✓ Toolbar |

- **Hide** the toolbar (review, step 3).
- **Display** the toolbar once again (review, step 2).

Exercise 30 continued...

View objects as small icons:

- **Click** (the Small Icons button).

  The icons are displayed using small icons in a left-to-right order.

💾 3½ Floppy (A:)	💾 (C:)
🖳 Control Panel	🖨 Printers
🌐 Dial-Up Networking	

⑥ **View objects in a list:**

- **Click** (the List button).

  The icons are displayed in a list and in a top-to-bottom order.

  - 💾 3½ Floppy (A:)
  - 💾 (C:)
  - 🖳 Control Panel
  - 🖨 Printers
  - 🌐 Dial-Up Networking

⑦ **View objects showing details:**

- **Click** (the Details button).

  The icons are displayed in a list with headings and information about each item in the list.

Name	Type	Total Size	Free Space
💾 3½ Floppy (A:)	3½ Inch Floppy Disk		
💾 (C:)	Local Disk	455MB	330MB
🖳 Control Panel	System Folder		
🖨 Printers	System Folder		
🌐 Dial-Up Networking	System Folder		

⑧ **View objects as large icons:**

- **Click** (the Large Icons button).

  The icons are displayed using large icons.

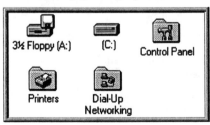

⑨ • **Close** My Computer.

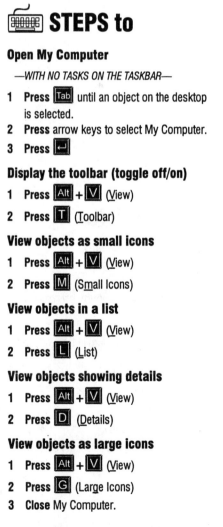

⌨ **STEPS to**

Open My Computer

—WITH NO TASKS ON THE TASKBAR—

1 **Press** `Tab` until an object on the desktop is selected.
2 **Press** arrow keys to select My Computer.
3 **Press** `↵`

Display the toolbar (toggle off/on)

1 **Press** `Alt` + `V` (View)
2 **Press** `T` (Toolbar)

View objects as small icons

1 **Press** `Alt` + `V` (View)
2 **Press** `M` (Small Icons)

View objects in a list

1 **Press** `Alt` + `V` (View)
2 **Press** `L` (List)

View objects showing details

1 **Press** `Alt` + `V` (View)
2 **Press** `D` (Details)

View objects as large icons

1 **Press** `Alt` + `V` (View)
2 **Press** `G` (Large Icons)
3 **Close** My Computer.

EXERCISE 31

Browse Folders Using Separate Windows

To browse folders opening a separate window for each object that is double-clicked.

— Terms and Notes —

*HINT: When browsing folders using separate windows, you can close the selected folder **and all its parent folders** by holding* Shift *while you click the Close button.*

 **STEPS to**

Open a new window with My Computer

—WITH MY COMPUTER OPEN AND WITH THE DEFAULT BROWSING OPTION SELECTED—

With toolbar displayed

1 **Press** Tab until an item in the workspace is selected.
2 **Press** arrow keys to select the desired object or folder.
3 **Press** ⏎

Without toolbar displayed

1 **Press** arrow keys to select the desired object or folder.
2 **Press** ⏎

Change My Computer's Browse Option

The Options dialog box in My Computer has a Browsing options section that lets you change the way windows open when you open objects or folders in My Computer. The two options are:

- **Browse** folders using a separate window for each folder.   Example: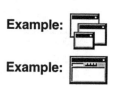

- **Browse** folders by using a single window that changes as you open each folder.   Example:

Begin with the desktop displayed and with no tasks on the taskbar.

1 • **Open** My Computer (review, Exercise 30).

2 **Change My Computer's browsing option:**

- **Click** View, then Options.
  The Options dialog box opens.
- **Click** Browse folders by using a separate window for each folder.
  The option button by the item is selected.
- **Click** [OK]

3 **Open the drive C: window:**

- **Double-click** 🖴 (the drive C: icon).
  (C:)
  The (C:) window opens.

4 **Open the Windows folder window:**

- **Double-click** 📁 (the Windows folder).
  Windows
  NOTE: You may have to scroll to find the Windows folder.
  A new window named Windows opens. Now three folder windows are open.
- **Arrange** the windows in a cascade order (review, Exercise 22).
  The windows are arranged in a cascade order.

5 **Close the Windows:**

- **Close** the Windows window.
- **Close** the (C:) window.
- **Size** My Computer so that the entire toolbar can be seen.
- **Close** My Computer.

Begin with the desktop displayed and with no tasks on the taskbar.

1 •   **Open** My Computer (review, Exercise 30).
   •   **Display** the toolbar if it is not already displayed (review, Exercise 30).
   •   **View** large icons in My Computer's workspace (review, Exercise 30).

2 **Change My Computer's browsing option:**
   •   **Click** View, then Options.
      The Options dialog box opens.
   •   **Click** Browse folders by using a single window that changes as you open each folder.
      The option button by the item is selected.
   •   **Click** [OK]

3 **Change folder (to drive C:) using a single window:**
   •   **Look** at the title bar.
      The name of the window is My Computer.
   •   **Double-click** 🖴 (the drive C: icon).
      [C:)
   or
   Right-click the drive C: icon and **click** Open.
      The window's title bar name changes to (C:).

4 **Change folder (to Windows) using a single window:**
   •   **Double-click** 📁 (the Windows folder).
      Windows
   or
   Right-click the Windows folder and **click** Open.
      The window's title bar name changes to Windows.

5 **Switch back to the My Computer window:**
   •   **Click** 🔼 (the Up One Level button).
      The window's title bar name changes to (C:).
   •   **Click** 🔼 (the Up One Level button).
      The window's title bar name changes to My Computer.

6 **Change My Computer's browsing options back to the default:**
   •   **Click** View, then Options.
      The Options dialog box opens.
   •   **Click** Browse folders using a separate window for each folder.
   •   **Click** [OK]

7 •   **Close** My Computer.

To switch to the single window method of browsing and then browse folders using a single window.

 **STEPS to**

Change My Computer window option

—WITH MY COMPUTER OPEN—

1   **Press** [Alt] + [V] (View)
2   **Press** [O] (Options)
   The Options dialog box opens.
3   Choose a way to browse:

   Browse with single window
   •   **Press** [N] to browse folder by using a single window that changes as you open each folder.
   or
   Browse with separate windows
   •   **Press** [S] to browse folders using a separate window for each folder.
4   **Press** [↵] to choose OK.

EXERCISE 33

My Computer Menus

To look at the menu bar menus in My Computer and other folder windows opened from My Computer.

Begin with the desktop displayed and with no tasks on the taskbar.

1
- **Open** My Computer (review, Exercise 30).
- **Display** the toolbar if it is not already displayed (review, Exercise 30).
- **View** Large Icons if not already displayed (review, Exercise 30).

2 **Examine Menu bar menus:**
- **Click** the File menu.
- **Move** the pointer over the Edit, View, and Help menus, examining each menu as it opens.
  Each menu opens.

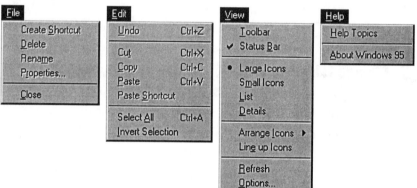

NOTE: If an object in the workspace is selected, the File menu will be different.
- **Click** outside the menu bar to deselect the menus.

3 **Examine File menu with drive C: selected:**
- **Click** the drive C: icon to select it.
- **Click** the File menu to open it.
  The menu items in the menu have changed to include commands that become available when an object is selected as well as a command that is appropriate only for a disk drive.
- **Click** outside the File menu to close it.

4 **Examine File menu with a folder selected:**
- **Double-click** the drive C: icon to open the (C:) window.
- **Maximize** the window.
- **Click** the Windows folder icon to select it.
  NOTE: You may have to scroll to find the Windows folder.
- **Click** the File menu to open it.
  The command options in the menu are appropriate for a folder.
- **Click** outside the File menu to close it.
- **Restore** the (C:) window.
- **Close** the (C:) window.
  The My Computer window is the only window remaining open.

5
- **Go on** to Exercise 34 without stopping.

 **STEPS to**

Examine My Computer menus

—WITH MY COMPUTER OPEN—

Open and close the File menu
1 Press `Alt` + `F` (File)
2 Press `Alt`

Open and close the Edit menu
1 Press `Alt` + `E` (Edit)
2 Press `Alt`

Open and close the View menu
1 Press `Alt` + `V` (View)
2 Press `Alt`

Open and close the Help menu
1 Press `Alt` + `H` (Help)
2 Press `Alt`

Continue from Exercise 33 without stopping.

1 **Examine the right-click menu for a drive:**
- **Right-click** the drive C: icon.
  A menu with file commands for disk drives opens.
- **Click** outside the menu to close it.

2 **Examine right-click menu for printers:**
- **Right-click** the Printers folder icon.
  A menu with File commands for printers opens.
- **Click** outside the menu to close it.

3 **Examine right-click menu for a folder:**
- **Double-click** the drive C: icon.
  The (C:) folder opens.
- **Right-click** the Windows folder icon.
  A menu with File commands for folders opens.
- **Click** outside the menu to close it.

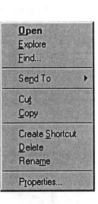

4 **Examine right-click menu for a data file:**
- **Double-click** the Windows folder icon to open its window.
- **Maximize** the Windows window.
- **Right-click** Argyle (a Paint data file).
  NOTE: If you cannot find Argyle, right-click any other ✎ *icon.*
  A menu with File commands for data files opens.
- **Click** outside the menu to close it.

5 **Examine right-click for the workspace:**
- **Right-click** an open area in the workspace.
  A menu with View commands for the current window opens.
- **Move** the mouse pointer over View, Arrange Icons, and New to open their cascading menus.
- **Click** outside the menu to close it.

6 **Exit the windows:**
- **Restore** the Windows window.
- **Close** the Windows window.
- **Close** the (C:) window.
- **Close** the My Computer window.

EXERCISE 34

My Computer Right-Click Menus

To look at the right-click menus (also called shortcut menus) in My Computer and other folder windows opened from My Computer.

--- **Terms and Notes** ---

NOTE: There are convenient right-click menus throughout Windows 95. Just right-click whenever you want a menu.

right-click menu
An easy-to-use menu that opens whenever you right-click an object or area, except in a dialog box (see *shortcut menu*).

shortcut menu
Another name for right-click menu (an easy-to-use menu that opens whenever you right-click an object or area). This book calls shortcut menus *right-click menus* because the term seems more specific and less confusing than *shortcut menu*.

 **STEPS to**

Display right-click (shortcut) menus for an object.
1 **Select** the desired object
2 **Press** Shift + F10

EXERCISE 35

Change Disk Drives with My Computer

To switch between drive C: and drive A: starting with My Computer.

— Terms and Notes —

NOTE: This exercise introduces a new way to change to a different object's folder window. Certain objects are listed in the Go to a different folder drop-down list box, and any object you click in the list box causes the current window to change to that object's folder (rather than open a new window—if you are browsing using separate windows).

 **STEPS to**

Change drives in My Computer

—WITH MY COMPUTER OPEN—

1 **Press** `Tab` until the Go to a different folder list box is selected.
2 **Press** `↓` to open the box.
3 **Press** arrow keys to select the desired item.
4 **Press** `↵`

Begin with the desktop displayed and with no tasks on the taskbar.

1
- **Open** My Computer (review, Exercise 30).
- **Display** the toolbar and large icons if not already displayed.

2 Change to drive C: without opening a new window:
- You can use the Go to a different folder drop-down list box to change to certain objects *without* opening a new window.
- **Click** `My Computer ▼` (the Go to a different folder drop-down list box).
- **Click** `(C:)` (the drive C: icon).
  The My Computer window changes to the (C:) window and no new window opens.

3 Change to drive A: without starting a new window:
- **Insert** your data disk in drive A:.
- **Click** the Go to a different folder drop-down list box.
- **Scroll** up to reveal the drive A: icon if necessary.
- **Click** the drive A: icon.
  The window changes to the (A:) window with your three Notepad documents and two WordPad documents displayed.

```
┌─ 3½ Floppy (A:) ──────────────────────────────────  _ □ ✕ ┐
│ File  Edit  View  Help                                      │
│ ┌ 3½ Floppy (A:)    ▼│ 🖿 🗁 🗀 ✂ 📋 📋 ↺ ✕ 🗐 📇 📶 📅   │
│                                                              │
│   📄       📄        📄        📄       📄       📄        │
│  Create1  Create2  richtext   saveas   savefile  winfun     │
│   └─────────┴──────────┘       └──────────┴─────────┘       │
│            │                             │                  │
│       WordPad files                 Notepad files           │
│                                                              │
│ 5 object(s)          │11.2KB                                │
└──────────────────────────────────────────────────────────┘
```

- **Notice** the difference between the Notepad file icons and the WordPad file icons.

4 Change back to drive C: without starting a new window:
- **Click** the Go to a different folder drop-down list box.
- **Click** the drive C: icon.
  The window changes back to the (C:) window.
- **Close** the (C:) window.

5 Change drives by opening new windows:
- **Open** My Computer.
- **Double-click** the drive A: icon.
  The drive A: folder opens in a new window.
- **Close** the drive A: folder.
- **Double-click** the drive C: icon.
  The drive C: folder opens in a new window.
- **Close** the drive C: folder.
- **Close** the My Computer folder.

Begin with the desktop displayed and with no tasks on the taskbar.

1
- **Open** My Computer (review, Exercise 30).
- **Display** the toolbar and large icons if not already displayed.

2 Change to the Windows folder:
- **Change** View options so you can browse folders using a single window (review, Exercise 32).
- **Double-click** the drive C: icon.
- **Double-click** the Windows folder.
- **Maximize** the Windows folder.

3 Arrange items by Name:
- **Right-click** the workspace (*not* an icon).
  The view menu appears.
- **Move** the pointer on Arrange Icons.
  The Arrange Icons menu appears.
- **Click** by Name.
  First all the folders and then all the files are arranged alphabetically from left to right.

4 Change the way the items are viewed:
- **Click** (the Small Icons button).
  The items are still listed alphabetically from left to right.
- **Click** (the List button).
  The items are still listed alphabetically from top to bottom.

5 Arrange items by Type:
- **Right-click** the workspace.
- **Move** the pointer on Arrange Icons.
- **Click** by Type.
  The items are listed alphabetically by type, and then alphabetically within type.
- **Scroll** through the window and see if you can find groups of identical icons.
  Since each program has a distinctive icon, you cannot recognize them as a special group.
- **Notice** the group of Paint data (bitmap image) icons.
  Paint data files are listed alphabetically.
- **Notice** the group of Help icons.
  Help program files are listed alphabetically.

Exercise 36 continued...

EXERCISE 36
Arrange Icons

To sort items in a folder window (or the Explorer) by name, type, size, or date.

 **STEPS to**

Arrange Icons
—WITH MY COMPUTER OPEN—
1 Press `Alt` + `V` (View)
2 Press `I` (Arrange Icons)
3 Choose a way to arrange icons:
- Press `D` (by Drive Letter)
- Press `T` (by Type)
- Press `S` (by Size)
- Press `F` (by Free Space)

Toggle Auto Arrange
1 Press `Alt` + `V` (View)
2 Press `I` (Arrange Icons)
3 Press `A` (Auto Arrange)
   When Auto Arrange is selected, a check mark appears in front of the item.

6 **View the items displaying information about the files:**

- **Click** ▦ (the Details button).

  Headings for the objects are displayed across the top of the workspace.

headings ⸺

file types

- **Scroll** the through the window and notice the different types of files and the icons that represent the file types. While there are a few icons that are not grouped together, notice that in the Type column all of the file types are grouped together.

  Some file types and their icons are listed below:

ICON	FILE TYPE	ICON	FILE TYPE
	Directory		DOS File
	Application (icon varies)		Help File
	Bitmap Image		Shortcut to MS-DOS Program
	Configuration Settings		Sound
	Cover Page Editor Document		Text Document
	DAT File		

7
- **View** Large Icons (review, Exercise 30).
- **Arrange** icons by Name (review, step 3).
- **Click** 🔼 (the Up One Level icon) to move to the (C:) window.
- **Click** 🔼 (the Up One Level icon) to move to the My Computer window.
- **Restore** the My Computer window.

8 **Auto Arrange icons:**

- **Move** the Control Panel icon about 1 inch (but not on another icon).
- **Move** the Control Panel icon back to its original position.
- **Right-click** the workspace and **move** the pointer on Arrange Icons.
- **IF** Auto Arrange does *not* have a check mark by it, **click** Auto Arrange to select it.
- **Move** the Control Panel icon about 1 inch.

  The icon jumps back to its original position (or possibly switches places with another icon).

- **Right-click** the workspace and **move** the pointer on Arrange Icons.

  The Arrange Icons item should have a check mark by it.

- **IF** Auto Arrange has a check mark by it (as it should), **click** Auto Arrange to deselect it.

9
- **Change** View options so you can browse folders using separate windows (review, Exercise 32).
- **Exit** My Computer.

Begin with the desktop displayed and with no tasks on the taskbar.

 • **Open** My Computer (review, Exercise 30).
   • **Display** the toolbar and large icons if not already displayed.

❷ Open the Explorer from My Computer:

• **Right-click** the drive C: icon, then **click** _E_xplore.
   or
   Click the drive C: icon, then **click** _F_ile, _E_xplore.
   The Explorer program opens with the title, **Exploring - (C:)**.

Exploring Drive C:

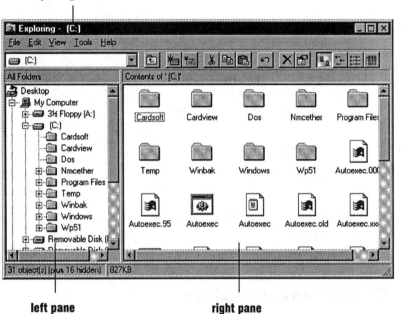

left pane
(All Folders)

right pane
(contents of selected folder in left pane)

The Explorer is similar to folder windows (including My Computer)—they have four menus in common and Explorer's right pane is like a folder window. The Explorer window is divided into two panes. The _left pane_ displays the Windows hierarchy (All Folders) and the _right pane_ displays the contents of the selected folder in the left pane. The title bar names the folder that is selected in the left pane. Explorer has one more menu on the menu bar than My Computer; the Tools menu. More about Explorer in Lesson Six.

❸ • **Click** My Computer in the left pane.

The title bar name changes to **Exploring - My Computer**.

• **Exit** the Explorer.
   • **Exit** My Computer.

❹ Open the Explorer from the desktop:

• **Right-click** My Computer.
   • **Click** _E_xplore.
   Explorer opens with the title, **Exploring - My Computer**.
   • **Exit** Explorer.
   • **Exit** My Computer if it is open.

EXERCISE 37
Start Explorer from My Computer

To open My Computer and then use My Computer to open Explorer.

 **STEPS to**

Open Explorer from My Computer

—WITH MY COMPUTER OPEN—

IF the toolbar is displayed
Press [Tab] until an item in the workspace is selected.

1 **Press** arrow keys to highlight an object.
   Explorer will open with the highlighted object also selected in its left pane.

2 **Press** [Alt] + [F] (_F_ile)
   or
   Press [Shift] + [F10]

3 **Press** [E] (_E_xplore)

EXERCISE 38

Start a Program from a Folder

To start a program from within a folder that you opened while browsing with My Computer (or Explorer).

Why Start a Program from a Folder?

This method of starting programs is useful for starting a program that is not accessible from the Start menu, or to start a program if you happen to be looking in a folder when you decide you want to start a program in that folder.

Begin with the desktop displayed and with no tasks on the taskbar.

1
- **Open** My Computer (review, Exercise 30).
- **Display** the toolbar and large icons if not already displayed.
- **Change** View options so you can browse folders using a single window (review, Exercise 32).

2 Change to folder that holds a program:
- **Open** the drive C: folder.
- **Open** the Program Files folder.
- **Open** the Accessories folder.
  The Accessories folder holds Mspaint and Wordpad.

3 Start and then exit WordPad:
- **Double-click** Wordpad.
  or
  Right-click Wordpad, then **click** Open
  WordPad opens.
- **Exit** WordPad.

4 Start and then exit Calculator:
- **Click** 🔼 (the Up One Level icon) until you return to the drive C: window (watch the title bar until it changes to (C:).
- **Open** the Windows folder.
- **Scroll** until you find the Calculator icon. 🖩
  Calc
- **Double-click** Calc.
  or
  Right-click Calc, then **click** Open.
  Calculator opens.
- **Exit** Calculator.

5
- **Change** View options so you can browse folders using separate windows (review, Exercise 32).
  The browsing option is returned to its default.
- **Close** the Windows window.

 **STEPS to**

Start a program with My Computer

—*WITH MY COMPUTER OPEN*—

IF toolbar is displayed

Press Tab until an item in the workspace is selected.

1 **Press** arrow keys to select the desired object or folder.
2 **Press** ↵ to open the folder.
3 **Repeat** steps 1-2 until the folder containing the program you want to start is open.
4 **Press** arrow keys to select the desired program file.
5 **Press** ↵ to open the program.

Why Open a Document from a Folder?

Opening a file from My Computer is convenient because Windows starts the associated program in addition to opening the file, and if you are browsing, it is nice to be able to open a document without delay.

Begin with the desktop displayed and with no tasks on the taskbar.

1
- **Open** My Computer (review, Exercise 30).
- **Display** the toolbar and large icons if not already displayed.

2 **Open documents on drive A:**
- **Double-click** the drive A: icon.
  or
  Right-click the drive A: icon and **click** <u>O</u>pen.
- **Double-click saveas**.
  or
  Right-click saveas and **click** <u>O</u>pen.
  *Notepad starts with **saveas** displayed.*
- **Exit** Notepad.
- **Close** the drive A: window.

3 **Open a drawing on drive C:**
- **Double-click** the drive C: icon.
- **Double-click** the Windows folder.
- **Scroll** until you find the **Autumn Leaves** icon; it should be near the beginning of the file icons.
- **Open Autumn Leaves** (either double-click its icon or right-click its icon and click open).
  NOTE: If you cannot find Autumn Leaves, open any other file with a  *icon. Paint opens with **Autumn Leaves** in it.*

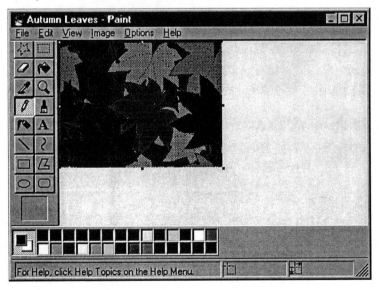

4
- **Exit** Paint.
- **Exit** the Windows window.
- **Exit** the (C:) window.
- **Exit** the My Computer window.

Open a Document from a Folder

To open a data file and its associated program from within a folder that you opened using My Computer or Explorer.

— Terms and Notes —

data file (document)
A file that consists of data that has been created in a program, such as a letter typed in WordPad or a picture drawn in Paint.

document (data file)
Any data you create with a program, for example, a report or a picture. A document and a data file are the same thing

NOTE: A document has traditionally been thought of as data created specifically in a word processor.

⌨ STEPS to

Open a document from a folder
—WITH MY COMPUTER OPEN—
IF toolbar is displayed
Press `Tab` until an item in the workspace is selected.
1 **Press** arrow keys to select the desired object or folder.
2 **Press** ⏎ to open the object's folder.
3 **Repeat** steps 1-2 until the folder containing the program you want to start is opened.
4 **Press** arrow keys to select the desired data file.
5 **Press** ⏎ to open the file.

EXERCISE 40

Create and Delete Folders

To make a new folder and name it, and to remove a folder.

Begin with the desktop displayed and with no tasks on the taskbar.

❶ • **Open** My Computer (review, Exercise 30).
• **Display** the toolbar and large icons if not already displayed.
• **Open** the Floppy (A:) folder window.

❷ Create a folder:
• **Click** File, then New, then Folder.
or
Right-click the workspace and **click** New, then Folder.
A new folder appears in the workspace and is named New Folder, a cursor is blinking at the end of the name.

• **Type:** My Folder
The original text disappears and My Folder becomes the folder's new name.
• **Press** ⏎
The folder is still selected.

❸ Open the new folder:
• **Press** ⏎ again.
or
Double-click My Folder.
The folder opens and it is empty.

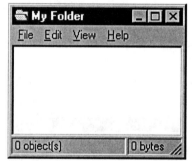

• **Close** the My Folder window.
The folder appears as an icon in the Floppy (A) window.

❹ Delete the new folder:
WITH THE NEW FOLDER ICON STILL SELECTED:
• **Click** File, then Delete.
or
Press Del
The Confirm Folder Delete dialog box opens asking: Are you sure you want to remove the folder 'My Folder' and all its contents?
• **Click** Yes.
The Deleting... dialog box briefly appears showing the folder flying into the Recycle Bin.

❺ Create My Folder again:
• **Follow** the directions in step 2 to create a My Folder again.
• **Go on** to Exercise 41 without stopping.

 **STEPS to**

Create a folder
—WITH THE DRIVE A: FOLDER WINDOW OPEN—
1 Press **F** (File)
2 Press **W** (New)
3 Press **F** (Folder)
4 **Type** a name for the folder.
5 Press ⏎

Delete a folder
—WITH THE DRIVE A: FOLDER WINDOW OPEN—
1 Press **Tab** until the folder to delete is selected.
2 Press **F** (File)
3 Press **D** (Delete)
The Confirm Folder Delete dialog box appears.
4 Press **Y** (Yes)

Continue from Exercise 40 without stopping

❶ • **Arrange Icons** by Name (review, Exercise 36).
   My Folder moves to the beginning of the list.

   • **Open** My Folder (review, step 3).

   • **Move** My Folder so you can view all the files in the workspace.

❷ ## Move a file into the My Folder window:

   • **Drag create1** into the My Folder window.
   The Moving... dialog box briefly appears showing the file flying into the folder.

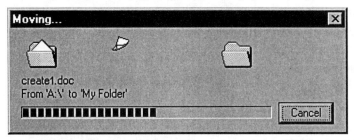

*The file, **create1**, has moved from the workspace in drive A: to the workspace in My Folder.*

❸ ## Move a file into My Folder using the icon:

   • **Drag create2** onto the My Folder icon.

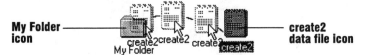

My Folder ——— icon   create2
                                                                          data file icon
              create2create2 create2   create2
              My Folder

Again, the Moving... dialog box briefly appears showing the file flying into the folder.

❹ • **Click** the My Folder window.
   or
   Click the My Folder task button on the taskbar.
   My Folder becomes the active window, and you can see the two files in My Folder.

   • **Arrange** the the icons by Name (review, Exercise 36).

   • **Close** the My Folder window.
   The My Folder window closes into the My Folder icon (which represents the window).

   • **Arrange** the icons in Floppy (A:) by Name (review, Exercise 36).
   The icons are arranged alphabetically with the folder first.

   • **Open** My Folder.
   The My Folder window opens, displaying the two files within it.

   • **Close** the My Folder window.

❺ • **Close** Floppy (A:).

   • **Close** My Computer.

EXERCISE 41

Move Files into a Folder

To drag files from one location into a folder.

 **STEPS to**

Move files into a folder
(within the same window)
   —*WITH THE DRIVE A: FOLDER WINDOW OPEN*—
   IF toolbar is displayed
   Press [Tab] until an item in the workspace is selected.

1 **Press** arrow keys to select the file to be moved.

2 **Press** [Ctrl]+[X] (Cut)
   The icon becomes dimmed.

3 **Press** arrow keys to select the folder into which you want to move the file.

4 **Press** [⏎] to open the folder.

5 **Press** [Ctrl]+[V] (Paste)

6 **Press** [Tab] until the Go to a different folder list box is selected.

7 **Press** [↓] to open the list box.

8 **Press** [↑] until Floppy A: is highlighted.

9 **Press** [⏎]
   The dimmed icon that is being moved has now disappeared.

EXERCISE 42

Use Quick View

To take a quick look at the contents of a data file.

— Terms and Notes —

Quick View
A simple program that displays the contents of the selected item; it will appear on the menu only if there is a *viewer* available for the type of file you select and if it has been installed (the typical install does not install Quick View).

NOTE: The Quick View program is not automatically installed when you install Windows 95. If it is not on your system, you may want to install this very useful program. Quick View requires 1.3 Mb of hard disk space.

WARNING: Do not do this procedure if the computer you are using is not your own computer.

STEPS To Install Quick View
1 **Click** the Start menu.
2 **Open** Settings.
3 **Open** Control Panel.
4 **Open** Add/Remove Programs.
5 **Click** the Windows Setup tab.
6 **Click** Accessories.
7 **Click** the Details button.
8 **Scroll** until you see Quick View.
9 **Click** the box by Quick View.
   A check mark appears in the box.
10 **Click** OK.
11 **Click** OK again.
   The Insert Disk dialog box asks for a certain Windows 95 disk.
12 **Insert** the disk and **click** OK.
   The Copying Files dialog box and then the Start Menu Shortcuts dialog box each appear for a short time as the files are added to Windows 95 on your computer.
13 **Close** the Control Panel.

 **STEPS to**

Use Quick View

—*WITH THE DRIVE A:FOLDER WINDOW OPEN*—
IF toolbar is displayed
Press `Tab` until an item in the workspace is selected.
1 **Press** arrow keys to select the file to be viewed.
2 **Press** `Ctrl` + `F` (File)
3 **Press** `Q` (Quick View)

74   Lesson Three — My Computer

WARNING: The Quick View program may not have been installed when Windows 95 was installed. If it was not, you can either follow the instructions in the left column to install Quick View, or you can skip this exercise.

Begin with the desktop displayed and with no tasks on the taskbar.

① • **Open** My Computer (review, Exercise 30).
   • **Display** the toolbar and large icons if not already displayed.
   • **Open** the drive A: folder window.

② Use Quick View to look at the winfun data file:
   • **Right-click** the **winfun** icon.
   • **Click** Quick View.
   The Quick View program opens with the text from winfun displayed.

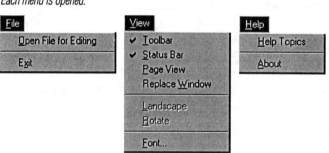

③ Look at the Quick View menus:
   • **Click** the File menu.
   • **Move** the pointer over the View and Help menus, examining each menu as you move over it.
   Each menu is opened.

File	View	Help
Open File for Editing	✔ Toolbar	Help Topics
Exit	✔ Status Bar	About
	Page View	
	Replace Window	
	Landscape	
	Rotate	
	Font...	

④ View the Quick View toolbar:
   • **Open** the View menu.
   • **Click** Toolbar if it does *not* have a check mark by it.
   or
   Click outside the menu to close it if Toolbar *does* have a check mark by it.
   The toolbar is displayed.

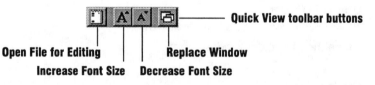

Exercise 42 continued...

Exercise 42 (continued)

⑤ Change the font size in the Quick View workspace:

- **Click** $\boxed{\text{A}}$ (the Increase Font Size button—the large A) twice.
  The text size increases noticeably.

- **Click** $\boxed{\text{A}}$ (the Decrease Font Size button—the small A) twice.
  The text returns to its original size.

- **Click** $\boxed{\text{A}}$ (the Decrease Font Size button—the small A) twice again.
  The text size decreases noticeably.

- **Click** $\boxed{\text{A}}$ (the Increase Font Size button—the large A) twice.
  The text returns to its original size.

  NOTES: The default font for Quick View is Arial 10 point.

  The font you select affects only Quick View, not the text in the file.

⑥ Open the file in Quick View:

- **Click** Open File for Editing button.
  Notepad opens with the winfun document in it.

- **Exit** Notepad.

- **Exit** Floppy (A:).
  My Computer remains open.

⑦
- **Open** the drive (C:) window.
- **Open** the Windows folder window.
- **Maximize** the Windows folder window.
- **Right-click** the Autumn Leaves icon (you may have to scroll to find it).

  NOTE: If you cannot find Autumn Leaves, open any other file with a 📝 icon.

- **Click** Quick View.
  *The Quick View program opens with the picture of **Autumn Leaves** displayed.*

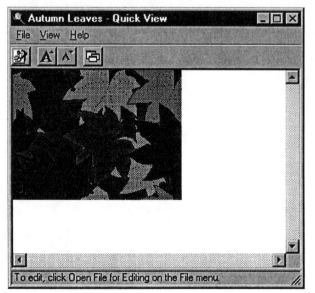

⑧
- **Exit** Quick View.
- **Restore** the Windows window.
- **Exit** the Windows window.
- **Exit** the (C:) window.
- **Exit** My computer.

EXERCISE 43

Print from a Folder

To make a hard copy of the information in a document (data file) that is in a folder.

Printing from a Folder

When you print a document (data file) from a folder window, Windows automatically:

- starts the associated program,
- opens the data file,
- prints the file, and
- then exits the program.

Begin with the desktop displayed and with no tasks on the taskbar.

1
- **Open** My Computer (review, Exercise 30).
- **Display** the entire toolbar and large icons if not already displayed.

2 **Print a document from a folder window:**
- **Open** Floppy (A:).
- **Right-click saveas.**

  or

  Click saveas, then <u>F</u>ile.
  Either the shortcut menu or the File menu opens; notice the similarity.

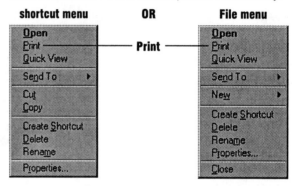

Exercise 43 continued...

 **STPEPS to**

Print a document from a folder

—*WITH MY COMPUTER OPEN*—

IF toolbar is displayed

Press `Tab` until an item in the workspace is selected.

1 **Press** arrow keys to select the desired object or folder.
2 **Press** `↵` to open the object's folder.
3 **Repeat** steps one and two until the folder containing the program you want to start is opened.
4 **Press** arrow keys to select the desired data file.
5 **Press** `Alt` + `F` (<u>F</u>ile)
6 **Press** `P` (<u>P</u>rint)

3 • **Make sure** the printer is ready to receive data.

   • **Click** Print.

   Notepad starts, **saveas** *opens and is printed, and Notepad closes.*

```
                            saveas


        Notepad is a program (also called an application) that is used
        to create and edit unformatted text files.  An unformatted text
        file is a file that contains only ASCII text characters (letters,
        numbers, and symbols) and a few codes such as a carriage return.

        WordPad is a simple word processor.  WordPad has automatic
        word wrap, so you do not have to press Enter at the end of each
        line (as you do in Notepad).  You press Enter only at the end
        of short lines and paragraphs in WordPad.

        The Save command either resaves a previously named document or
        opens the Save As dialog box so you can name and save a new
        document.

        The Save As... command opens a dialog box to let you either name
        and save a new document or rename and save a previously named
        document.


















                            Page 1
```

4 • **Close** Floppy (A:).

   • **Close** My Computer.

EXERCISE 44

Practice

**Lesson Three
My Computer**

Tasks Reviewed:
- Use My Computer
- Browse Using Separate Windows
- Browse Using a Single Window
- Examine My Computer Menus
- Examine My Computer Right-Click Menus
- Change Disk Drives with My Computer
- Arrange Icons

Begin with the desktop displayed and with no tasks on the taskbar.

1
- **Open** My Computer.
- **Browse** folders using separate windows.
  NOTE: Just check to see that the Browse folders using a separate window for each folder option is selected; if it is not, then select it.

2
- **Hide** the toolbar.
- **Display** the toolbar.

3
- **View** objects as Small Icons.
- **View** objects in a List.
- **View** objects showing Details.
- **View** objects as Large Icons.

4
- **Look** at the Edit menu.
- **Look** at the View menu.
- **Look** at the File menu.

5
- **Select** (click once) the drive (C:) icon.
- **Look** at the File menu.
- **Select** (click once) the Control Panel icon.
- **Look** at the File menu.
- **Right-click** the Control Panel icon and examine the menu.
- **Right-click** the workspace and examine the menu.

6
- **Insert** your data disk into drive A:.
- **Open** the drive A: folder.
- **Open** the My Folder folder.
- **Close** the My Folder and drive A: windows.

7
- **Change** the browse option to *browse* folders using a *single* window.
- **Open** the drive C: folder.
- **Open** the Windows folder.
- **Move** up one level to the drive C: window.
- **Move** up one level to the My Computer window.
- **Open** the drive C: folder.
- **Open** the Windows folder.

8
- **Maximize** the Windows window.
- **Arrange** the icons by Name.
- **View** the icons in a List.

9
- **Arrange** the icons in the Windows workspace by Type.
- **Scroll** through the window and notice all the file types.

Exercise 44 continued...

10 • **View** the icons showing <u>D</u>etails.
• **Scroll** through the window.

11 • **View** the icons as Large Icons.
• **Arrange** the icons by <u>N</u>ame.

12 • **Restore** the window.
• **Change** the browse option to browse folders using separate windows.
• **Exit** the Windows window.
There should be no windows left open now.
• **Remove** your data disk from drive A:.

13 • **Open** My Computer.
• **Browse** folders using separate windows.
NOTE: Just check to see that the Browse folders using a separate window for each folder option is selected; if it is not, then select it.
• **Go on** to Exercise 45 without stopping.

EXERCISE 45

Practice

Lesson Three
My Computer

Tasks Reviewed:
- Start Explorer from My Computer
- Start a Program from a Folder
- Open a Document from a Folder
- Create and Delete Folders
- Move Files into a Folder
- Use Quick View
- Print from a Folder

Begin with the desktop displayed and with no tasks on the taskbar.

1
- **Open** the drive C: folder.
- **Open** the Windows folder.
- **View** objects in a List.
- **Arrange** the icons by Name.

2
- **Scroll** until the Notepad program is visible.
- **Start** Notepad from the Windows window.
- **Exit** Notepad.

3
- **Find** and **start** Explorer from the Windows window.
- **Exit** Explorer.

4
- **Find** and **open** the picture, **Zig Zag**.

  NOTE: If you cannot find Zig Zag, open any other file with a [icon] icon.

- **Exit** Paint.
- **Exit** the Windows window, then the drive (C:) window.

5
- **Insert** your data disk into drive A:.
- **Open** the drive A: folder.
- **View** objects as Large Icons.
- **Open** the document, **winfun**.
- **Exit** Notepad.

6
- **Create** a folder; name it **Practice**.
- **Open** the Practice folder.
- **Move winfun** into the Practice folder.
- **Close** the Practice window.

7
- **Move savefile** into the Practice folder without opening the folder.
- **Open** the Practice folder. (Are two files in the folder?)

8
- **Move winfun** back to the drive A: window.
- You may need to size or move the Practice window so the workspace of both the Practice and drive A: windows are visible.
- **Switch** back to the Practice folder.
- **Move savefile** back to the drive A: window.

9
- **Switch** back to the Practice folder.
- **Close** the Practice window.
- **Delete** the Practice folder (in the (A:) window).
- **Arrange** icons by Name.

Exercise 45 continued...

NOTE: *If Quick View is not installed on your computer, skip steps 10, 11, and 12.*

  • **Use** Quick View to look at **saveas**.
  • **Maximize** Quick View.
  • **Restore** Quick View.

11 • **Increase** font size once.
  • **Decrease** font size once.
    The text returns to its original size.

12 • **Open** the file from Quick View.
  • **Exit** Notepad.

13 • **Print winfun** from within the Floppy A: folder window.

```
                          winfun


        Windows is a user-friendly program.




















                          Page 1
```

  • **Close** the drive A: window.
  • **Close** My Computer.
  • **Remove** your data disk from drive A:.

Exercise 45 continued...

Lesson Three Worksheets (9–11) are in Appendix D

Lesson Four
Help

Table of Contents

TOPIC 15
Help

— Terms and Notes —

Help Topics program
The Windows 95 Help program; it has three sections to help you locate Help topics: Contents, Index, and Find. There is a main Help Topics program for Windows in general, and there are smaller Help Topics programs for Windows Accessory programs such as WordPad and Paint.

Help topics
Information about a Windows subject. A Help topic usually begins with a title and contains information about a particular task, command, or dialog box.

Help Topics button
A button at the top of a Help topic that returns you to the Help Topics program.

Contents
An area of the Help Topics program that displays organized categories (books) that you look through to find and then choose the Help topic you want.

Index
An area of the Help Topics program that displays a list of words and phrases that you can search to find a related Help topic.

Find
An area of the Help program that lets you search for the actual words contained in all the Help topics for a given program. When you use Find for the first time, Windows must create the list of words.

Back button
A button at the top of a Help topic that returns you to the previous Help topic. Use this button to backtrack through the topics you have viewed so far.

Options button
A button at the top of a Help topic that lets you work with the Help topic. You can Annotate, Copy, Print, change Font, Keep Help on Top, or Use System Colors for the current Help topic.

Related Topics button ▨
A shortcut box you click to go to a Help topic related to the one you are currently viewing.

Click here button ▣
A shortcut box you can click to start the program or open the window related to the current Help topic.

There Are Many Ways to Get Help in Windows 95

Windows makes it easy for you to get help. Below are some of the different Help features available:

buttons	To display a button's name, rest the pointer on it.
menus	To display a short definition of a menu option on the status bar, select the option.
dialog boxes	To get information about dialog box controls, click ? at the top right corner of the box and then click the item you want information about.
What's This?	Right-click an item about which you want information in a dialog box and then click What's This?
Windows 95 tour	A 10-minute tutorial to get you started using Windows 95.
	(You may need to install the Windows tutorial component or run it from a CD-ROM if Windows 95 is on CD-ROM).
Help Topics program	The Help Topics program has three parts which direct you to Help topics:

- **Contents** A categorized list of Help topics.
- **Index** An alphabetized list of subjects leading to related Help topics.
- **Find** A list of all the words in the Help topics for a particular program.

The Help Topics Program

Index tab
Contents tab
Find tab

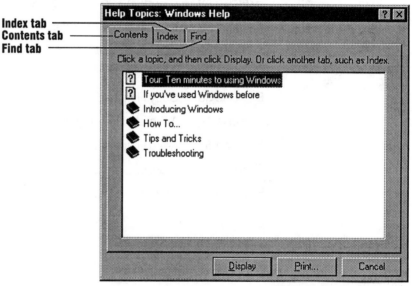

Help Topic with a Click Here Button

Help Topic with a Related Topics Button

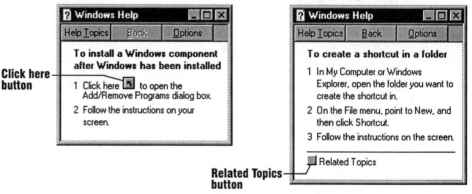

Click here button

Related Topics button

The Contents Section of Help Topics

The Contents section of Help Topics arranges Help topics by logical categories. When you first select the Contents section of Help Topics, four categories are displayed as closed books (see illustration on previous page).

Double-click a book to open it and display other categories (represented by closed books) or Help topics (represented by a piece of paper with a question mark on it). All the categories (books) are listed in the right column. *(See illustration below)*

To open a Help topic, double-click it or select it and then click [Display]. There are about 160 Help topics in the Contents section of the Windows Help Topics program.

Contents Tab with Some Open Books and Topics Displayed

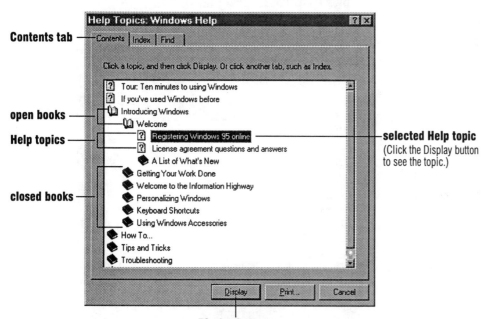

Contents tab

open books

Help topics

closed books

selected Help topic
(Click the Display button to see the topic.)

Display button
(Changes to Open, Close, or Display, depending on what is selected.)

Topic 15 (continued)

HELP

— **Terms and Notes** —

Contents categories [book] only
You open a category (book) to find Help topics.

Introducing Windows
Welcome
    A List of What's New
Getting Your Work Done
Welcome to the Information Highway
Personalizing windows
Keyboard Shortcuts
Using Windows Accessories
    For General Use
    For Writing and Drawing
    For Communicating with Others
    For Sound and Video
    For Using with Two Computers
    For Maintaining Your Computers

How To...
Run Programs
Work with Files and Folders
Print
Use a Network
Communicate with Others
Safeguard Your Work
Change Windows Settings
    Change How Windows Looks
    Customizing My Computer or Windows
        Explorer
    Change Taskbar Settings
    Add or Remove Fonts
    Change Keyboard Settings
    Change Mouse Settings
    Change Multimedia Settings
    Set Up Windows for Multiple Users
Set Up Hardware
Maintain Your Computer
Use a Portable Computer with Windows
Set Up Windows Accessibility Features
    Change Keyboard Settings
    Change Mouse Settings
    Change How Windows Looks
    Use Sound
    Set Up Windows for Multiple Users
Use Help

Tips and Tricks
For Setting Up the Desktop Efficiently
For Maintaining Your Computer
For Running Programs
For Working with Files and Folders
For Printing
For Networking
Tips of the Day

Troubleshooting

The Index Section of Help Topics

The Index is the area of the Help Topics program that displays a list of words and phrases that you can search to find a related Help topic. You can get to an Index entry two ways:

- Type the first few letters of the word you're looking for in the text box. With the first letter you type, Windows jumps to the first word containing that letter and continues moving to find a match for the other letters you type as you type them.

- Scroll through the list and click the entry you want to find topics about.

Once an entry is selected, you can double-click it (or click Display), and either the Topics Found window displays all the related Help topics, or if only one related Help topic exists, that Help topic is automatically displayed.

Index Tab of the Windows Help Topics Program

Topics Found dialog box for *about new features* topic

The Find Section of Help Topics

The Find section of Help Topics is a complex topic searching feature in which Windows builds (or rebuilds) a list (database) of words from all (or selected) help files. Find performs a **full-text search**. The first time you select the Find tab, the Find Setup Wizard dialog box opens with the *Minimize database size (recommended)* option selected (it is the default). Keep *Minimize database size* selected and follow directions in the dialog box to build the Find list.

Once the Find list is built, you can find a Help topic by either typing the word you are looking for in box 1, or scrolling through box 2 and clicking the word you want. All the Help topics that contain the word you typed in box 1 or selected in box 2 are displayed in box 3. You can then select the desired Help topic from box 3 and display it.

The Options button opens the Find Options dialog box from which you can change the way the Find program searches for words.

The Find Tab of the Windows Help Topics Program and Find Options Box

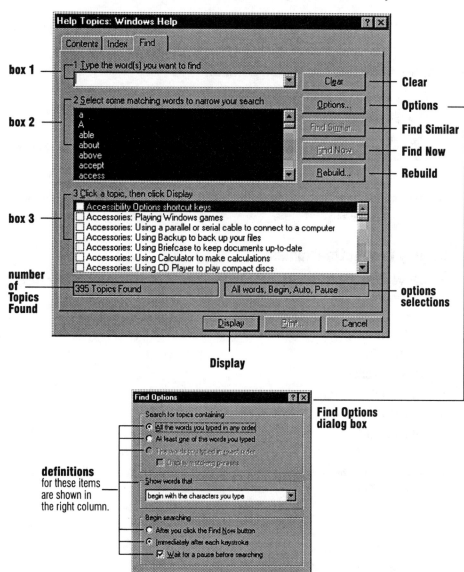

Display

Find Options dialog box

definitions for these items are shown in the right column.

Files

NOTE: Most of the options noted are defined in the right column.

Topic 15 (continued)
HELP

Information about Find options

Type the word(s) you want to find
Provides a space for you to type the word(s) or phrase you want to find in the Help topics. You can type a few characters and use the word list below to see if any words match what you type.
If you want to specify more than one word, separate them with a space.

Clear
Removes the characters you typed in the text box.

Options...
Click this to specify how and when to search for your word(s) or phrase.

Find Similar...
Searches for Help topics that are related to those you marked as relevant to your search.
If this button is unavailable, your word list was not set up to support similarity searches. You can recreate the word list by clicking Rebuild.

Find Now
Searches for Help topics that contain the words or phrase you specified. If this button is not available, the search happens automatically after you type the word or phrase. If you want to use the Find Now button instead, click Options and change the setting.

Rebuild...
Click this to recreate the word list.

Display
Displays the Help topic you selected.

All the words you typed in any order
Specifies that you want to find all Help topics containing all of the words you specify.

At least one of the words you typed
Specifies that you want to find all Help topics containing at least one of the words you specify.

The words you typed in exact order
Specifies that you want to find all Help topics containing the exact phrase you specify. If this option is unavailable, it means that your word list was not set up to support phrase searching. You can recreate the word list and specify that you want to include phrase searching.

Show words that
Determines how to match the characters you type to the words in the Help file.

After you click the Find Now button
Begins searching for topics when you click Find Now, rather than as you type.

Immediately after each keystroke
Begins searching for topics as soon as you begin typing.

Wait for a pause before searching
Begins searching for topics after a pause in your typing.

Files...
Click this if you want to specify the Help files, associated with the current Contents and Index, to search.

EXERCISE 46

Identify Button Names

To rest the pointer on a button until its name appears.

Begin with the desktop displayed and with no tasks on the taskbar.

1 • **Start** WordPad.

• **Display** the toolbar, format bar, and status bar if they are not already displayed. If necessary, resize the window to show all the format bar buttons.

NOTE: If any of the bars listed above are not displayed, click View, then click by the bar that is not displayed; repeat the procedure for each bar that needs to be displayed.

toolbar ——

format bar ——

status bar ——

2 ## Display each toolbar button's name:

• **Rest** the mouse pointer on the last button on the Format Bar

The name of the last button on the Format bar appears below the button.

button
Bullets — button name

• **Move** the pointer left on the Format Bar, resting it on each button until its name appears.

3 ## Display task button names:

• **Move** the pointer and **rest** it on the WordPad task button (on the taskbar).
No name appears above the button.

Note: If a task button's entire name is showing, no name box will appear when you rest the pointer on the button.

• **Start** Paint.
• **Start** Notepad.
• **Start** Notepad again.
• **Start** Calculator.
• **Start** Explorer.
There are six buttons on the taskbar; only the Calculator button displays its full name.

• **Move** the pointer over each task button and **rest** it on the button until its name appears.
A name appears for every task button except Calculator.

4 • **Exit** all the programs except WordPad.
• **Go on** to Exercise 47 without stopping.

Continue from Exercise 46 without stopping

 • **Maximize** WordPad.
 • **Look** at the left side of the Status bar.
  The left side of the status says: **For Help, press F1**
 • **Click** the Format menu.
  The Format menu drops down.

Format
Font...
Bullet Style
Paragraph...
Tabs...

2 **Display information about a menu item:**
 • **Rest** the pointer on Paragraph...

Format
Font...
Bullet Style
Paragraph...
Tabs...

 • **Look** at the status bar.
  The left side of the status bar displays information about Paragraph.

selected menu item

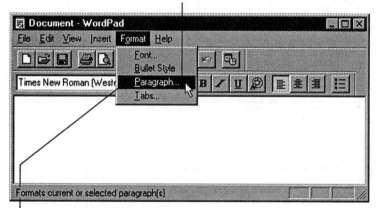

information about menu item

 • **Move** the pointer on Bullet Style and **look** at the information about it on the status bar.
 • **Move** the pointer on Tabs and **look** at the information about it on the status bar.

3 **Examine information for other menus:**
 • **Look** at the information about the File menu items.
 • **Look** at the information about the Edit menu items.
 • **Look** at the information about the View menu items.
 • **Look** at the information about the Insert menu items.

4 • **Restore** and **exit** WordPad.

EXERCISE 47
Identify Menu Information

To look at the status bar to see information about the selected menu option.

— Terms and Notes —

status bar
The bar at the bottom of a program; it displays information about the program, and it can be turned on and off from the View menu.

 **STEPS to**

Identify menu information

Display information about paragraph formats in WordPad
1 **Open** WordPad.
2 **Press** [Alt] + [O] (Format)
3 **Press** [P] (Paragraph)
4 **Look** at the Status Bar.

EXERCISE 48

Use Dialog Box Help

To use the dialog box Help features to identify the function of the dialog box controls.

Begin with the desktop displayed and with no tasks on the taskbar.

①
- **Start** WordPad.
- **Display** the Toolbar, Format Bar, and Status Bar if they are not already displayed.

② Use ? in a dialog box:
- **Open** the Open dialog box (select File, Open).
  The Open dialog box appears.

Help question mark

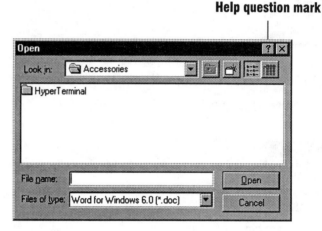

- **Click** ? (the Help question mark).
  A question mark attaches to the pointer.

- **Click** the workspace.
  A pop-up window appears with information about the workspace.

- **Read** the information in the pop-up window.
- **Click** the pop-up window.
  The window disappears.

③ Use ? to get more information:

With the Open dialog box still displayed in WordPad:
- **Click** ? (the Help question mark).
  A question mark attaches to the pointer.

- **Click** Look in:
  A pop-up window appears with information about the Look in drop-down list box.
- **Read** the information in the pop-up window.
- **Click** the pop-up window to close it.

Exercise 48 continued...

④ Use What's This? button to get help in a dialog box:

The **right-click** method of getting help is very similar to the **?** Help feature.
With the Open dialog box still displayed in WordPad:

* **Right-click** File _n_ame.
  The What's This? button appears.

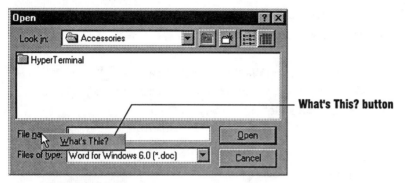

         What's This? button

* **Click** [What's This?]
  A pop-up window appears with information about the File name text box.

* **Click** the pop-up window to close it.

⑤
* **Right-click** [_O_pen]
* **Click** [What's This?]
  A pop-up window appears with information about the Open button.
* **Click** the pop-up window to close it.

⑥ What do you get when you right-click the workspace:

This is an area in which right-clicking will get a different result than using
the **?** (question mark) Help feature.

* **Right-click** the workspace in the Open dialog box.
  A right-click menu appears.
* **Click** outside the menu to close it.

⑦
* **Close** the Open dialog box.
* **Close** WordPad.

⌨ STEPS to

Get help in a dialog box

Display information about controls in the Open dialog box in WordPad

1 **Open** WordPad
2 **Press** [Alt] + [F] (_F_ile)
3 **Press** [O] (_O_pen)
   The Open dialog box appears with the cursor in the File _n_ame text box.
4 **Press** [Tab] until the desired control or button is selected.
5 **Press** [F1] (Help)
   A pop-up box appears with information about the selected item.
6 **Press** [Esc] to close the pop-up window.
7 **Press** [Alt] + [F] (_F_ile), then [O] (_O_pen) to return to the Open dialog box.

NOTE: This method may not work for Notepad. Press Alt + Tab in Notepad to return to the Open dialog box.

EXERCISE 49

Use Help Topics, Contents

To look through categories (books) to find Help Topics.

— Terms and Notes —

Contents
An area of the Help Topics program that displays organized categories (books) that you look through to find and then choose the Help topic you want.

Help Topics button
A button at the top of a Help topic that returns you to the Help Topics program.

Help topics
Information about a Windows subject. A Help topic usually begins with a title and contains information about a particular task, command, or dialog box.

NOTE: When you go from a Help topic back to the Help Topics program, the Windows Help window (which contains the Help topic) remains open.

 **STEPS to**

Use Help Topics, Contents
—WITH HELP OPEN—

Select the Contents tab

1 **Press** `Tab` or `Shift` + `Tab` until the current tab is selected.

2 **Press** `←` to move left one tab.

3 **Repeat** steps 1 and 2 once more if necessary to reach the Contents tab.

Open and close books

1 **Press** `Tab` to move to the list area.

2 **Press** `↑` or `↓` to select a book.

3 **Press** `↵` (to toggle between opening and closing the selected book).

Open a Help topic
—WITH A BOOK OPEN—

1 **Press** `↑` or `↓` to select a Help topic.

2 **Press** `↵` to open the topic.

Return to Help from Windows Help
—WITH WINDOWS HELP OPEN—

• **Press** `T` (Help Topics)

Close a Windows Help topic and Help
—WITH WINDOWS HELP OPEN—

• **Press** `Alt` + `F4`

92   Lesson Four — Help

Begin with the desktop displayed and with no tasks on the taskbar.

① Access the Contents tab in Help Topics:

• **Click** 🗔 Start , then Help.
  The Help Topics: Windows Help program opens.

• **Click** the Contents tab if it is not already in front.

② Open a book (category):

• **Double-click** Introducing Windows.
  or
  Click Introducing Windows, then **click** ⎸ Open ⎸
  The Introducing Windows book opens and several new books appear.

• **Double-click** Getting Your Work Done
  The Getting Your Work Done book opens and several Help topic pages appear.

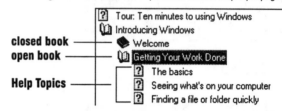

③ Close a book (category):

• **Double-click** Getting Your Work Done.
  or
  Click Getting Your Work Done, then **click** ⎸ Close ⎸
  The Getting Your Work Done book closes.

④ Open a Help Topic:

• **Open** the Using Windows Accessories book, then the For General Use book.

• **Double-click** Calculator: for making calculations.
  or
  Click Calculator: for making calculations, then **click** ⎸ Display ⎸
  The Windows Help window appears with instructions for using the Calculator.

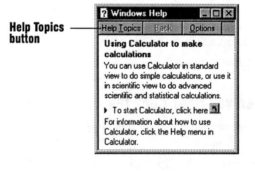

⑤ Return to Help Topics program:

• **Click** ⎸ Help Topics ⎸
  The Help Topics window reappears.

• **Double-click** Windows games.
  The Windows Help window appears with instructions for playing Windows games.

⑥ Close the Windows Help window:

• **Click** ⊠
  The Windows Help window closes and the Help Topics program closes.

Begin with the desktop displayed and with no tasks on the taskbar.

❶ Access the Index tab in Help Topics:

- **Click** Start, then <u>H</u>elp.
  The Help Topics: Windows Help program opens.
- **Click** the Index tab if it is not already in front.
  The Index section moves to the front; the cursor is blinking in the text box.

❷ Search for information about grouping programs:

- **Type:** g
  The index entries jump to the highlighted entry, games.
- **Type:** r
  The index entries jump to the highlighted entry, graphics.
- **Type:** o
  The index entries jump to the highlighted entry, grouping programs.
- **Press** ⏎ to activate the already selected [Display]
  The Topics Found dialog box opens with three entries; the top entry, Adding a new submenu to the Programs menu, is highlighted.
- **Press** ⏎ to activate the already selected [Display] again.
  The Windows Help window opens with information about how to add a submenu to the Programs menu.
- **Click** [Help Topics] to return to the Index section of Help.

❸ Search for information about changing your computer's date:

- **Scroll** the Index entries until *date* appears.
- **Double-click** changing your computer's date.
  The Windows Help window appears. It has a click here button and a Related Topic button.

Click here button ——
Related Topics button ——

[Windows Help window illustration]
? Windows Help
Help Topics | Back | Options
To change your computer's date
1 Click here 🖱 to display Date/Time properties.
2 In the Date area, click the correct month, year, and day.
Note
• Windows uses the date setting to identify when files are created or modified.
▪ Related Topics

- **Click** 🖱 (the click here button) to open the Date/Time properties.
  The Date/Time Properties dialog box opens with today's date and the correct time (if they are set correctly).
- **Click** [Cancel] to close the Date/Time properties dialog box without making changes.
- **Click** ▪ (the Related Topics box).
  The Topics Found dialog box opens with the Changing your computer's time topic.
- **Close** the Topics Found dialog box.

❹ • **Close** the Windows Help window.

EXERCISE 50

Use Help Topics, Index

To locate Help topics by searching through alphabetized entries for subjects that are related to those Help topics.

— Terms and Notes —

Index
An area of the Help Topics program that displays a list of words and phrases that you can search to find a related Help topic.

 **STEPS to**

Use Help Topics, Index
—WITH HELP OPEN—
Select the Index tab
1 **Press** [Tab] or [Shift] + [Tab] until the current tab is selected.
2 **Press** [←] or [→] to move to the Index tab.

Search for a subject
• **Type** the first few letters of the word you're looking for.
  or
  Press [Tab] to move to the entries list and use arrow keys to locate and select the desired entry.

Display the topic or list of Topics Found
• **Press** [⏎]
  IF the Topics Found dialog box opens:
  1 **Select** the desired topic.
  2 **Press** [⏎]

Return to Help from Windows Help
—WITH WINDOWS HELP OPEN—
• **Press** [T] (Help <u>T</u>opics)

Close a Windows Help topic and Help
—WITH WINDOWS HELP OPEN—
• **Press** [Alt] + [F4]
  or
  • **Press** [Alt] + [Space]
  • **Press** [C] (<u>C</u>lose)

EXERCISE 51

Use Help Topics, Find

To locate Help topics by searching through a list of all the words that are contained in a Help Topic file (or group of files).

— Terms and Notes —

Find
An area of the Help program that lets you search for the actual words contained in all the Help topics for a given program. When you use Find for the first time, Windows must create the list of words.

STEPS to

Create a Find list
—WITH HELP OPEN—
Select the Find tab
1 **Press** `Tab` or `Shift` + `Tab` until the current tab is selected.
2 **Press** `→` to move right one tab.
3 **Repeat** steps 1 and 2 once more if necessary to reach the Find tab.

Create a Find list
—WITH THE FIND TAB IN FRONT—
1 **Press** `Alt` + `R` (Rebuild)
2 **Press** `↵` to go to the Next> step and accept the default of Minimize database size (recommended).
3 **Press** `↵` to finish.

Find a Help topic using the text box
1 **Type** the word(s) you want to find. *One or more topics are found.*
2 **Press** `Tab` to move to the topics area.
3 **Press** `↑` or `↓` to select the desired topic.
4 **Press** `↵` to display the topic.

Return to Help from Windows Help
• **Press** `T` (Help Topics)

Close a Windows Help topic and Help
• **Press** `Alt` + `F4`
  or
  • **Press** `Alt` + `Space`
  • **Press** `C` (Close)

Begin with the desktop displayed and with no tasks on the taskbar.

❶ Access the Find Setup Wizard:
• **Click** Start, then Help.
  The Help Topics: Windows Help program opens.
• **Click** the Find tab if it is not already in front.
  Either the Find section moves to the front, or, if a list has not been created previously, a window appears to walk you through the process of creating a list (database) of words from your help file(s).

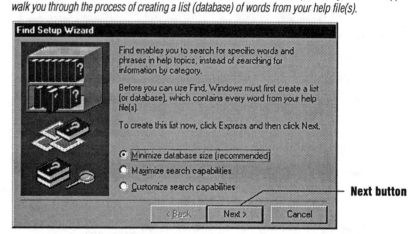

Next button

IF you do NOT have a window that matches the illustration above:
• **Click** `Rebuild...`
  A window that matches the illustration above appears.

❷ Create (or recreate) a word list:
• **Click** `Next >` to accept the Minimize database size option.
• **Click** `Finish`
  A Creating Search Index message appears for a short time, and then the Find section of Help Topics appears with the cursor blinking in the text box.

The space to type the word(s) you want to find in the Help topics. ——

A list of all the words found in the Help topic files(s) when the Find list was created. ——

A list of all the Help topics from which the list of search words (above) were gathered. ——

The number of topics found that contain one of the highlighted words above. ——

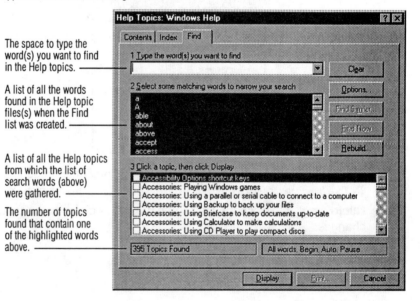

Exercise 51 continued...

❸ Find a Help topic about games:

- **Type:** Games (if you don't type a capital "G" two entries appear).
  One entry appears in the word list and one topic is found.

- **Press** 🔲 to activate [Display] and open the topic.
  A window containing instructions for Playing Windows games appears.

- **Click** [Help Topics] to return to the Help Topics program.

❹ Find Help topics about dates:

- **Click** [Clear]
  The information in the text box disappears and all the words are highlighted again.

- **Type:** date
  Two entries appear in the word list and seven topics are found.

- **Click** the first entry—date.
  Now only four topics are found.

- **Double-click** the last entry—Changing your computer's date.
  A window containing instructions to change your computer's date appears.

❺ Go back to the previous Help topic:

- **Click** [Back]
  The window containing instructions for Playing Windows games reappears and the Back button is dimmed, indicating that you can't go back any more.

- **Click** [Help Topics] to return to the Help Topics program.

❻ Find Help topics that contain the word, rest:

- **Click** [Clear]
- **Type:** rest
  Several words are highlighted, all beginning with the letters, rest
- **Scroll** through all the words that start with rest.
- **Click** the first word, rest.
  Now just three topics are found.
- **Click** Tips: Using Help.
- **Click** [Display]
  The Using Help topic appears.
- **Read** the Using Help tips.
- **Look** for the word, rest, in the Help topic (it's in the last bulleted item).
- **Click** [Help Topics] to return to the Help Topics program.

❼
- **Display** the topic: Network backup: Enabling automatic backup on your computer (double-click the topic or click it and then click Display).
- **Look** for the word, rest, in the Help topic.
- **Click** [Help Topics] to return to the Help Topics program.

❽
- **Click** [Clear] to clear the text box.
- **Close** the Help Topics program.
- **Close** the Windows Help window.

— Terms and Notes —

Three ways to display a Help topic
1 Double-click a topic
2 Click a topic, click Display
3 Click a topic, press 🔲
  (Because the Display button is selected, pressing 🔲 activates it.)

Wizard
A feature found throughout Windows in which step-by-step instructions walk a user through unfamiliar procedures

Back button
A button at the top of a Help topic that returns you to the previous Help topic. Use this button to backtrack through the topics you have viewed so far.

EXERCISE 52

Print Help Topics

To make a hard copy of Help topics (and books of Help topics from the Contents section of the Help Topics program).

— Terms and Notes —

NOTE: Line endings on your printout may not match those in the book (on the right) because of a slight variation in printers (even when they are using printing TrueType fonts).

 **STEPS to**

Print a Help topic

—FROM A WINDOWS HELP WINDOW—

1   **Press** [O] (Options)

2   **Press** [P] (Print Topic...)
    The Print dialog box appears.

3   **Press** [↵]

Print a Book

—FROM THE CONTENTS SECTION OF HELP—

1   **Select** the desired closed book
    (see Exercise 49 STEPS for directions).

2   **Press** [Alt] + [P] (Print...)
    The Print dialog box appears.

3   **Press** [↵]

Begin with the desktop displayed and with no tasks on the taskbar.

❶
- **Start** Help (review, Exercise 49, step 1).
- **Click** the Contents tab to bring it to the front.
- **Open** the Tips and Tricks book.
- **Open** the Tips of the Day book.
- **Display** Getting your work done.

❷ **Print a Help topic:**
- **Make sure** your printer is ready to receive data.
- **Right-click** the Help topic workspace.
  A shortcut menu appears.
- **Click** P̲rint Topic...
  The Print dialog box appears.
- **Click** [OK]
  The Help topic is printed.

> **Getting your work done**
> - To start a program, you just click the Start button, point to the folder your program is in, and then click the program.
> - You can minimize all open windows at once; just use your right mouse button to click an empty area on the taskbar, and then click Minimize All Windows.
> - To select more than one file or folder, hold down CTRL while you click each item.
> - Deleted files and folders are saved in the Recycle Bin until you empty it.
> - To open a document quickly, you can double-click its icon.
> - The Shut Down command on the Start menu enables you to safely shut down your computer.
> - You can minimize neck strain by positioning your monitor at eye level.
> - When you type, you should keep your wrists elevated or use a wristpad to minimize strain.
> - Even if you don't shut down your computer at night, you can turn off your monitor to save power.

- **Return** to the Help topic program (review, Exercise 49, step 4).

❸ **Print a book:**

You should be in the Contents section of Help Topics and the Tips and Tricks book should be open.
- **Click** the For Printing book.
- **Click** [Print...]
  The Print dialog box appears.
- **Click** [OK]
  The two topics in the For Printing book are printed.

> **To view printing status**
> ▶ Use your right mouse button to click the printer icon next to the clock on the taskbar.
>   When your document is finished printing, the printer icon disappears.
> **Tip**
> - You can double-click the printer icon on the taskbar to get information about the documents printing on the printer.

> **To put a shortcut on the desktop**
> 1   Click the program, folder, printer, or computer you want to create a shortcut to.
> 2   On the File menu, click Create Shortcut.
> 3   Drag the shortcut icon onto the desktop.
> **Tips**
> - You can use the shortcut as a fast way to open the item.
> - To change any settings for the shortcut, such as what kind of window it starts in or what key combination is used to access it, use your right mouse button to click the shortcut, and then click Properties.
> - To delete a shortcut, drag it to the Recycle Bin. The original item will still exist on the disk where it is stored.
>
> Related Topics

❹
- **Close** the Windows Help window

Begin with the desktop displayed and with no tasks on the taskbar.

❶
- **Start** Help (review, Exercise 49).
- **Click** the Contents tab if it is not already in front.
- **Open** the How To... book, then the Use Help book.
- **Display** Copying information from a Help topic.

❷ Copy a Help topic:
- **Right-click** the Help Windows workspace (not the desktop) then Copy.
  or
  Click ⌷ Options ⌷, then Copy.
  The menu disappears and, although nothing else seems to happen, the information from the Help topic is put into a part of the computer's memory, waiting to be pasted into a program.

❸ Paste a Help topic into WordPad:
- **Open** WordPad .
  The Help window remains on top of WordPad.
- **Change** to Rich Text Format (click File, New, Rich Text Document, OK).
- **Change** to Wrap text to ruler (click View, Options, the Rich Text tab, Wrap to ruler, OK) if it is not already selected.
- **Click** Edit, then Paste.
  The information from the Help topic appears in WordPad and the Help Topic stays on top, but it is not selected, that is, it is not active.

❹ Copy and paste part of a Help topic:
- **Switch** to the Help topic (click the Windows Help window or its task button on the taskbar).
- **Click** ⌷ Help Topics ⌷
- **Display** Printing a Help topic.
- **Move** the pointer around in the workspace.
  The pointer becomes an I-beam.
- **Move** the I-beam pointer just above *Tips*.
- **Drag** the I-beam pointer to the bottom right corner of the window.
  The text is highlighted.

- **Click** Options, then Copy.
- **Switch** to WordPad (click its window or the Document - Wordpad button).
- **Right-click** the workspace, then **click** Paste.
- **Press** ⏎ three times.
- **Type:** CONTENTS
- **Press** ⏎
- **Switch** to Windows Help (make it active).
- **Click** ⌷ Help Topics ⌷

Exercise 53 continued...

EXERCISE 53

Copy Help Topics

To copy the data in a Help topic and paste it into another program, such as WordPad.

 **STEPS to**

Use Help Topics, Index
—WITH HELP OPEN—
Select the Index tab
1 **Press** [Tab] or [Shift] + [Tab] until the current tab is selected.
2 **Press** ⬅ or ➡ to move to the Index tab.
Search for a subject
- **Type** the first few letters of the word for which you are looking.
  or
  Press [Tab] to move to the entries list and use arrow keys to locate and select the desired entry.
Display the topic or list of Topics Found
- **Press** ⏎
  IF the Topics Found dialog box appears:
  1 **Select** the desired topic.
  2 **Press** ⏎
Close a Windows Help topic
—WITH WINDOWS HELP OPEN—
1 **Press** [Alt] + [Space]
2 **Press** [C] (Close)
Return to Help Topics
—WITH WINDOWS HELP OPEN—
- **Press** [T] (Help Topics)

— **Terms and Notes** —

*NOTE: If filename extentions appear, for example, **help.rtf** instead of **help**, it is because the **Hide MS-DOS file extensions** command is not selected; the default is for it to be selected. (See Topic 22).*

5 **Copy and paste the text from a pop-up information window:**

- **Right-click** the Contents workspace, and then **click**
  or

  Click the question mark, and then **click** the Contents workspace.
  A pop-up window appears with information about the Contents section of Help Topics.

- **Right-click** the pop-up window.
  A small right-click menu appears.

  > Displays Help topics organized by category. Double-click a
  > book icon to see what topics are in that category. To see a
  > topic, double-click its icon.
  >
  > You can close a book by double-clicking it.
  >
  >   Copy
  >   Print Topic...

  — **small right-click menu**

- **Click** C̲opy.
- **Switch** to WordPad.
  WordPad moves to the front and part or all of Help is hidden.
- **Click** E̲dit, then P̲aste.
  or
  Right-click the workspace, then **click** P̲aste.

6 **Save the document in My Folder and print the copied Help text:**

- **Insert** your data disk in drive A:.
- **Click** F̲ile, then S̲ave.
- **Access** drive A:.
- **Open** My Folder.
- **Change** the Save as t̲ype box to Rich Text Format (RTF).
- **Click** the File n̲ame text box.
- **Delete** the text.
- **Type** the filename, **help**.
- **Click** [Save]
- **Print** the file.

To copy information from a Help topic

1   In the Help topic window, click the Edit menu or the Options button, and then click Copy.
      You can also use the right mouse button to click inside the topic or pop-up window.
2   In the document where you want the information to appear, click the place where you want to put the information.
3   On the Edit menu, click Paste.

Tip

    If you want to copy only part of a topic, select the part you want to copy before you click the Copy command.

Tips

You can print a group of related topics by clicking a book in the Help Contents and then clicking Print.
    To print the Help in a pop-up window, use your right mouse button to click inside the pop-up window, and then click Print Topic.

CONTENTS
Displays Help topics organized by category. Double-click a book icon to see what topics are in that category. To see a topic, double-click it.
You can close a book by double-clicking it.

---

7 - **Close** WordPad.
- **Close** Help Topics: Windows Help.
- **Close** the Windows Help window.

Begin with the desktop displayed and with no tasks on the taskbar.

① • **Start** Help (review, Exercise 49).
  • **Click** the Find tab if it is not already in front.
  • **Type:** ann
    The word, Annotate, appears in the word list.
  • **Click** [Display]

② **Annotate a Help topic:**
  • **Right-click** the workspace.
    or
    Click [Options]
  • **Click** <u>A</u>nnotate.
    The Annotate window appears.

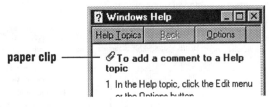

  • **Type:** An annotation is a note or comment that you add to a Help topic.
  • **Click** [Save]
    A paper clip is added in front of the topic name.

paper clip ——

  ③ **Open an annotation:**
  • **Click** the paper clip.
    or
    Click <u>O</u>ptions, then <u>A</u>nnotate.
    The Annotate window appears.

④ **Delete an annotation from a Help topic:**
  • **Click** [Delete]
    The Annotation window closes and the paper clip disappears from the Help topic.

⑤ • **Close** the Windows Help window.

Annotate Help Topics

To add a note or comment to Help topics.

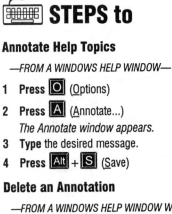

⌨ STEPS to

Annotate Help Topics
  —FROM A WINDOWS HELP WINDOW—
  1 **Press** [O] (<u>O</u>ptions)
  2 **Press** [A] (<u>A</u>nnotate...)
    The Annotate window appears.
  3 **Type** the desired message.
  4 **Press** [Alt] + [S] (<u>S</u>ave)

Delete an Annotation
  —FROM A WINDOWS HELP WINDOW WITH A PAPER CLIP—
  1 **Press** [O] (<u>O</u>ptions)
  2 **Press** [A] (<u>A</u>nnotate...)
    The Annotate window appears.
  3 **Press** [Alt] + [D] (<u>D</u>elete)

EXERCISE 55

Keep Help on Top

To make Help topics stay in front of other windows.

— Terms and Notes —

Keep Help on Top Options
Default
The Default option came with the Help file and may include different settings for different types of Help windows.

On Top
All Help windows in the current Help file stay on top.

Not On Top
None of the Help windows in the current Help file stay on top.

 **STEPS to**

Keep Help windows on top
—*FROM A WINDOWS HELP WINDOW*—

1 Press 🅾 (Options)
2 Press 🅚 (Keep Help on Top)
3 Press 🅾 (On Top)

Keep Help windows NOT on top
—*FROM A WINDOWS HELP WINDOW*—

1 Press 🅾 (Options)
2 Press 🅚 (Keep Help on Top)
3 Press 🅽 (Not On Top)

Use the default
—*FROM A WINDOWS HELP WINDOW*—

1 Press 🅾 (Options)
2 Press 🅚 (Keep Help on Top)
3 Press 🅳 (Default)

Why keep Help Windows on Top?

You may want to keep a Help window on top when you are trying to follow the Help topic's step-by-step directions while you perform a particular task.

Begin with the desktop displayed and with no tasks on the taskbar.

❶
- **Start** Help (review, Exercise 49, step 1).
- **Click** the Find tab if it is not already in front.
- **Type:** Top
  Three entries appear in the word list and 136 topics are found.
- **Click** the entry, Top.
  Now one topic is found and it is selected.
- **Click** [Display]

❷ Keep Help windows on top:
- **Right-click** the Help topic workspace.
- **Click** Keep Help on Top.
- **Click** On Top.

❸ Open programs to test the Keep On Top command:
- **Open** Notepad.
  The Help topic stays on top.
  NOTE: This may be the same result you had previously because the Default option is set to **On Top** *for some Help windows and to* **Not On Top** *for other windows.*
- **Open** Calculator.
- **Move** Calculator about halfway through the Help topic.
  Even though Calculator is still active, the Help topic stays on top.

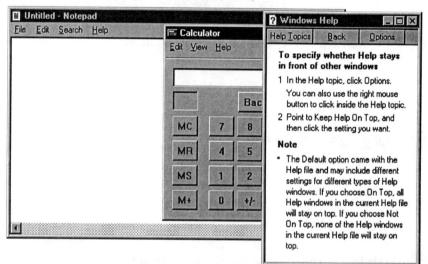

- **Click** [Help Topics]
  The Help Topics program appears; notice that the Help topic stays in back this time.
- **Close** the Help Topics program.
  The screen remains similar to the illustration above; Notepad, Calculator, and Windows Help are all open.

Exercise 55 continued...

4 **Keep Help windows in back:**

- **Right-click** the Help topic workspace.
- **Click** Keep Help on Top.
- **Click** Not On Top.
- **Click** the Calculator.
  The Calculator moves to the front; the Help topic goes in back.
- **Click** Notepad.
  Notepad moves to the front; the Help topic moves to the back. Calculator may be completely hidden.
- **Click** the Calculator task button.
  Calculator moves to the front; the Help topic remains in back.

[Screenshot showing Notepad, Calculator, and Help windows]

- **Click** the Windows Help task button.
  Now the Help topic moves to the front; the screen is similar to the illustration on the previous page.

5 **Use the default setting:**

The Default option may include different settings for different types of Help windows.

- **Right-click** the Help topic workspace.
- **Click** Keep Help on Top.
- **Click** Default.
- **Click** Notepad.
  The Help topic window remains in front.
- **Click** the Calculator task button.
  The Help topic window remains in front.

NOTE: The default for Windows' main Help Topics program is to keep Help topics on top.

6 • **Close** Windows Help, Calculator, and WordPad.

EXERCISE 56

Practice

**Lesson Four
Help**

Tasks Reviewed:
- Identify Button Names
- Identify Menu Information
- Use Dialog Box Help
- Use Help Topics, Contents
- Use Help Topics, Index
- Use Help Topics, Find

Begin with the desktop displayed and with no tasks on the taskbar.

1
- **Open** My Computer; display the entire toolbar and status bar.
- **Identify** the toolbar button names.
- **Identify** information about the <u>U</u>ndo option in the <u>E</u>dit menu.
- **Identify** information about each of the other commands on the <u>E</u>dit menu.
- **Close** My Computer.

2
- **Open** Notepad.
- **Click** <u>S</u>earch, then <u>F</u>ind—the Find dialog box appears.
- **Get** information (open a pop-up window) about:
  - Fi<u>n</u>d what
  - Match <u>c</u>ase
  - Direction
  - <u>F</u>ind Next
  - Cancel
- **Close** the Find dialog box and Notepad.

3
- **Start** Help.
- **Access** the Contents section.
- **Open** the How To... book, then the Work with Files and Folders book.
- **Display** the topic, Finding a file or folder.
- **Return** to the Help Topics program.

4
- **Display** the topic, Copying a file or folder.
- **Close** the Windows Help window.

5
- **Start** Help.
- **Access** the Index section.
- **Search** for information about shortcuts.
- **Display** the subtopic, about shortcuts.
- **Open** each of the *related topic buttons* displayed.
- **Return** to the Help Topics program.

6
- **Access** the Find section.
- **Rebuild** the word list.

7
- **Search** for information about help.
- **Click** the word entry, helps.
- **Display** the help topic, Troubleshooting hardware conflicts.
- **Open** the related topics button, "Display an overview of the process."
- **Go back** to the previous Help Topic.
- **Close** the Windows Help window.

Begin with the desktop displayed and with no tasks on the taskbar.

①
- **Start** Help.
- **Access** the Find section.
- **IF** the text box has a word in it, **click** [Clear]
- **Click** the word, able.
  Nine topics are found.
- **Display** the topic, Viewing information about a device driver.
- **Print** the Help topic.

Tasks Reviewed:
- Print Help Topics
- Copy Help Topics
- Annotate Help Topics
- Keep Help On Top

To view information about a device driver

1 Click here [ ] to display Device Manager.
2 Click the plus sign next to the type of hardware, and then double-click the hardware.
3 Click the Driver tab, and then click the device driver you want information about.

Tip
- Some devices don't have a Driver tab. In this case, you may be able to view information about the driver by double-clicking the icon in Control Panel that is specific to that type of hardware. See your hardware documentation for more information.

Related Topics

- **Return** to the Help Topics program.

②
- **Access** the Contents section of Help Topics.
- **Open** the Troubleshooting book.
- **Display** the topic, If you need more disk space.
- **Copy** the topic.

③
- **Open** WordPad.
- **Click** File, then New, then Rich Text Document, then [OK]
- **Click** View, then Options, then the Rich Text tab, then Wrap to ruler, then [OK]

④
- **Paste** the topic into WordPad.
- **Switch** back to the Help topic.
- **Return** to the Help Topics program.

⑤
- **Display** the topic, If you have trouble starting Windows.
- **Highlight** and **copy** the first section, Windows Startup Troubleshooter (but not the section, What do you want to do?).
- **Paste** the copied text into WordPad.
- **Press** [↵] twice.

⑥
- **Click** Format, then Paragraph.
  The Paragraph dialog box appears.
- **Get** information about the Alignment command.
- **Copy** the information in the pop-up window.
- **Close** the dialog box and **paste** the information into WordPad.

Exercise 57 continued...

7 • **Save** the document in My Folder on drive A: using the Rich Text Format (RTF); name it **help2**

• **Print** the document.

> Disk Space Troubleshooter
>
> This troubleshooter helps you solve problems you may encounter if you run out of disk space. To free up disk space, just click a method you want to try, and then carry out the suggested steps.
>
> ◇ Empty the Recycle Bin
> ◇ Use ScanDisk to check for errors that may be using up disk space
> ◇ Back up unneeded files and remove them from your hard disk
> ◇ Remove Windows components that you don't use
> ◇ Create more disk space by using DriveSpace disk compression
>
> ◇ See more ways to free up disk space
>
> Windows Startup Troubleshooter
>
> If you have trouble starting Windows, you can use several methods to start your computer with or without starting Windows or the network. After you identify and resolve the problem, you can restart your computer as you usually do.
>
> Lists the alignments available for the selected paragraph.
>
> Left: Aligns text at the left indent.
>
> Right: Aligns text at the right indent.
> Center: Centers the text between margins.

• **Close** WordPad without saving, if asked.

• **Click** the workspace of the Help topic to deselect the text.

8 • **Annotate** the Help Topic.

• **Type:** Making an annotation creates a paper clip icon in the topic to remind you that there is a note there.

• **Save** the annotation.

• **Open** the annotation and **delete** it.

9 • **Open** the Calculator and move it halfway through the Help topic. Which window stays on top? The Calculator or the Help topic?

• **Click** the Help topic and **change** the Keep Help on Top option to On Top.

10 • **Switch** to the Calculator; the Help topic should remain on top.

• **Switch** back to the Help topic and **change** the Keep Help on Top option to Not On Top.

• **Switch** to the Calculator; the Calculator should remain on top now.

11 • **Change** the Keep Help on Top option to Default.

• **Switch** to the Calculator. Which window stays on top?

12 • **Close** the Windows Help window and Calculator.

Exercise 57 continued...

Lesson Four Worksheet (12)
is in Appendix D

Lesson Five
The Desktop

Table of Contents

TOPIC 16
The Desktop

— Terms and Notes —

desktop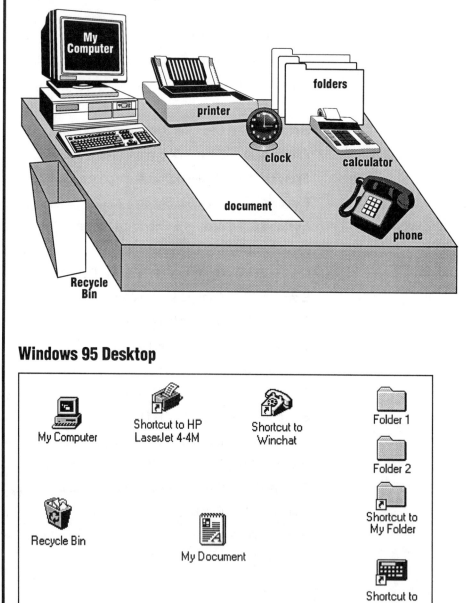
The simple opening screen in Windows 95 that contains a few objects, the Start menu, and a taskbar.

NOTE: The computer system is naturally structured with many levels (a hierarchy); but, by using shortcuts on the desktop, the structure seems to disappear. You can design a logical structure (grouping of files) to meet your individual needs.

The Desktop is Heart of Windows 95

The Windows 95 **desktop** is more than:

*   the large area you see when you start Windows,
*   the hierarchical structure managed by the shell, or
*   the background upon which a few graphical objects and a taskbar appear.

The desktop is the heart of Windows 95. The idea behind the Windows 95 desktop is that you can use it pretty much the way you use your personal desktop at home—to keep important items at your fingertips. If you put your computer, printer, clock, phone, folders, and documents on your real desktop, you can do the same with your Windows 95 desktop. You can decorate it to fit your mood *(see Exercise 15)*, and even scan (if you have a scanner) your favorite picture and put it on the desktop.

A Traditional Desktop

Windows 95 Desktop

Shortcuts are Powerful and Efficient

A **shortcut** is an icon you create that contains a pointer (a direct route) to a specific object (the **target**). The target object might be a document, program, folder, disk drive, or printer. A shortcut can always be identified by the **jump-arrow** that appears in the lower-left corner of its icon. You can think of a shortcut as simply being a different name to refer to an object, for example, a different name for *Calculator* might be *Shortcut to Calc* (both names will open the Calculator).

Shortcuts are powerful because they let you have quick access to all the objects you need while Windows does all the work of keeping track of what you are doing. Shortcuts are efficient because when you use a shortcut to jump from one place to another you do NOT have to:

- remember multiple folder and subfolder names,
- work through a lot of menus,
- open multiple folders, or
- type out long path names.

Creating a shortcut can be as easy as using Find to locate the object you want and then dragging the object onto the desktop. While you can place shortcuts in just about any location, a practical place to put shortcuts to the objects you use most often is on the desktop, where they are handy.

While shortcuts let you jump to different locations without appearing to follow a logical path, behind the scenes, Windows keeps precise track of your movements, as you can see in the shortcut's Properties dialog box below. To locate the path, open the shortcut's **property sheet**, click the Shortcut tab, and look at the Target box.

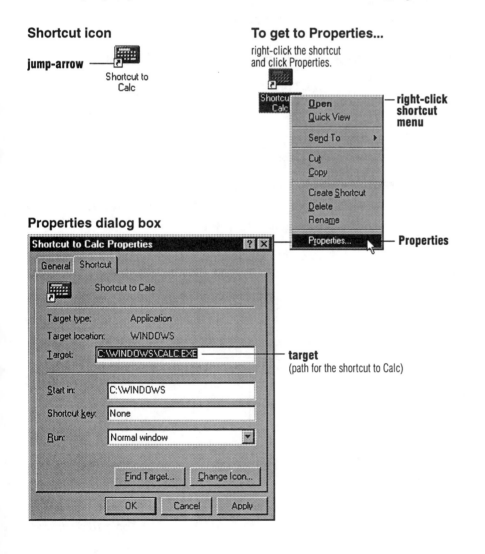

Shortcut icon

jump-arrow ——— Shortcut to Calc

To get to Properties...

right-click the shortcut and click Properties.

Shortcut to Calc

| Open |
| Quick View |
| Send To ▶ |
| Cut |
| Copy |
| Create Shortcut |
| Delete |
| Rename |
| Properties... |

—— right-click shortcut menu

—— Properties

Properties dialog box

Shortcut to Calc Properties [?][X]

General / Shortcut

Shortcut to Calc

Target type: Application
Target location: WINDOWS
Target: C:\WINDOWS\CALC.EXE —— **target** (path for the shortcut to Calc)

Start in: C:\WINDOWS
Shortcut key: None
Run: Normal window

Find Target...   Change Icon...

OK   Cancel   Apply

— Terms and Notes —

shortcut
An icon containing a direct route to a specific object and displaying a small jump-arrow in the lower-left corner. Double-click a shortcut to quickly open the file or program it represents. You can customize your desktop by creating shortcuts for the programs you use most often.

jump-arrow ↗
A small arrow that appears in the lower-left corner of *shortcut* icons thereby distinguishing them from other icons.

target
The name of the object to which a shortcut is pointing (the name includes the path to the object).

property sheet
A special kind of dialog box that groups the settings for an object's properties.

property
A characteristic of an object; many properties can be changed by using a control in a Properties dialog box.

*NOTES: Do not confuse **shortcuts** with the term shortcut as it is used in **right-click shortcut menus**, and **keyboard shortcuts**.*

You can create more than one shortcut to an object, and you can even create a shortcut to a shortcut.

TOPIC 18
Documents

document (data file)
Any data you create with a program, for example, a report or a picture. A document and a data file are the same thing

NOTE: Traditionally a document has been thought of as data created specifically in a word processor.

document-centric
A system that focuses on documents and their contents rather than the programs used to create the documents.

Documents are Central

If the desktop is the heart of Windows 95, and if shortcuts are powerful and efficient, then **documents** can be characterized as the *center of activity*. Most of what you do on your computer system revolves around producing documents of one kind or another. Realizing this, Microsoft designed Windows 95 to be **document-centric**, that is, centered around documents (rather than the programs used to create documents).

Different Ways to Open a Document

Using the Document menu:
- open the Start menu,
- open Document menu, and
- click the document (if listed as one of the fifteen documents last used).

Using the File menu:
- open a program,
- click the File menu, and
- click the document (if listed as one of the four documents last used).

Using the Open dialog box:
- open a program
- click File, then Open
- find the folder the document is in, and finally,
- click the filename, then OK.

Double-clicking a document file:
- double-click a document anywhere you see it.

Different Kinds of Actions You Might Perform on a Document

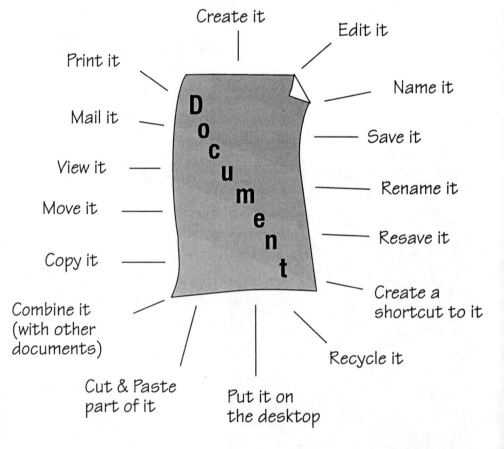

Topic 18 continued...

The Documents Menu

On the Start menu, Documents are listed before Programs (when moving up), and when you open the Documents menu, up to 15 of the most recently used documents are listed.

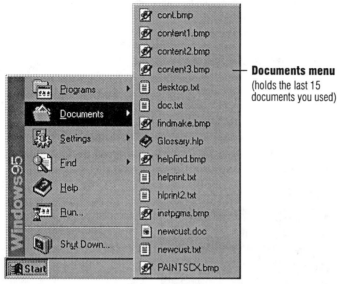

Documents menu
(holds the last 15 documents you used)

Documents on the File Menu

The last four documents you open are listed on the File menu in WordPad. Simply click a document listed on the File menu to open it.

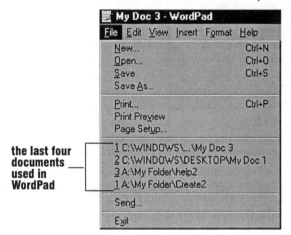

the last four documents used in WordPad

Double-click a Document File

The illustration below shows documents in a folder window.

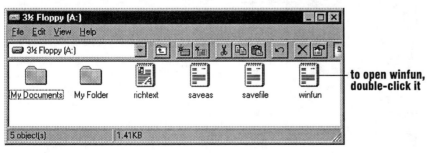

to open winfun, double-click it

EXERCISE 58

Clear the Documents Menu

To access the Taskbar Properties dialog box and empty the Documents menu.

— Terms and Notes —

YOU MAY WANT TO COMPLETE LESSON FIVE IN ONE SESSION

IMPORTANT: If you are in a training environment and if you do not have a separate user profile (see Appendix B), you should complete Lesson Five in one session.

 **STEPS to**

Clear the Documents menu

1 Press `Ctrl` + `Esc` (Start menu)
2 Press `S` (Settings)
3 Press `T` (Taskbar)
4 Press `Shift` + `Tab` to select the Taskbar Options tab.
5 Press `→` select the Start Menu Programs tab.
6 Press `Alt` + `C` (Clear)
7 Press `↵`

Begin with the desktop displayed and with no tasks on the taskbar.

① Look at the documents in the Documents menu:

- **Open** the Start menu.
- **Open** the Documents menu.
  The Documents menu displays up to 15 of the last documents used (see Topic 18).
- **Click** outside the menus to close them.

② Open the Taskbar Properties dialog box:

- **Right-click** the taskbar.
- **Click** Properties.

③ Clear the Documents menu:

- **Click** the Start Menu Programs tab.
  The Start Menu Programs section moves to the front.

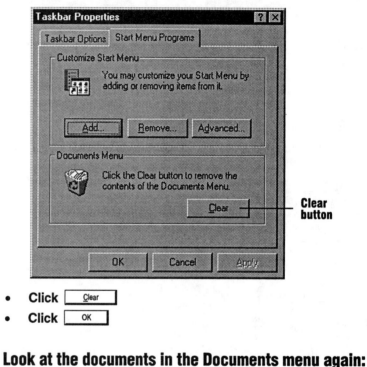

Clear button

- **Click** [Clear]
- **Click** [OK]

④ Look at the documents in the Documents menu again:

- **Open** the Start menu.
- **Open** the Documents menu.
  The Documents menu is empty.

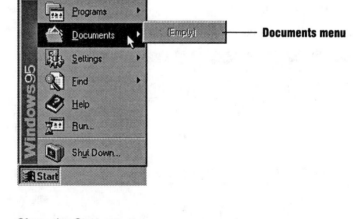

Documents menu

⑤ · Close the Start menu.

Begin with the desktop displayed and with no tasks on the taskbar.

1
- **Start** WordPad.
- **Click** File, then New, then Rich Text Document, then [OK]
- **Make sure** word wrap is set to Wrap to ruler (review, Exercise 28).

2 Create a document:
- **Type:** Most of what you do on your computer system is centered around producing documents of one kind or another. Microsoft designed Windows 95 to be document-centric, that is, centered around documents rather than the programs used to create documents.
- **Press** [Ctrl] + [S] (Save).

  or

  Click [💾] (the Save button on toolbar).
  The Save As dialog box opens.

3 Save the document on the desktop using a long filename:
- **IF** Desktop is not displayed in the Save in list box,

  click [📁] until Desktop is displayed in the Save in list box.
- **Change** Save as type to Rich Text Format (RTF) if it is not already there.
- **Delete** the information in the File name text box.
- **Type:** My Doc 1
  The Save As dialog looks something like this.

Desktop ——

- **Click** [Save]

4
- **Print My Doc 1** (review, Exercise 20).

> Most of what you do on your computer system is centered around producing documents of one kind or another. Microsoft designed Windows 95 to be document-centric, that is, centered around documents rather than the programs used to create documents.

5
- **Close** WordPad.

  *The document, **My Doc 1**, appears somewhere on the desktop.*

  My Doc 1

  WARNING: If the icon name appears as My Doc 1.rtf, then:
  - ***Right-click** My Computer, click Explore, then View, then Options.*
  - ***Click** Hide MS-DOS file extensions for file types that are registered.*
  - ***Click** [OK], then **exit** Explorer.*

EXERCISE 59
Save a Document on the Desktop

To choose the desktop in the Save in list box of the Save As dialog box.

— Terms and Notes —

long filename
A filename that is up to 255 characters long and can contain spaces and most symbols.
*NOTES: A filename is classified as **long** when it is longer than eight characters, contains a space, and/or contains any of the following characters: [ ]+=;, . (Not the period; it is used only to add a filename extension of a period and up to three letters to a filename, whether it is long or short.)*
*When you save a file with a **long filename**, Windows saves not only the long filename, but a **short filename** that meets the conventional filenaming rules (see Topic 11).*

⌨ STEPS to

Save a document on the desktop
1 **Open** WordPad (or other program).
   IF WordPad...
   change to Rich Text Format:
   - **Press** [Alt] + [F] (File)
   - **Press** [N] (New)
   - **Press** [↓] to select Rich Text Document.
   - **Press** [↵]
   Change wrap option to wrap to ruler:
   - **Press** [Alt] + [V] (View)
   - **Press** [O] (Options)
   - **Press** [A] (Wrap to ruler)
   - **Press** [↵]
2 **Create** a document.
3 **Press** [Alt] + [F] (File)
4 **Press** [A] (Save As)
5 **Press** [Alt] + [I] (Save in)
6 **Press** [↓] to open the list.
7 **Press** [Page Up] to select Desktop.
8 **Press** [↵]
9 **Press** [Alt] + [N] (File name)
10 **Type** a filename.
11 **Press** [↵]
12 **Exit** WordPad (or other program).

EXERCISE 60

Create a Document on the Desktop

To start the process of creating a document when you are in the desktop area.

— Terms and Notes —

WARNING: A comment about the warning at the bottom of the previous exercise:

If MS-DOS file extensions are displayed, this exercise will not perform as expected; when you try to change the filename, you will get a WARNING dialog box. If you DO get a warning dialog box about changing the filename extension, click No *, press* Esc *, press* Del *, and click* Yes *Do the procedure at the end of Lesson 59, and start this exercise again. Hiding and displaying MS-DOS file extensions is covered in Lesson Six.*

Begin with the desktop displayed and with no tasks on the taskbar.

1 Create a new document from the desktop:

- **Right-click** an empty spot on the desktop.
  The right-click shortcut menu appears.
- **Click** New, then Text Document.
  *The **New Text Document** icon appears on the desktop with the icon selected and the cursor blinking at the end of the highlighted name.*

2 Change the document's name:

While the text is still highlighted:

- **Type:** My Doc 2 and **press** ⏎
  The original text disappears, the new text appears, and the icon is still highlighted.

- **Click** a blank spot on the desktop.
  The highlighting disappears, but the text still has a dotted line around it.

 — **dotted line** (a sign that this was last icon selected)

- **Click My Doc 1.**
  My Doc 1 *is selected, and the dotted line disappears from **My Doc 2**.*

My Doc 2 — **no dotted line**

3 Open the newly created, empty document:

- **Double-click** the **My Doc 2** icon.
  or
- **Right-click** the **My Doc 2** icon and **click** Open.
  Notepad opens with an empty screen and a title of My Doc 2 - Notepad

4 Edit the document and save it:

- **Type:** The idea behind the Windows 95 desktop is that you can use it ⏎ pretty much the way you use your personal desktop. You can put ⏎ your computer, clock, phone, folders, and documents on the ⏎ Windows 95 desktop. You can decorate it to fit your mood, and ⏎ even scan your favorite picture and put it on the desktop.
- **Click** File, then Save.
  The document is saved on the desktop.

5 • **Exit** Notepad.

Begin with the desktop displayed and with no tasks on the taskbar.

① Create a shortcut by right-clicking an object:

- **Open** My Computer.
- **Browse** folders using a single window (review, Exercise 32).
- **Open** the Printers folder.
- **Identify** the icon for the printer that is currently connected to your computer system; if there is more than one printer, pick the printer you want to use.
- **Right-click** the printer icon.
- **Click** Create Shortcut.
  A Shortcut dialog box appears.

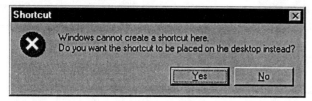

- **Click** Yes.
- **Close** the Printers folder.
  The Shortcut to printer is displayed on the desktop.

Shortcut to HP
LaserJet 4-4M ——— **your printer's name**

② Create a shortcut by left-dragging an object:

- **Open** My Computer, then drive C:, then Windows.
- **Find** Calc (the Calculator program).
- **Move** the Windows folder so that the top right corner of the desktop is visible.
- **Drag** Calc to the top right corner of the desktop.
  A Shortcut icon appears on the desktop.

- **Click** outside the icon to deselect it.
- **Close** the Windows folder.

③ Create a shortcut by right-dragging an object:

- **Open** My Computer.
- **Insert** your disk in drive A:.
- **Open** the Floppy (A:) folder.
- **Right-drag** (drag using the right mouse button) **savefile** to the desktop.
  A right-click menu appears.
- **Click** Create Shortcut(s) Here.
  The Shortcut to saveas icon is created.
- **Browse** folders using separate windows (review, Exercise 31).
- **Close** the Floppy (A:) folder.

Exercise 61 continued...

EXERCISE 61

Create a Shortcut

To create an new icon that points to an object.

— Terms and Notes —

common ways to create shortcuts:
- right-drag an object
- left-drag an object
- right-click an object
- right-click the desktop or a folder's workspace

NOTE: Although there are several ways to create a shortcut, not every method works for every object.

shortcut
An icon containing a direct route to a specific object and displaying a small jump-arrow in the lower-left corner. Double-click a shortcut to quickly open the file or program it represents. You can customize your desktop by creating shortcuts for the programs you use most often.

NOTE: The procedure to create a shortcut may be slightly different depending upon where the object (for which you are creating the shortcut) is located.

right-drag (mouse action)
- Move the pointer on an item.
- Hold down the *right* mouse button.
- Slide the pointer to a new location.
- Release the mouse button.

NOTES: Notice that the filename in the Command line text box includes a three letter filename extension (see Topic 11). Most files are assigned a filename extensior even though they are usually not visible to you.

Windows 95 uses filename extensions to recognize file types. Filename extensions are covered in Lesson Six.

 **STEPS to**

STEPS to are on the next page.

CREATE A SHORTCUT

— Terms and Notes —

command line
A place where you enter the path to a file.

path
The route to a folder or file; it consists of the disk drive, folder, subfolders (if any), and the filename (if the path is to a file). For example, C:\WINDOWS\CALC is the path to the Calculator program. If long folder names or filenames are used in a path, the path must be enclosed in quotes ("). For example, "A:\My Folder\help2.rtf" is the path to the document file, help2 on drive A:.

 **STEPS to**

Create a shortcut

For the Printer
1 **Open** My Computer *(see page 61)*.
2 **Open** the Printers *folder (see page 62)*.
3 **Select** the desired printer.
4 **Press** `Alt` + `F` (File)
5 **Press** `S` (Create Shortcut)
6 **Press** `Y` (Yes)
7 **Close** all the open folders.

For the Calculator
1 **Open** My Computer *(see page 61)*.
2 **Turn** on the toolbar if it's not already on:
   • **Press** `Alt` + `V` (View)
   • **Press** `T` (Toolbar)
3 **Press** `Tab` until you select the Go to a different folder drop-down list box.
4 **Press** `↓` to open the list.
5 **Press** `Page Up` to select Desktop.
6 **Press** `↵`
7 **Press** `Alt` + `F` (File)
8 **Press** `W` (New)
9 **Press** `S` (Shortcut)
10 **Press** `Alt` + `R` (Browse)
11 **Open** the Windows folder:
   • **Press** `Tab` until a dotted line appears around a folder in the workspace.
   • **Press** arrow keys until you find and highlight the Windows folder.
   • **Press** `↵`
12 **Press** `C` until Calc is highlighted.
13 **Press** `↵` three times.
14 **Close** the open folders *(see page 61)*.

---

4 **Create a shortcut by right-clicking the desktop:**

• **Right-click** a blank area of the desktop.
  The right-click menu opens.

• **Click** New, then Shortcut.
  The Create Shortcut dialog box opens with the cursor blinking in the Command line text box.

[Create Shortcut dialog box]

Type the location and name of the item you want to create a shortcut to. Or, search for the item by clicking Browse.

Command line: ——— **Command line**

Browse... ——— **Browse button**

< Back   Next >   Cancel

• **Click** [Browse...]
  The Browse dialog box opens; it looks just like the Open dialog box.

• **Open** the drive A: folder (click Look in, then Floppy (A:)).

• **Change** Files of type to All Files.

• **Open** My Folder.
  The files within My Folder appear in the workspace.

[Browse dialog box]

Look in ——— Look in: My Folder

files in My Folder ———
create1
create2
help
help2

File name: Open

Files of type ——— Files of type: All Files   Cancel

• **Click help2**, then [Open]
  The name of the item (or target) that the shortcut points to appears in the Command line in the Create Shortcut dialog box.

path ———
Command line:
"A:\My Folder\help2.rtf"

• **Click** [Next >]
• **Click** [Finish]
  The help2 shortcut appears on the desktop.

help2

① Look at the Calculator shortcut's property sheet:

- **Right-click** the Shortcut to Calc icon.
- **Click** Properties.
  The Shortcut to Calc Properties dialog box is opened.

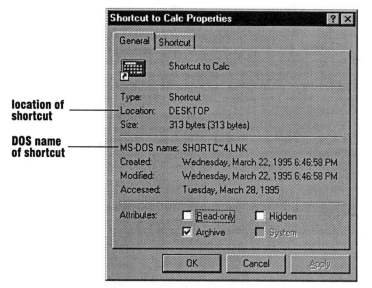

location of shortcut —

DOS name of shortcut —

- **Click** the Shortcut tab.
  The Shortcut tab moves to the front.

Target ——
The target is the entire path to the file the shortcut is pointing to (the filename is CALC.EXE).

② Use on-line help to get information about properties:

- **Click** [?], then **Target**.
  A pop-up window opens with information about the Target type.
- **Read** the information.
- **Right-click** Target location, then **click**  What's This?
  A pop-up window opens with information about the Target location.
- **Get** on-line help for the remaining items using the method you prefer.
- **Close** the Shortcut to Calc Properties dialog box.

Exercise 62 continued...

EXERCISE 62

Look at a Shortcut's Property Sheet

To open a shortcut's properties dialog box and examine the shortcut's properties.

— Terms and Notes —

property sheet
A special kind of dialog box that groups the settings for an object's properties.

target
The name of the object to which a shortcut is pointing (the name includes the path to the object).

some properties for shortcuts are:
- type of file
- location of file
- size of file
- MS-DOS name of file
- date file was created
- date file was modified
- date file was last accessed
- attributes for the file
- target file's type
- target file's location
- target file's name
- folder to start in (contains the original item)
- shortcut's shortcut key
- kind of window the file will run in; normal, maximized, or minimized

⌨ **STEPS to**

Look at a Shortcut's Property Sheet
For a Shortcut on the Desktop

1 **Press** [Tab] until an item on the desktop is selected.
2 **Press** arrow keys to select the desired shortcut.
3 **Press** [Alt] + [↵]
4 **Press** [Ctrl] + [Tab] until the Shortcut tab moves forward.
5 **Press** [Esc] to cancel the property sheet.

LOOK AT A SHORTCUT PROPERTY SHEET

— Terms and Notes —

NOTES: Examining shortcut properties helps you understand shortcuts.

Notice that the filename in the Target item of the Properties dialog box includes a three letter filename extension (see Topic 11). Most files are assigned a filename extension even though they are usually not visible. Windows 95 uses filename extensions to associate a file with a program.

3 **Look at a document shortcut's property sheet:**

- **Right-click** the Shortcut to savefile.
- **Click** Properties.
  The Shortcut to savefile Properties dialog box is opened.
- **Click** the Shortcut tab.
  The Shortcut section moves to the front.

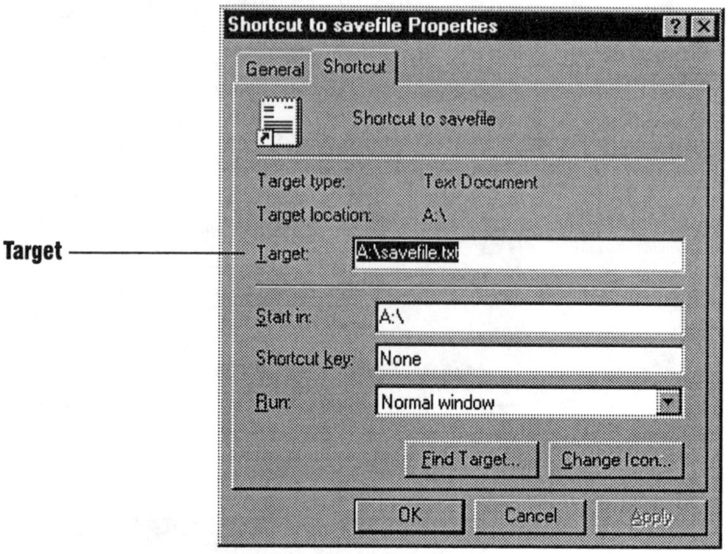

Target ——

Shortcut to savefile Properties	? X
General Shortcut	

Shortcut to savefile

Target type:	Text Document
Target location:	A:\
Target:	A:\savefile.txt

Start in:	A:\
Shortcut key:	None
Run:	Normal window

Find Target...   Change Icon...

OK   Cancel   Apply

- **Look** at the information.
- **Close** the dialog box.

4 **Look at a printer shortcut's property sheet:**

- **Right-click** the Shortcut to (your printer).
- **Click** Properties.
  The Shortcut to (your printer) Properties dialog box is opened.
- **Click** the Shortcut tab.
- **Look** at the information.
- **Close** the dialog box.

Begin with the desktop displayed and with no tasks on the taskbar.

1 **Drag and drop a document from the desktop onto the printer:**

- **Make** sure the printer is ready to receive data.
- **Drag My Doc 2** onto your printer's shortcut icon.

  My Doc 2 is printed. (If you watch, you will see Notepad open, My Doc 2 open, the document get sent to the printer, and Notepad close.

My Doc 2

The idea behind the Windows 95 desktop is that you can use it
pretty much the way you use your personal desktop. You can put
your computer, clock, phone, folders, and documents on the
Windows 95 desktop. You can decorate it to fit your mood, and
even scan your favorite picture and put it on the desktop.

Page 1

---

2 **Drag and drop a document shortcut from drive A: onto the printer:**

With your data disk still in drive A:

- **Drag** Shortcut to savefile onto your printer's icon.

  Savefile is printed.

---

savefile

Notepad is a program (also called an application) that is used
to create and edit unformatted text files. An unformatted text
file is a file that contains only ASCII text characters (letters,
numbers, and symbols) and a few codes such as a carriage return.

WordPad is a simple word processor. WordPad has automatic
word wrap, so you do not have to press Enter at the end of each
line(as you do in Notepad). You press Enter only at the end
of short lines and paragraphs in WordPad.

The Save command either resaves a previously named document or
opens the Save As dialog box so you can name and save a new
document.

Page 1

EXERCISE 63

Use Drag and Drop to Print

To drag a document and deposit it on the printer shortcut so it can be printed.

— Terms and Notes —

drag and drop
A procedure in which you drag a document and drop it on an object so the object can do something useful to the document, for example, move, copy, delete, or print it.

NOTE: The drag and drop procedure has been used in previous exercises without calling it drag and drop. For example, in Exercise 4 you were instructed to move a file into a folder by using the drag and drop procedure.

EXERCISE 64

Create a Folder on the Desktop

To make a new folder on the desktop.

Begin with the desktop displayed and with no tasks on the taskbar.

1 **Create a new folder on the desktop:**

- **Right-click** an empty spot on the desktop.
  The right-click shortcut menu appears.
- **Click** New, then Folder.
  The New Folder icon appears on the desktop with the icon selected and the cursor blinking at the end of the highlighted name.

New Folder

- **Type:** My Tools and **press** ↵
  The My Tools folder icon appears selected on the desktop.

My Tools

2 **Create a folder from the Save As dialog box:**

- **Open** Notepad.
- **Type:** You can create a new folder when you save a document. When you ↵ are in the Save As dialog box, simply right-click the workspace, ↵ and then click New, then Folder.
- **Click** File, then Save As.
- **Click** 🔼 until Desktop appears in the Save in box.
- **Click** the List button if it is not already pressed.
- **Right-click** the workspace, and then **click** New, then Folder.
- **Type:** My Documents and **press** ↵
  The My Documents folder appears in the workspace and it is selected.

My Documents

- **Double-click** the My Documents folder to open it.
- **Type:** My Doc 3 in the File name text box.
- **Click** [Save]
- **Exit** Notepad.
  The My Documents folder appears somewhere on the desktop.

My Documents

3 **Open the newly created folder:**

- **Double-click** My Documents (or right-click it, then click Open).
  *My Documents opens and displays the newly created document (file), **My Doc 3**.*

- **Close** My Documents.

 **STEPS to**

Create a folder on the desktop

1 **Open** My Computer (*see page 61*).
2 **Turn** on the toolbar if it's not already on:
  - **Press** Alt + V (View)
  - **Press** T (Toolbar)
3 **Press** Tab until you select the Go to a different folder drop-down list box.
4 **Press** ↓ to open the list.
5 **Press** Page Up to select Desktop.
6 **Press** ↵
7 **Press** Alt + F (File)
8 **Press** W (New)
9 **Press** F (Folder)
10 **Type** a new folder name, if desired.
11 **Press** ↵
12 **Press** Alt + F4

Begin with the desktop displayed and with no tasks on the taskbar.

Arrange the Desktop

To move objects around on the desktop and line up the icons.

1 **Move objects around on the desktop:**

- **Drag** the objects you have created in this lesson (documents, folders, and shortcuts) to the top right area on the desktop so they look something like this:

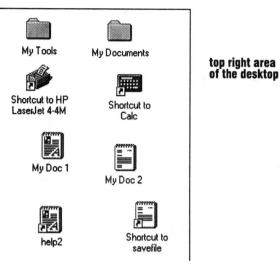

top right area of the desktop

2 **Line up the icons on the desktop:**

- **Right-click** an empty area on the desktop.
- **Click** Line up Icons.

The icons are evenly aligned. You may need to adjust the icons a second time and line them up again.

aligned icons

EXERCISE 66

Capture the Screen

To copy an image of the entire screen and paste it in a program.

Begin with the desktop displayed and with no tasks on the taskbar.

1 **Copy an image of the desktop:**

- **Press** ▦ (Print Screen).

  Nothing seems to happen, but if all went well, an image of the screen was copied.

2 **Paste the screen image into WordPad:**

- **Open** and **maximize** WordPad.
- **Click** <u>E</u>dit, then <u>P</u>aste.

  The captured screen image appears in the WordPad workspace.

  NOTES: When you paste the image into WordPad, the workspace scrolls to the bottom of the image. To view the top of the image, you can click the up arrow in the scroll bar until you reach the top of the document.

  If you click anywhere inside the image, lines surround the image and small squares appear at the corners and middle of the lines. If you click the left edge of the screen, the image reverses colors. Press Ctrl *+* Home *to deselect the image.*

3 **Print the screen image:**

- **Make** sure the printer is ready to receive data.
- **Click** 🖨 (the Print button) (or click <u>F</u>ile, <u>P</u>rint, OK).

  The screen capture is printed; your image may be slightly different.

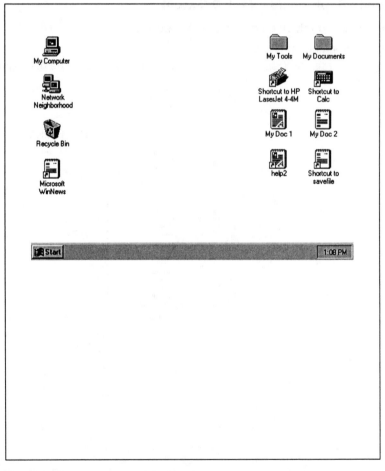

- **Exit** WordPad without saving the document.

 **STEPS to**

Capture the screen

- **Press** ▦ (Print Screen)

Print the Capture

1 **Open** WordPad.
2 **Press** Ctrl + V (Paste)
3 **Print** the document.
4 **Exit** WordPad.

Begin with the desktop displayed and with no tasks on the taskbar.

1 Open a window:

- **Open** the My Documents folder.
- **Display** the toolbar and status bar if they are not already displayed.
- **Size** the window wide enough to show the entire status bar and about 2.5 inches high.

2 Capture a window:

With the title bar of My Documents highlighted:

- **Press** [Alt] + [Print Scrn] (hold down [Alt], tap [Print Scrn] and then release [Alt]).

  Nothing seems to happen, but if all went well, an image of the window was copied.

3 Paste the image into WordPad:

- **Open** WordPad.
- **Click** [icon] (the Paste button) (or click Edit, Paste).

  The screen image appears in the WordPad workspace.

4 Print the window image:

- **Make** sure the printer is ready to receive data.
- **Click** [icon] (the Print button) (or click File, Print, OK).

  The screen capture is printed.

```
My Documents                                    _ □ ✕
File  Edit  View  Help

My Documents         ▼  [toolbar icons]

  [document icon]
  My Doc 3

1 object(s)            4.50KB
```

- **Exit** WordPad without saving the document.
- **Close** the My Documents folder.

Capture a Window

To copy an image of the active window.

 **STEPS to**

Capture a window

1 **Open** or **select** the desired window.

2 **Press** [Alt] + [Print Scrn]

Print the capture

1 **Open** WordPad.

2 **Press** [Ctrl] + [V] (Paste)

3 **Print** the document.

4 **Exit** WordPad.

EXERCISE 68

Undo
an Action

To reverse a file operation
or series of file operations.

 **STEPS to**

Select a file or folder
1 **Open** My Folder (*see page 61*).
2 **Turn** on the toolbar if it's not already on:
   - **Press** `Alt` + `V` (View)
   - **Press** `T` (Toolbar)
3 **Press** `Tab` until you select the Go to a different folder drop-down list box.
4 **Press** `↓` to open the list.
5 **Press** `Page Up` to select Desktop.
6 **Press** `↵`
7 **Press** `Tab` to move to the workspace.
8 **Press** arrow keys to select a file or folder.

Make a change
Rename an icon
1 **Press** `Alt` + `F` (File)
   or **Press** `Shift` + `F10`
2 **Press** `M` (Rename)
3 **Type** the new name.
4 **Press** `↵`
Delete an icon
1 **Press** `Alt` + `F` (File)
   or **Press** `Shift` + `F10`
2 **Press** `D` (Delete)
3 **Press** `Y` (Yes)
NOTE: You cannot undo a deleted folder.
Copy/paste a shortcut or document
1 **Press** `Ctrl` + `C` (Copy)
2 **Change** to a new location, if desired.
3 **Press** `Ctrl` + `V` (Paste)
Move a shortcut or document
1 **Press** `Ctrl` + `X` (Cut)
   The icon dims.
2 **Open** a different folder.
3 **Press** `Ctrl` + `V` (Paste)
   The icon appears in the folder.
4 **Return** to the first folder.
   The original icon has disappeared.
Undo an action
1 **Press** `Alt` + `E` (Edit)
2 **Press** `U` (Undo)
IF undoing a copy: **Press** `Y` (Yes)
Close the open folders
- **Press** `Alt` + `F4` to close each folder.

❶ Change a shortcut's name, then undo the change:
- **Click** the **help2** shortcut icon.
- **Click** the name itself so you can rename the icon.
- **Type:** Get Help and **press** `↵`
- **Right-click** an empty area on the desktop.
  The right-click menu appears.

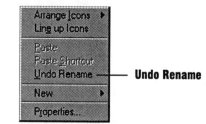

  Arrange Icons ▶
  Line up Icons

  Paste
  Paste Shortcut
  Undo Rename ——— **Undo Rename**

  New ▶

  Properties...

- **Click** Undo Rename.
  The shortcut's name returns to help2

❷ Perform several file operations:
CHANGE AN ICON'S NAME
- **Click** the **help2** shortcut icon, then the name itself.
- **Type:** Get More Help and **press** `↵`
PUT A DOCUMENT IN A FOLDER
- **Drag and drop My Doc 1** on the My Documents folder.
DELETE A DOCUMENT
- **Right-click My Doc 2**, then **click** Delete.
  or
  Click My Doc 2, then **press** `Del`
  *The Confirm File Delete dialog box appears, asking if you are sure you want to send **My Doc 2** to the Recycle Bin.*
- **Click** Yes.

❸ Undo a series of actions:
UNDO THE LAST ACTION (DELETE)
- **Right-click** an empty area on the desktop.
  The right-click menu appears with an Undo Delete option.
- **Click** Undo Delete.
  My Doc 2 appears in the first empty spot on the desktop.
UNDO THE MIDDLE ACTION (MOVE)
- **Right-click** an empty area on the desktop.
  The right-click menu appears with an Undo Move option.
- **Click** Undo Move.
  My Doc 1 appears in the first empty spot on the desktop.
UNDO THE FIRST ACTION (RENAME)
- **Right-click** an empty area on the desktop.
  The right-click menu appears with an Undo Rename option.
- **Click** Undo Rename.
  *The shortcut's name returns to **help2**.*

❹
- **Drag My Doc 1** and **My Doc 2** back to their previous positions, on the right side of the desktop.
- **Line up** the documents (review, Exercise 65).

Begin with the desktop displayed and with no tasks on the taskbar.

1 Empty the Recycle Bin:

- **Right-click** the Recycle Bin.
- **Click** Empty Recycle Bin, then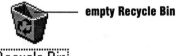
- **IF** the Recycle Bin is already empty, click outside the menu to close it.
  An empty Recycle Bin is displayed.

 — **empty Recycle Bin**

Recycle Bin

2 Put a document in the Recycle Bin:

- **Drag and drop** the **help2** shortcut on the Recycle Bin.
  The shortcut disappears, and the Recycle Bin now has something in it.

— **something is in the Recycle Bin**

Recycle Bin

3 Put a group of objects in the Recycle Bin:

HINTS:

When you select a group of objects, start with the pointer outside the objects rather than on an object (if you start too close to an object, it will move).

When you drag the group, drag an object rather than the space between objects. If you deselect the group when you try to drag it, try the procedure again.

When you drop the group, be sure the Recycle Bin's name is highlighted before you release the mouse button.

- **Drag** the pointer to select (highlight) several objects as illustrated below:

start here —

drag the pointer diagonally
to this corner

- **Drag and drop** the group of selected objects on the Recycle Bin as illustrated below.

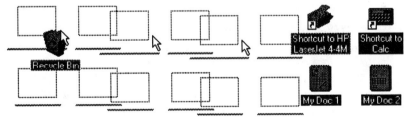

Exercise 69 continued...

EXERCISE 69

Use the Recycle Bin

To put objects to be deleted in the Recycle Bin, to empty the Recycle Bin, or to restore objects in the Recycle Bin.

— Terms and Notes —

About the Recycle Bin, Undo, and delete:

- When you delete an object, it goes into the Recycle Bin and you must confirm the deletion.
- When you put an object in the Recycle Bin, you do not need to confirm the deletion (as you do when you delete it).
- When an object is in the Recycle Bin, you can use the Undo command to restore it.
- Once you empty the Recycle Bin, you cannot restore (or undo) any objects that were in it.

STEPS to

—WITH THE DESKTOP SHOWING—

Empty the Recycle Bin
1 Press `Ctrl` + `Esc`, `Esc`, `Tab`, `Tab`.
2 Press arrow keys until the Recycle Bin is highlighted.
3 Press `↵` to open the Recycle Bin.
4 Press `Alt` + `F` (File)
5 Press `B` (Empty Recycle Bin), `Y` (Yes)
6 Press `Alt` + `F` (Close)

Put an object in the Recycle Bin
1 Press `Tab` until an object on the desktop is selected.
2 Press arrow keys until the desired object is highlighted.
3 Press `Del` (Delete), `Y` (Yes)

Restore an object
1 Press `Ctrl` + `Esc`, `Esc`, `Tab`, `Tab`.
2 Press arrow keys until the Recycle Bin is highlighted.
3 Press `↵` to open the Recycle Bin.
4 IF Toolbar is displayed, Press `Tab` until an object in the workspace is selected.
5 Press arrow keys until the desired object is highlighted.
6 Press `Alt` + `F` (File)
7 Press `E` (Restore), `Y` (Yes)
8 Press `Alt` + `F` (File), `C` (Close)

NOTE: Objects in the Recycle Bin take up space on your hard disk. If you need more disk space, empty your Recycle Bin. Even if you do not need more space, it is a good idea to check and empty the Recycle Bin periodically.

Exercise 69 (continued)

④ Open the Recycle Bin:

- **Right-click** the Recycle Bin, then **click** <u>O</u>pen.

  or

  Double-click the Recycle Bin.
- **Display** the toolbar (if not already displayed) and large icons (if not already selected).

  The Recycle Bin folder appears with the toolbar and the deleted items displayed as large icons.

  ```
  Recycle Bin                                        _ □ ✕
   File  Edit  View  Help
   Recycle Bin           ▼  🔼  ✂  📋📋  ↶  ✕  📄  📊  ▦  ▤

     help2      My Doc 1   My Doc 2   Shortcut to   Shortcut to HP
                                        Calc        LaserJet 4-4M

   5 object(s)              10.1KB
  ```

⑤ Restore objects in the Recycle Bin:

- **Drag** the pointer to select the last two objects in the Recycle Bin.

  NOTE: You can just drag across the icons rather than surround them.

  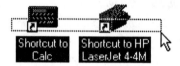

- **Click** <u>F</u>ile, then <u>R</u>estore.

  The two objects disappear from the Recycle Bin, and are returned to the desktop.
- **Drag** the pointer to select **My Doc 1** and **My Doc 2**.
- **Drag** the documents from the Recycle Bin to the desktop.

  One object remains in the Recycle Bin, help2

⑥ Empty the Recycle Bin:

- **Click** <u>F</u>ile, then Empty Recycle <u>B</u>in.

  The Confirm File Delete dialog box appears.
- **Click** [Yes]
- **Close** the Recycle Bin folder.

⑦
- **Move** the recycled objects back to the top right corner of the desktop.

  NOTE: When objects are recycled to the desktop, they usually move into the first available spot. However, sometimes an icon may move on top of another icon. If you look closely, you can usually spot these doubled-up icons. Simply drag one icon off the other icon. Occasionally objects are so closely aligned that it is hard to see that there are two icons together, but if you are sure there should be another icon, you can try dragging some to see if another icon exists under them.
- **Line up** the icons.

Organizing Your Desktop

Organizing the desktop can put the many objects you use most often within easy reach without cluttering your desktop. Simply create a few folders and move documents (and shortcuts to document) into folders as desired; for example, you may want to put all the documents relating to a certain project in one folder. You may even want to create subfolders (folders within a folder) to further organize your documents.

Begin with the desktop displayed and with no tasks on the taskbar.

1 **Move documents and shortcuts to document into My Documents:**

- **Drag and drop** Shortcut to savefile on My Documents.
- **Select My Doc 1** and **My Doc 2**.
- **Drag and drop My Doc 1** and **My Doc 2** on My Documents.

2 **Move objects into My Tools:**

- **Drag and drop** the Shortcut to (your printer) and Shortcut to Calc on My Tools.

The destop is cleaned up.

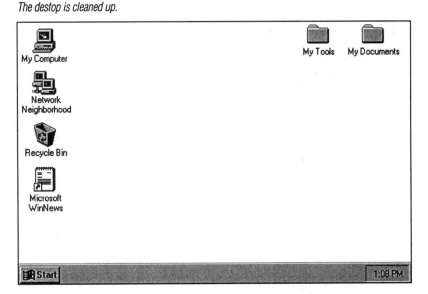

3 **Create a subfolder and move a document into it:**

- **Open** My Documents.
- **Create** a folder in My Documents (review, Exercise 40).
- **Name** the new folder Misc (review, Exercise 40).
- **Drag and drop** Shortcut to savefile on MISC.
- **Arrange** the remaining icons by <u>N</u>ame (review, Exercise 36).

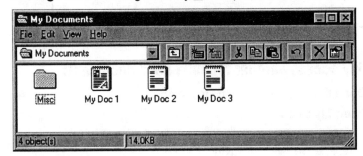

- **Close** the open folder(s).

EXERCISE 70

Organize the Desktop

To arrange files on the desktop in a useful order by putting them in folders.

EXERCISE 71

Use the Documents Menu

To quickly open a recently used document by using the Documents menu.

— Terms and Notes —

NOTE: *When you open a document from the Documents menu, it opens into the program that its file type is associated—which is not necessarily the program it was created in.*

Begin with the desktop displayed and with no tasks on the taskbar.

❶ Quickly access a recently used document:

- **Open** the Start menu, then <u>D</u>ocuments.
  The document menu displays the documents you used since you cleared the document menu in Exercise 58.

- **Click My Doc 3.**
  The document opens in Notepad, the program in which it was created.

❷ Print the document:

- **Make** sure the printer is ready to receive data.
- **Print My Doc 3.**

```
                            My Doc 3


        You can create a new folder when you save a document.  When you
        are in the Save As dialog box, simply right-click the workspace,
        and then click New, then folder.

















                                 Page 1
```

- **Exit** Notepad (without saving, if asked).

❸ Quickly access another recently used document:

- **Open** the Start menu, then <u>D</u>ocuments.
- **Open My Doc 2.**
  The document opens in Notepad, the program in which it was created.
- **Exit** Notepad (without saving, if asked).

NOTE: *Notepad found **My Doc 2** even though it had been moved into a folder after it was created.*

STEPS to

Use the Documents menu

1 Press `Ctrl` + `Esc`
2 Press `D` (Documents)
3 Press `↑` and `↓` to highlight the desired document.
4 Press `⏎`

Begin with the desktop displayed and with no tasks on the taskbar.

❶ Create a WordPad shortcut on the desktop:

- **Richt-click** the desktop, then **click** New, then Shortcut.
  The Create Shortcut dialog box appears.

- **Type:** `"c:\program files\accessories\wordpad.exe"`
  (with the quotes)

- **Click** `Next>` , then `Finish`
  A WordPad shortcut appears on the desktop.

❷ Create a WordPad document and save it on the desktop:

- **Double-click** the WordPad shortcut to start WordPad.

- **Type:** WordPad remembers the last four documents you used with it. You can easily open one of those documents by using the File menu.

- **Click** File, then Save.

- **Click** until Desktop appears in the Save in box.

- **Save** the document using the Word for Windows 6.0 format (not the Rich Text Format usually used); **name** it **filemenu**.

- **Exit** WordPad.
  *The new document, **filemenu**, appears on the desktop.*

❸ Open recently used documents using WordPad's File menu:

- **Start** WordPad by double-clicking its icon.

- **Click** File.

Document - WordPad

File Edit View Insert Format Help

New...	Ctrl+N
Open...	Ctrl+O
Save	Ctrl+S
Save As...	
Print...	Ctrl+P
Print Preview	
Page Setup...	
1 C:\WINDOWS\DESKTOP\filemenu	
2 C:\WINDOWS\DESKTOP\My Doc 1	
3 A:\help2	
4 A:\help	
Send...	
Exit	

the last four documents used in WordPad

- **Click** C:\WINDOWS\DESKTOP\filemenu
  Filemenu opens into WordPad.

- **Exit** WordPad.

❹ Open a document by dragging it onto a program:

- **Locate** both the WordPad shortcut and **filemenu** document on the desktop.

- **Drag filemenu** on the WordPad shortcut and **drop** it.
  Filemenu opens into WordPad.

❺
- **Exit** WordPad.
- **Put** the WordPad shortcut and **filemenu** document into the recycle bin.
- **Empty** the recycle bin.

Open a File Menu Document

To start a program and use the File menu to open one of the last document used quickly.

— Terms and Notes —

NOTE: When you start WordPad (and many other programs), you can easily open one of the last documents you used by clicking the desired document in the File menu. Notepad is one of the programs whose File menu does not display recently used documents.

NOTE: You are asked to use the Word for Windows 6.0 document format in this exercise rather than Rich Text because Rich Text Format documents cannot be opened from the File menu if the filename or any or the folder names in its path have a space in them. Even though most users will not have spaces in any folder names, it could happen if you use a profile and have a space in the users profile's folder name.

 **STEPS to**

Open a File menu document
1 **Open** a program.
2 **Press** `Alt` + `F` (File)
3 **Press** `↓` until the desired document is highlighted.
4 **Press** `↵`

EXERCISE 73

Wrap Up Lesson Five

Delete the My Tools folder and the two shortcuts in it; open My Documents, delete Misc, close My Documents; and move the folder and the three files in it to drive A:

— Terms and Notes —

NOTES: Exercises in this book are designed to leave no permanent changes to Windows 95. Lesson Five is the longest section in which changes to Windows 95 remain in place.

In step 2, you could copy My Documents to an <u>open</u> Floppy (A:) window by simply dragging and dropping My Documents in the window.

Begin with the desktop displayed and with no tasks on the taskbar.

❶ Delete My Tools:

- **Drag and drop** My Tools on the Recycle Bin.
  My Tools, along with the printer and Calculator shortcuts in it, are removed from the desktop.

❷ Delete the Misc folder inside My Documents:

- **Open** My Documents.
- **Drag and drop** the Misc folder on the Recycle Bin.
  Misc and the shortcut in it are removed from the desktop.
- **Close** My Documents.

❸ Copy the My Documents folder to drive A:

This method of moving or copying can be very handy.

- **Open** My Computer, then Floppy (A:) and then **close** My Computer.
- **Minimize** the Floppy (A:) folder.
  Floppy (A:) shrinks into its task button on the taskbar.

<u>Do the next three actions as one movement:</u>

- **Drag and rest, but do not release** the My Documents folder on the Floppy (A:) task button.
- **Pause** until the Floppy (A:) folder opens, and then
- **Continue dragging, then drop** My Documents in the open Floppy (A:) window.

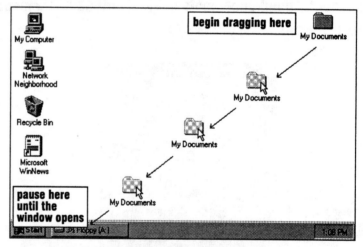

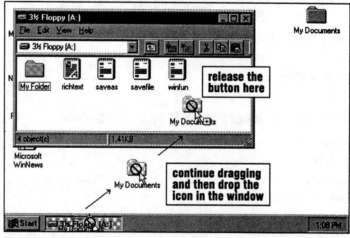

The Moving... window appears for a short time, then the My Documents folder appears in the Floppy (A:) window.

Exercise 73 continued...

4 **Arrange icons in Floppy (A:):**

- **Arrange** the icons in Floppy (A:) by <u>N</u>ame.
  The My Documents folder moves to the front of the other objects in the window.

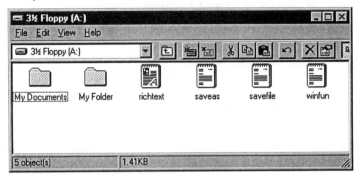

- **Open** My Documents.
  My Doc 1, ***My Doc 2***, and ***My Doc 3*** *are displayed in the window.*
- **Close** My Documents and Floppy (A:) (if it is open).

5 **Delete My Documents from the desktop:**

- **Drag and drop** My Documents in the Recycle Bin.
  My Documents, along with the documents in it, are removed from the desktop.

6 **Empty the Recycle Bin:**

- **Right-click** the Recycle Bin.
- **Click** Empty Recycle <u>B</u>in, then [<u>Y</u>es]
  The desktop is cleared of all the object used in this lesson.

— Terms and Notes —

NOTE: Windows lets you both copy and move files between folders, but not disk drives--you can only copy files between disk drives. This is a safety feature that is meant to keep you from accidently losing files.

EXERCISE 74

Practice

Lesson Five
Using the Desktop

Tasks Reviewed:
- Clear the Document Menu
- Save a Document on the Desktop
- Create a Document on the Desktop
- Create a Shortcut
- Look at a Shortcut Property Sheet
- Use Drag and Drop to Print
- Create a Folder on the Desktop
- Arrange the Desktop
- Capture the Screen

Begin with the desktop displayed and with no tasks on the taskbar.

1
- **Clear** the Documents menu.

2
- **Create** a shortcut on the desktop to your printer.
- **Create** a shortcut on the desktop to the document, **help**, that is in My Folder on drive A:.
- **Close** all the folder windows.

3
- **Start** and **maximize** Notepad.
- **Type:** On the Start menu, Documents are listed before Programs (as you⏎ move up). When you open the Documents menu, you will find a⏎ list of up to 15 of the most recently used documents.⏎
- **Save** the file on the desktop; name it **DOC1**.
- **Exit** Notepad.

4
- **Right-click** the desktop and create a New Text Document; name it **DOC2**.
- **Open DOC2** and **Maximize** Notepad.
- **Type:** Shortcuts are powerful because they let you have quick access to⏎ all the objects you need. Meanwhile, Windows does all the work⏎ of keeping track of what you are doing.⏎
- **Save** the document and **Exit** Notepad.

5
- **Use** drag and drop to print **DOC1**.

DOC1

On the Start menu, Documents are listed before Programs (as you move up). When you open the Documents menu, you will find a list of up to 15 of the most recently used documents.

Page 1

Exercise 74 continued...

6 • **Start** and **maximize** WordPad.
   • **Click** <u>F</u>ile, then <u>N</u>ew, then Rich Text Document, then `  OK  `
   • **Click** <u>V</u>iew, then <u>O</u>ptions, then Wra<u>p</u> to ruler, then `  OK  `

7 • **Type:** When you start WordPad (and many other programs), you
       can easily open one of the last documents you used. Simply
       click File, then click the desired document.
   • **Save** the document on the desktop as a Rich Text format; name it **DOC3**.
   • **Print DOC3.**

> When you start WordPad (and many other programs), you can easily open one of the last documents you
> used. Simply click File, then click the desired document.

   • **Exit** WordPad.

8 • **Look** at the property sheet for Shortcut to help.
   • **Click** the Shortcut tab and examine the information.
   • **Close** the Shortcut to help property sheet.

9 • **Create** a folder on the desktop; name it **My Things**.
   • **Move** the objects created in this exercise to the top right corner of
       the desktop:

DOC1	Shortcut to help
DOC2	Shortcut to printer
DOC3	My Things

   • **Line up** the icons.
   • **Capture** an image of the screen.
   • **Print** the screen capture.

   • **Exit** WordPad without saving.

EXERCISE 75

Practice

Lesson Five
Using the Desktop

Tasks Reviewed:
- Capture a Window
- Undo an Action
- Use the Recycle Bin
- Organize the Desktop
- Use the Documents Menu
- Open a File Menu Document
- Wrap Up the Practice

Begin with the desktop displayed and with no tasks on the taskbar.

1
- **Open** My Computer.
- **Capture** the My Computer window.
- **Close** My Computer.
- **Print** the window capture.

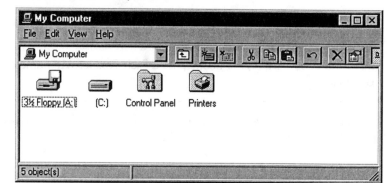

- **Exit** WordPad without saving.

2
- **Change** Shortcut to help's name to `help is coming.`
- **Undo** the change you just made.

3
- **Change** Shortcut to help's name to `help is on the way.`
- **Put DOC2** in the My Things folder.
- **Undo** the last two changes (move and rename).
- **Move DOC2** back to its previous position.

4
- **Empty** the Recycle Bin if it has anything in it.
- **Put** Shortcut to help in the Recycle Bin.

5
- **Select DOC1** and **DOC2**.
- **Put** them in the Recycle Bin.

6
- **Open** the Recycle Bin.
- **Drag DOC1** to the desktop.
- **Select DOC2**.
- **Click** File, then Restore.

7
- **Use** the File menu to empty the Recycle Bin.
- **Close** the Recycle Bin.
- **Move DOC1** and **DOC2** back to their previous positions.

8
- **Use** the Documents menu to open **DOC2**.

Exercise 75 continued...

9 • **Print DOC2**, and **exit** Notepad.

```
                              DOC2




        Shortcuts are powerful because they let you have quick access to
        all the objects you need.  Meanwhile, Windows does all the work
        of keeping track of what you are doing.


















                              Page 1
```

10 • **Create** a WordPad shortcut on the desktop (review, Exercise 72).
• **Open** WordPad using its shortcut.
• **Type:** I'm going to create a document, save it on the desktop, close WordPad, and open the document using the File menu.
• **Save** the document on the desktop using the Word 6 format; name it **myfile**.
• **Exit** WordPad.

11 • **Start** WordPad.
• **Open myfile** using the File menu.
• **Exit** WordPad.

12 • **Open myfile** by dragging it on the WordPad shortcut.
• **Exit** WordPad.
• **Put** the WordPad shortcut and **myfile** in the Recycle Bin.
• **Empty** the Recycle Bin.

13 • **Organize** the desktop by putting **DOC1**, **DOC2**, **DOC3** and Shortcut to printer in the My Things folder.

Exercise 75 continued...

(14)
- **Open** My Things.
- **Put** Shortcut to printer in the Recycle Bin.
- **Close** My Things.

(15)
- **Open** the drive A: folder (Floppy (A:)).
- **Copy** My Things to drive A:.
- **Close** the open folder windows.

(16)
- **Put** My Things in the Recycle Bin.
- **Empty** the Recycle Bin.

Lesson Five Worksheet (13) is in Appendix D

Lesson Six
The Explorer

Table of Contents

TOPIC 19
The Explorer

— Terms and Notes —

Explorer
The Windows 95 program that you can use to explore your computer system, including remote computers if your system is networked.

folder window
A window that displays the contents of a folder (or certain other objects, such as disk drives). Folder windows offer many of the same folder managing features as the Explorer. Double-click a folder to open its window and see what is in it.

folder
A structure that holds files and/or other folders that are stored on a disk. A folder can also hold other objects, such as printers and disk drives. (Folders have traditionally been called *directories*.)

file
A set of data or program instructions that is saved on a disk as a named unit.

hierarchy
A system of things (or people) ranked one above the other. On computers, the term *hierarchy* describes the multilevel structure of folders and subfolders on a disk; or, in the case of Windows 95, it describes a multilevel structure of objects on the entire computer system. The structure is also referred to as a *tree*.

shell
A program, such as Explorer, that lets you control your system.

browse
To look at files, folders, disks, printers, programs, documents, and other objects on your computer system.

tree
A representation of the hierarchy (structure) on a computer system (especially a horizontal representation).

NOTE: While files and folders on the computer are naturally structured with many levels (a hierarchy), by using shortcuts, that structure seems less apparent and is less important to the user. Still, it is useful to understand the structure.

The Explorer is Your Eyes to Your Computer's Resources

The Explorer lets you see where your computer's resources are located. The Explorer window is divided into two panes. The left pane displays the Windows' hierarchy; it is labeled *All Folders*. The right pane displays the objects in the folder that is selected in the left pane; it is labeled *Contents of 'foldername'* (where *foldername* is the name of the selected folder in the left pane).

The Explorer is similar to folder windows; its right pane, in particular, resembles a folder window's workspace.

Listed below are some of the similarities between folder windows and Explorer:

- You can view objects the right pane as Large Icons, Small Icons, List, or Details.
- You can arrange icons in the right pane by name, size, type, or modification date.
- You can start programs.
- You can open documents.
- You can use Quick View (if it is installed).
- You can create and delete folders.
- You can move, copy, and delete files and folders.
- The File, Edit, View, and Help menus are the same.
- Right-click menus are the same.

Listed below are some of the differences between folder windows and Explorer:

- Explorer has a left pane that displays the Windows 95 hierarchy.
- Explorer has a Tools menu.
- The Options dialog box (opened from the View menu) has different items.

The Explorer lets you perform file management tasks such as:

- browse folders and files
- copy and move folders and files
- sort folders and files
- create folders and shortcuts
- format disks
- copy disks

Lesson Six emphasizes features that folder windows do not have and reviews some of the features covered in Lesson Three (My Computer).

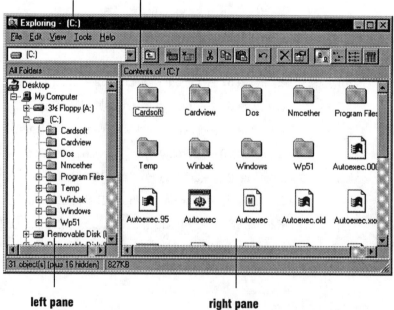

exploring drive C: contents of drive C:

left pane
(All Folders)

right pane
(contents of selected folder in left pane)

The Left Pane of Explorer Shows the Computer's Structure

As described in Lesson Three, disk structure is nothing more than a hierarchy of folders and subfolders. There is a *top* folder on every disk (traditionally called the *root directory*). The top folder contains other folders that are sometimes called *subfolders*. Folders *in* the top folder are the second level of folders. Folders *in* second level folders are third level folders, and so forth.

NOTE: Folders were called directories before the release of Windows 95.

Windows 95 has created a logical hierarchy of **objects** *above* the disk drives. The object immediately above the disk drives is called *My Computer*. The object that is immediately above My Computer is called the *Desktop*. The left pane of the Explorer shows the computer's structure.

The illustrations of the Explorer windows below have been sized to show only the left pane and they do not display the toolbar as the illustration on the previous page does. Notice that even though the left pane is labeled *All Folders*, it contains other objects—Desktop, My Computer, Network Neighborhood, Recycle Bin and disk drives. Many of these objects are called *system folders*. Notice that the desktop is always at the top of the structure in the left pane.

A plus sign (+) beside an object means that the object contains additional folders. Click an object's plus sign to **expand** it (show its subfolders).

A minus sign (-) beside an object means that it has been expanded to show its subfolders. Click an object's minus sign to **collapse** it (hide its subfolders).

The structure in this illustration is collapsed as much as possible. Your structure may be slightly different when fully collapsed.

Left Pane of Explorer

The structure in this illustration has one object expanded—My Computer. My Computer holds your disk drives, the Control Panel, and Printers. When drive C: is expanded, many more folders will be displayed *(see the next page)*. Your structure may be different.

Left Pane of Explorer

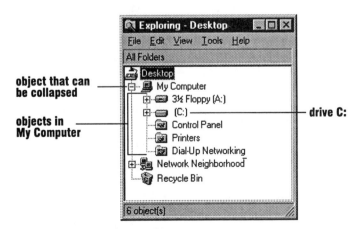

— Terms and Notes —

Explorer's left pane
The part of the Explorer that displays the hierarchical structure on your computer system (including remote computers if your system is networked).

object
One of the many *things* that you use when working with the computer system—items such as:

- files
- programs
- folders
- shortcuts
- disk drives
- Control Panel tools
- My Computer
- Network Neighborhood
- The Recycle Bin
- My Briefcase

NOTE: As used here object is really just another catch-all term for an item, element, thing, whatcha-ma-call-it, or thing-a-ma-jig. The terms object and object-oriented have a more formal computer-related meaning that is not used in this book.

expand
To display unseen folders in an object displayed in the left pane of Explorer. Objects that can be expanded have a plus sign (+) beside them.

collapse
To hide the folders that are displayed in an object that is in the left pane of Explorer. Objects that can be collapsed have a minus sign (-) beside them.

TOPIC 21

A Look at Structure

Windows 95's Method of Showing the Computer's Structure

This is how Windows 95 depicts the computer's hierarchical structure in the left pane of the Explorer. The illustration below shows all of the objects (mostly folders) expanded except drive A: and Network Neighborhood.

You can see that this representation of the structure takes less room and is more practical to create in the Explorer than the horizontal representation of the same structure on the next page. The different levels of the structure are pointed out below. The structure on individual computers will vary.

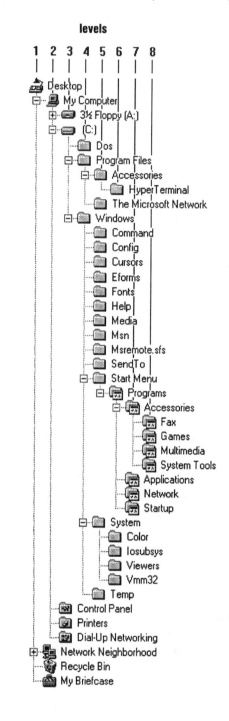

Topic 21 continued...

The Traditional Way of Showing the Computer's Structure

This is how the structure on the previous page would look if it were depicted horizontally—somewhat like the hierarchy of an organizational chart for a company.

Some people can visualize the computer's structure better when looking at this type of illustration, however. When you turn it upside down, you can imagine a tree, with the Desktop being the root and with folders branching off of the root. Thus the traditional name for the structure—tree. The different levels of the structure are pointed out below. A heavy line shows the way from the desktop to the Start Menu.

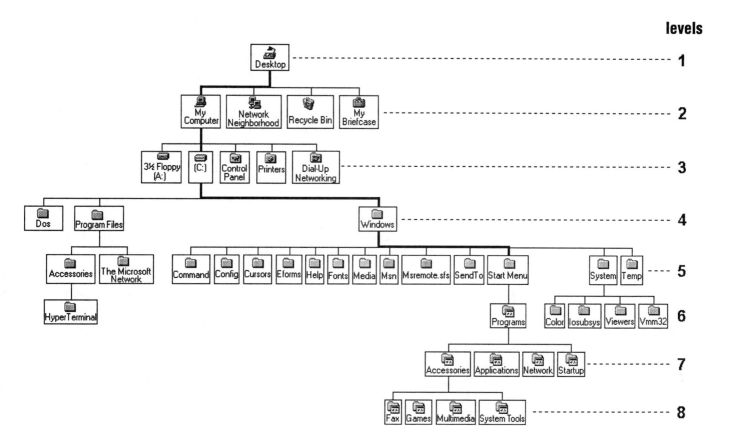

TOPIC 22
Explorer Options

— Terms and Notes —

associated file
A file type that has been identified as belonging to a certain program, such as .TXT with Notepad, .BMP with Paint, or .DOC with Word 6. When you open an associated file, the program related to the file opens automatically.

Two of Explorer's Options Produce Notable Changes

Two of Explorer's options produce changes that should be noted. One of these options is **Hide MS-DOS file extensions for file types that are registered**. The other option is **Hidden files**. Since it is easy to change these options, you should be aware of what they mean and what their consequences are.

Hide MS-DOS File Extensions for File Types That are Registered

When selected (checked), the *Hide MS-DOS file extensions for file types that are registered* option hides filename extensions (this is the default).

Filename extensions **associate** a document file with a specific program. While the computer system must use filename extensions to identify document types, you may prefer to use document icons to identify document types. Some users like to display filename extensions, others feel they just add clutter.

Hide MS-DOS file extentions for file types that are registered ———

This is how the filename, **create1.rtf**, appears when Hide MS-DOS file extensions... **is selected**

create1 — the filename extention is not displayed

This is how the filename, **create1.rtf**, appears when Hide MS-DOS file extensions... **is *not* selected**

create1.rtf — a filename extention of .rtf is displayed

Also, when the *Hide MS-DOS file extensions...* option is selected, Windows 95 automatically adds a filename extension when you *rename* a file. However, when this option is deselected (unchecked), you must provide the filename extension when you *rename* a file, and if you do not (or if you change it), a dialog box warns that if you change a filename extension, the file may become unusable. This can affect the exercises in this book in which you *rename* files.

Topic 22 continued...

Hidden Files

The other option of note is **Hidden files**. In the Hidden files section, you must select either **Show all files** or **Hide files of these types**.

Hidden files ⎯⎯⎯⎯
Show all files ⎯⎯⎯⎯
Hide files of these types ⎯⎯⎯

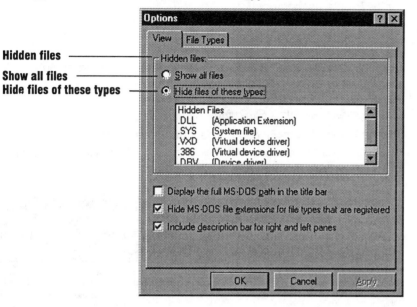

Something that is not apparent is that folders can have hidden **attributes** just as files can. Some of the folders that have a hidden attribute are: Recycled (under C:), and Inf, Pif, Recent, ShellNew, spool, and Sysbackup (all under Windows). Another folder that is hidden with this command is Desktop (under Windows)—even though the folder does not have a hidden attribute. Below is the Inf Properties dialog box showing a selected Hidden attribute.

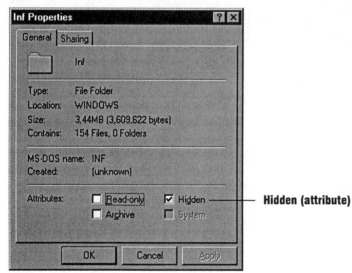

Hidden (attribute)

The default for Hidden files is Hide files of these types. Folders that have the hidden attribute are used by the computer system, and unless you have special reasons for using them, they are best left hidden.

— Terms and Notes —

hidden files
Files and/or folders that have a hidden attribute.

NOTE: You can see if a file or folder has a hidden attribute by choosing to Show all files (in the Options dialog box), then display a file's properties, and finally, look to see if the Hidden attribute has a check mark by it.

attribute
A characteristic (such as read-only, archive, hidden, or system) that changes how a file or folder can be used or displayed.

Show all files
An option that specifies that all files and folders should be displayed (including hidden and system files and folders).

Hide files of these types
An option that specifies that certain files and folders should not be displayed (including hidden files and folders and files with certain extensions that are listed in a box below the option).

EXERCISE 76

Start Explorer

To use a variety of methods to open the Explorer program.

— Terms and Notes —

NOTE: When you start Explorer by right-clicking a folder, it opens with that folder selected. When you open Explorer from the Program menu, it opens with drive C: selected. When you start Explorer by right-clicking the Start button, it opens with the Start Menu folder selected.

 STEPS to

Start Explorer

—USING THE START MENU—

1   Press `Ctrl` + `Esc` (Start menu)

2   Press `P` (Programs)

3   Press `W` (Windows Explorer)

   IF Explorer does not open, **press** `W` until Windows Explorer is highlighted and **press** `↵`

—USING THE RIGHT-CLICK MENU—

1   Press `Ctrl` + `Esc`, `Esc`, `Tab`, `Tab`

2   **Press** arrow keys to select one of the following:
   My Computer
   Recycle Bin
   Network Neighborhood

3   **Press** `Shift` + `F10` to open the right-click (shortcut) menu.

4   **Press** `E` (Explore)

Begin with the desktop displayed and with no tasks on the taskbar.

1 **Start Explorer using the Start menu:**

- **Click** 🏁 Start
- **Open** the Programs menu.
- **Click** 🔍 Windows Explorer
  The Explorer opens with drive (C:) in the title bar.
- **Display** the toolbar if it is not already displayed (review, Exercise 60).
- **Click** [▫▫] (the Large Icons button).
- **Notice** Explorer's title. Is it *Exploring - (C:)*?
- **Notice** the name of the right pane. The same object is in both titles.
  Explorer looks something like the illustration below; the contents of your Explorer window will be different.

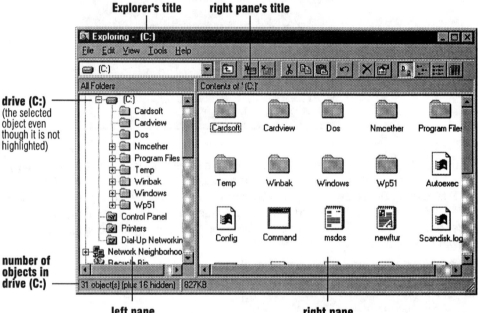

- **Exit** Explorer.

2 **Start Explorer using the right-click menu:**

- **Right-click** 🏁 Start
- **Click** Explore.
  The Explorer opens with Start Menu in its title and the right pane's title.
- **Exit** Explorer.

3 **Start Explorer using the right-click menu and My Computer:**

- **Right-click** the My Computer icon on the desktop.
- **Click** Explore.
  The Explorer opens with My Explorer in its title and the right pane's title.
- **Exit** Explorer.

NOTE: Right-clicking the Start button or My Computer is a quick way into Explorer. You can easily change the selected folder and browse once you are in Explorer. You can also start Explorer by right-clicking the Recycle Bin, Network Neighborhood or any folder on the desktop.

Begin with the desktop displayed and with no tasks on the taskbar.

1 • **Start** Explorer.

   • **Click** (the Large Icons button).

2 ## Move the split between panes:

   • **Move** the pointer on the split line between the panes until the pointer becomes a double-headed arrow.

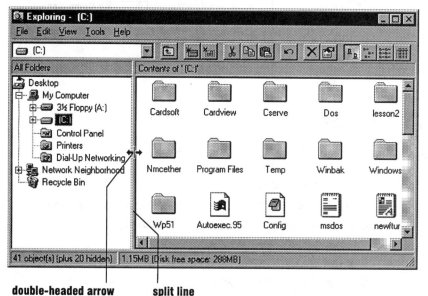

double-headed arrow   **split line**

   • **Drag** the split line until the left pane is about one inch wide.
     A scroll bar appears at the bottom of the left pane.

   • **Drag** the split line right until there is no scroll bar at the bottom of the left pane.

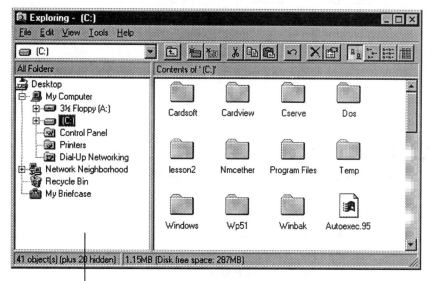

the wider left pane has no scroll bar at the bottom

3 • **Exit** Explorer.

EXERCISE 77

Resize Explorer's Panes

To move the split line between the left and right panes of Explorer.

EXERCISE 78

Expand and Collapse Folders

To display and hide the folders within a folder or object.

— Terms and Notes —

expand
To display unseen folders in an object displayed in the left pane of Explorer. Objects that can be expanded have a plus sign (+) beside them.

collapse
To hide the folders that are displayed in an object that is in the left pane of Explorer. Objects that can be collapsed have a minus sign (-) beside them.

NOTE: When you start Explorer by right-clicking a specific folder, Explorer will open with the necessary folders expanded to display that folder. When you start Explorer using the Program menu, it starts with drive (C:) expanded.

 **STEPS to**

Expand a folder

—*FROM THE EXPLORER*—

1 Press **Tab** until a folder in the left pane is selected.

2 Press **↑** or **↓** until you reach the desired folder with a plus sign (+) beside it.

3 Press **→** to expand the folder.

Collapse a folder

—*FROM THE EXPLORER*—

1 Press **Tab** until a folder in the left pane is selected.

2 Press **↑** or **↓** until you reach the desired folder with a minus sign (-) beside it.

3 Press **←** to compress the folder.

Begin with the desktop displayed and with no tasks on the taskbar.

❶ • **Right-click** My Computer and **click** <u>E</u>xplore.

Explorer opens with My Computer in the title bar and a structure in the left pane that resembles the illustration below.

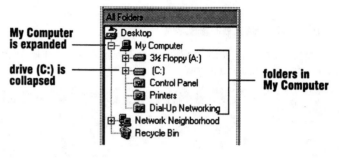

❷ Expand a folder:

• **Click** the plus sign (+) beside ⊞–💾 (C:)
  The folders on drive C: are displayed.

• **Maximize** the Explorer.

• **Scroll** through the structure until the Windows folder appears.

• **Click** the plus sign (+) beside ⊞–📁 Windows
  The folders in Windows are displayed.

• **Expand** the Start Menu folder.

• **Expand** the Programs folder.

• **Expand** the Accessories folder.
  The plus sign by each folder becomes a minus sign showing that each folder is expanded and can now be collapsed.

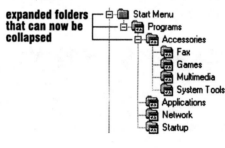

❸ Collapse a folder:

• **Click** the minus sign (-) beside ⊟–📁 Accessories
  The folders in Accessories are now collapsed.

• **Click** the minus sign (-) beside ⊟–📁 Programs
  The folders in Accessories are now collapsed.

• **Collapse** the Start Menu folder.

• **Collapse** the Windows folder.

• **Collapse** the drive (C:) folder.

• **Collapse** My Computer.
  The minus sign by each folder becomes a plus sign showing that each folder is collapsed and can now be expanded. The structure is entirely collapsed now.

❹ • **Restore** Explorer.
  • **Exit** Explorer.

Begin with the desktop displayed and with no tasks on the taskbar.

① • **Start** Explorer.
 • **Make sure** that toolbar and status line are displayed (both items should be checked in the View menu).
 • **Click** ▤ (the List button).
 • **Expand** (C:), Windows, Start Menu, and Programs (review, Exercise 78). You may have to scroll to find some of the folders.
 • **IF** there is a scroll bar at the bottom of the left pane, **Scroll** as far right as possible.

② **Select a folder:**

 • **Click** 📁 Start Menu (either the folder or the name).
 • **Adjust** the split line if necessary to view both sides.
   The folder opens, the contents of the folder appear in the right pane, the number of items in the folder appears in the left side of the status line, and the space used by the items in the folder and the remaining space on the disk appears to the right.

selected folder →

number of objects in selected folder →

contents of selected folder

amount of space used by objects in the right pane

free space on disk

 • **Click** in the right pane.
   The highlighting disappears from the Start Menu folder, but the folder remains open.
 • **Click** the Programs folder (in left pane) to select it.
   The Programs folder opens.
 • **Click** the Accessories folder (in left pane) to select it.
   The Accessories folder opens; it appears something like the illustration below.

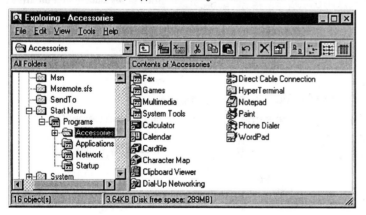

③ • **Exit** Explorer.

To open a folder (or other object) in the left pane of Explorer, which will cause its contents to be displayed in the right pane.

 **STEPS to**

Select a folder

—*FROM THE EXPLORER*—

1 **Press** `Tab` until a folder in the left pane is selected.
2 Choose from the following cursor movements to select a folder:

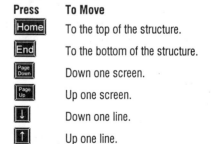

Press	To Move
`Home`	To the top of the structure.
`End`	To the bottom of the structure.
`Page Down`	Down one screen.
`Page Up`	Up one screen.
`↓`	Down one line.
`↑`	Up one line.

EXERCISE 80

Browse Your Data Disk

To move through the folders on drive A: and examine the files in the right pane of the Explorer.

— Terms and Notes —

NOTE: Because drive C: holds many important files, people sometimes become protective of it. They fear—not unreasonably—that information might inadvertently be deleted or somehow lost. In Windows 95 it is as easy as dragging the pointer over a few folders (purposely or accidently) to rearrange the folders on a disk. Therefore, this book instructs you to move and copy folders and files on your data disk in drive A: rather than on drive C: most of the time.

 **STEPS to**

Browse your data disk

—FROM THE EXPLORER—

1 **Press** `Tab` until a folder in the left pane is selected.

2 **Insert** your data disk in drive A:.

3 **Press** ⬆ or ⬇ until Floppy (A:) is selected and look at the objects in the right pane.

4 **Press** ➡ to expand Floppy (A:).

5 **Press** ⬇ to select the first folder under Floppy (A:), and look at the objects in the right pane.

6 **Repeat** step 5 two more times to examine objects in the remaining two folders.

Your Correct Data Disk is Needed for Lesson Six

Since the data disk you have been saving on will be used for many of the exercises from this point on, it is important that it have all the necessary folders and files. If your disk does not match the illustrations below, see Appendix F for instructions on how to prepare a data disk that is appropriate. If you desire, you can order a data disk from DDC Publishing with the required folders and files.

Begin with the desktop displayed and with no tasks on the taskbar.

①
- **Start** Explorer.
- **Insert** your data disk into drive A:.
- **Select** Floppy (A:) (review, Exercise 79).
- **Click** 🔲 (the List button).
- **Expand** drive A: (review, Exercise 78)
- **Do** you have the same files and folders in the right pane as in the illustration below?

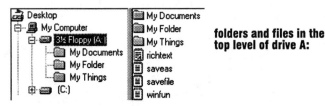

folders and files in the top level of drive A:

NOTE: Your icons that represent Rich Text Documents may be different than those in the illustrations.

②
- **Select** My Folder (in the left pane).
- **Do** you have the same files as in the illustration below?

files in My Folder on drive A:

③
- **Select** My Documents (in the left pane).
- **Do** you have the same files as in the illustration below?

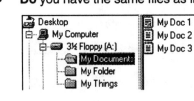

files in My Documents on drive A:

④
- **Select** My Things (in the left pane).
- **Do** you have the same files as in the illustration below?

files in My Things on drive A:

⑤
- **Exit** Explorer.
- **Remove** the data disk or go on to the next exercise.

Copying Your Data Disk

The Copy Disk procedure must be done using two disks of the same **size** and **density**. The disk you are copying is called the Copy from (or source) disk and the disk you are copying to is called the Copy to (or destination) disk.

To complete this exercise, you will need a disk that matches your data disk in size and density (see Exercise 92). This disk must either be blank or have unimportant data on it that you do not mind losing. The book will refer to this disk as your duplicate data disk because it will be an exact copy of your data disk. You will use your duplicate data disk in the exercises that follow, and if you make errors in the procedures, you can copy the original data disk again and start the exercises over.

Begin with the desktop displayed and with no tasks on the taskbar.

1 • **Start** Explorer.

2 • **Copy your data disk:**

   • **Right-click** Floppy (A:), then **Copy Disk** .
   The Copy Disk dialog box opens.

   ```
   ┌─ Copy Disk ──────────────────────── ? ✕ ┐
   │  Copy from:              Copy to:         │
   │  ┌─────────────────┐     ┌───────────────┐│
   │  │ 3½ Floppy (A:)   │     │ 3½ Floppy (A:) ││
   │  │                 │     │               ││
   │  └─────────────────┘     └───────────────┘│
   │  ┌────────────────────────────────────┐   │
   │  └────────────────────────────────────┘   │
   │              ┌─ Start ─┐  ┌─ Close ─┐      │
   │              └─────────┘  └─────────┘      │
   └───────────────────────────────────────────┘
   ```

   • **Keep** the default of Copy from Floppy (A:) and Copy to Floppy (A:).
   • **Write protect** your original data disk. (Slide the tab so the hole is open on a 3½" disk; place a write-protect tab over the cut-out notch on a 5¼" disk).
   • **Click** [Start]
   A dialog box asks you to insert the disk you want to copy from and click OK.
   • **Insert** your data disk in drive A: and **click** [OK]
   The Copy Disk dialog box says "Reading source disk" and reports its progress.

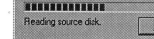 ── **the dialog box reports progress**

   A dialog box asks you to insert the disk you want to copy to and click OK.

   • **Remove** your source disk (data disk).
   • **Insert** your destination disk (also called target disk) in drive A:.
   • **Click** [OK]
   The Copy Disk dialog box says "Writing to destination disk" and reports its progress.

 ── **the dialog box reports progress**

   The Copy Disk dialog box reports "Copy completed successfully."

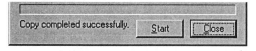

   • **Click** [Close]

3 • **Exit** Explorer.
   • **Remove** the duplicate data disk from drive A:.

EXERCISE 81
Copy a Disk

To copy the entire contents of a floppy disk to another floppy disk of the same size and density.

— Terms and Notes —

floppy disk size
The physical size of floppy disks; typically they come in two sizes, 5¼" and 3½".

floppy disk density
Density refers to the surface coating on a disk; the closer together the particles on the disk, the higher the disk's capacity.
Typically, 3½" floppy disks come in two densities: DD (double density)—720 Kb and HD (high density)—1.44 Mb.
Typically 5¼" floppy disks come in two densities: DD (double density)—360 Kb and HD (high density)—1.2 Mb.

bytes (b), kilobytes (Kb), and megabytes (Mb)
The size of computer memory and storage units is measured in *bytes*. A byte is the amount of space needed to hold one character.
1 byte = One character.
1 kilobyte = About 1,000 characters.
1 megabyte = About 1,000,000 characters.

*WARNING: Any existing data on the **Copy to** (destination) disk will be destroyed when the information from the **Copy from** (source) disk is copied to it, so be sure there is no important data on the **Copy to** (destination) disk before starting to copy data to it.*

⌨ STEPS to

Copy a disk
   —FROM THE EXPLORER—
   1 **Press** [Tab] until a folder in the left pane is selected.
   2 **Press** [↑] or [↓] until Floppy (A:) is selected.
   3 **Press** [Shift] + [F10] (shortcut menu)
   4 **Press** [Y] (Copy Disk).
     The Copy Disk dialog box appears.
   5 **Press** [↵] to start the disk copy.
   6 **Insert** your data disk in drive A:.
     A dialog box reports the progress.
   7 **Remove** the source disk.
   8 **Insert** the destination disk.
     A dialog box reports the progress.
   9 **Press** [↵] to close disk copy.
   10 **Remove** the duplicate disk.

EXERCISE 82

Select Objects in the Right Pane

To highlight one object, multiple connecting objects, or multiple separate objects. Once objects are selected, you can copy, move, or delete them.

 STEPS to

Select an object in the right pane

—FROM THE EXPLORER—

1 Press `Tab` until an object in the right pane is selected.

2 Press ⬆ or ⬇ until you reach the object you want to select.

Select multiple connected objects

—FROM THE EXPLORER—

1 Press `Tab` until an object in the right pane is selected.

2 Press ⬆ ⬇ ⬅ ➡ until you reach the first object you want to select.

3 Press `Shift` + ⬆ ⬇ ⬅ ➡ until you reach the last object you want to select.

Select multiple separate objects

—FROM THE EXPLORER—

1 Press `Tab` until an object in the right pane is selected.

2 Press ⬆ ⬇ ⬅ ➡ until you reach the first object you want to select.

3 Press and hold `Ctrl` while you:

a) Press ⬆ ⬇ ⬅ ➡ until you reach the next object you want to select.

b) Press `Space` to select the object.

c) Repeat steps a-b until all the desired objects are selected.

Begin with the desktop displayed and with no tasks on the taskbar.

1
- **Start** Explorer.
- **Insert** your duplicate data disk into drive A:.
- **Select** Floppy (A:) (review, Exercise 79).
- **Click** ▦ (the List button—so your screen matches the illustration below).
  A screen similar to the illustration below appears.

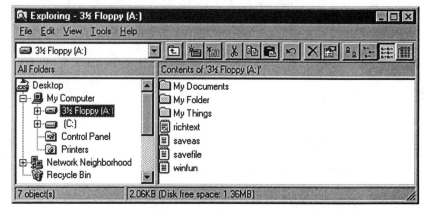

2 ## Select an object in the right pane:
- **Click** 📁 My Documents (in the right pane).
  The My Documents folder is highlighted.
- **Click** 📄 saveas
  *The file, **saveas**, is highlighted and the folder, My Documents, is deselected.*

3 ## Select multiple connected objects:
- **Click** 📁 My Folder
  The My Folder folder is highlighted.
- **Press** `Shift` while you **click** 📄 savefile
  *All the objects between and including My Folder and **savefile** are selected.*

4 ## Deselect objects:
- **Click** outside the objects.
  The highlighting disappears from the objects.

Exercise 82 continued...

⑤ Select multiple separate objects:

- **Click** 🗀 My Documents (in the right pane).
  The My Documents folder is highlighted.
- **Press** Ctrl while you **click** 🗀 My Things
- **Press** Ctrl while you **click** 📄 saveas
- **Press** Ctrl while you **click** 📄 winfun

  The separate objects are all selected.

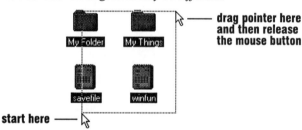

- **Click** outside the objects to deselect them.

⑥ Use the drag action to select multiple connected objects:

*HINTS: When you **select** a group of objects, start with the pointer outside the objects rather than on an object (if you start too close to an object, you will move it). If you do accidently move, copy, or delete an object or objects, remember that you can undo the action by using the Edit menu or a right-click menu in the workspace.*

- **Click** 🔳 (the Large Icons button).
- **Drag** the pointer to select (highlight) several objects as illustrated below.
  NOTE: Your arrangement may be different.

  ```
                          ┌── drag pointer here
                          │   and then release
                          │   the mouse button
  ```

  start here ──── ⬉

- **Release** the mouse button.

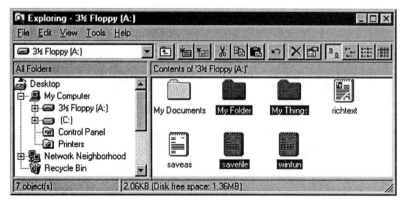

⑦ • **Click** outside the objects to deselect them.
- **Exit** Explorer; remove your data disk or go on to the next exercise.

EXERCISE 83

Invert Selection

To reverse which objects are selected and which are not.

— Terms and Notes —

NOTE: This feature is useful when you want to select all but a few objects of a large number of objects. You select the few objects you do not want selected, and then invert the selection.

Begin with the desktop displayed and with no tasks on the taskbar.

1
- **Start** Explorer.
- **Insert** your duplicate data disk into drive A:.
- **Select** Floppy (A:) (review, Exercise 79).
- **Click** (the List button).
- **Select** 📄 saveas and 📄 savefile (review, Exercise 82).
  A screen similar to the illustration below appears.

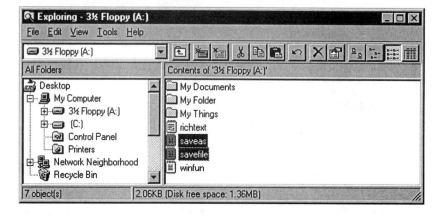

2 **Invert the selection:**
- **Click** <u>E</u>dit, then <u>I</u>nvert Selection.
  The selected objects and unselected objects are reversed.

> ■ My Documents
> ■ My Folder
> ■ My Things
> ▓ richtext
> 📄 saveas
> 📄 savefile
> ▓ winfun

3
- **Click** <u>E</u>dit, then <u>I</u>nvert Selection again.
  The selected and unselected objects return to their previous states.

> ■ My Documents
> ■ My Folder
> ■ My Things
> 📄 richtext
> ▓ saveas
> ▓ savefile
> 📄 winfun

4
- **Click** outside the objects to deselect them.
- **Exit** Explorer.
- **Remove** your data disk or go on to the next exercise.

 **STEPS to**

Invert selection

—*FROM THE EXPLORER*—

1 **Select** objects that you do NOT want selected (see keyboard steps for Exercise 82).

2 **Press** 🄰🄻🅃 + 🄴 (Edit)

3 **Press** 🄸 (Invert Selection)

Begin with the desktop displayed and with no tasks on the taskbar.

- **Start** Explorer.
- **Insert** your duplicate data disk into drive A:.
- **Select** Floppy (A:) (review, Exercise 79).
- **Click** 🔳 (the List button).
  A screen similar to the illustration below appears.

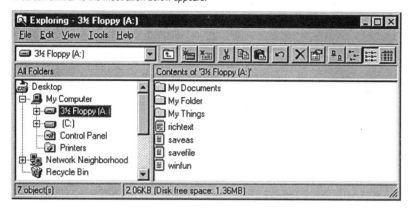

❷ Select all objects:

- **Click** Edit, then Select All.
  All the objects in the right pane are selected.

My Documents
My Folder
My Things
richtext
saveas
savefile
winfun

❸ Deselect objects:

- **Press** [Ctrl] while you **click** 📁 My Things
- **Press** [Ctrl] while you **click** 📄 saveas
  The two files are deselected.

- **Click** outside the objects to deselect them.
- **Exit** Explorer.
- **Remove** your data disk or go on to the next exercise.

EXERCISE 84

Select All Objects

To select all the items in the right pane.

 **STEPS to**

Select all objects

—FROM THE EXPLORER—

- **Press** [Ctrl] + [A] (Select All)

Deselect objects

—WITH ALL OBJECTS SELECTED—

- **Press and hold** [Ctrl] while you:
  a) **Press** [↑] [↓] [←] [→] until you reach an object you want to deselect.
  b) **Press** [Space] to deselect the object.
  c) **Repeat** a-b until all the desired objects are deselected.

EXERCISE 85
Move Objects

To transfer object(s) from one location to another and remove the object(s) from the original location.

— Terms and Notes —

There are many ways to move objects
There are many variables that you can change when moving, for example you can:
- Move a file using drag and drop.
- Move a file using cut and paste.
- Move a file using the Edit menu.
- Undo a Move.
- Move a folder and its contents.
- Move multiple objects

> *NOTE: Single objects are used in this exercise, but you can also select multiple objects and then use the procedures shown in this exercise to move them.*

- Move works the same for objects whether they are represented as large icons, small icons, list, or details (any of the view modes).

STEPS to

Move objects

—FROM THE EXPLORER—

1 **Select** the object(s) to be moved *(see keyboard steps for Exercise 82).*
2 **Press** `Ctrl` + `X` (Cut)
3 **Select** the object to which you want to move the cut object(s).
4 **Press** `Ctrl` + `V` (Paste)

Undo move

—FROM THE EXPLORER—

After an object has been moved:

1 **Press** `Alt` + `E` (Edit)
2 **Press** `U` (Undo Move)

Begin with the desktop displayed and with no tasks on the taskbar.

1
- **Start** Explorer and **insert** your duplicate data disk into drive A:.
- **Select** Floppy (A:) and **click**  (the List button).
- **Expand** Floppy (A:).

2 **Move a file using drag and drop:**

- **Drag winfun** to the folder, My Things, and **drop** it.

*The Moving dialog box appears briefly and shows **winfun** flying into My Things. Then the Explorer reappears without **winfun** at the bottom of the list.*

```
📁 My Documents
📁 My Folder
📁 My Things
📄 richtext
📄 saveas
📄 savefile
```
winfun is gone

- **Select** the My Things folder in the left pane.
The My Things folder opens, and the files in it are displayed in the right pane.

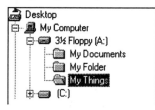 — **winfun is moved to My Things**

3 **Move a file by dragging it to an object into the left pane:**

- **Drag winfun** to Floppy (A:) and **Drop** it.

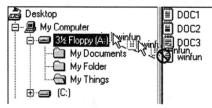

***Winfun** disappears from the right pane.*

- **Select** Floppy (A:).
***Winfun** is back where it started, in drive A: but not in any folder.*

4 **Move a file by using cut and paste:**

- **Right-click richtext**, then **click** Cut.
*The icon for **richtext** fades.*

Exercise 85 continued...

- **Select** the My Things folder in the left pane.
- **Right-click** the workspace in the right pane, then **click** <u>P</u>aste.
  Richtext appears in the right pane (in My Things).
- **Select** Floppy (A:).
  Richtext no longer appears in the top level of drive A:.

⑤ Undo a move:

- **Right-click** the workspace in the right pane, then **click** <u>U</u>ndo Move.
  Richtext appears at the bottom of the list in the right pane.
- **Sort** the right pane by name (right-click the workspace, point to Arrange <u>I</u>cons, and click by <u>N</u>ame).
  Richtext is put in the correct alphabetical order in the list.

⑥ Move a folder and its contents:

NOTE: You can use several methods to perform this action. You can:
- *drag a folder in the left pane to another folder in the left pane,*
- *drag a folder in the right pane to another folder in the right pane,*
- *drag a folder in the right pane to another folder in the left pane, or*
- *use cut and paste.*

You are instructed to drag the folder from the right pane to the left pane here.

- **Drag** My Things (in the *right* pane) to My Documents (in the *left* pane).

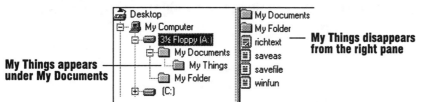

My Documents appears with a plus sign (+) beside it since it now contains a folder.
My Things disappears from the right pane.

- **Expand** My Documents.
  My Things is displayed under My Documents.

My Things appears under My Documents

My Things disappears from the right pane

- **Select** My Things.
  The documents in My Things appear in the right pane.

  DOC1
  DOC2   **documents in My Things**
  DOC3

- **Right-click** the right pane, then **click** <u>U</u>ndo Move.
  The objects on the desktop are displayed in the right pane.
- **Select** Floppy (A:)
  The objects in the top level of drive A: are displayed in the right pane.

⑦
- **Exit** Explorer.
- **Remove** your data disk or go on to the next exercise.

EXERCISE 86

Copy Objects

To transfer object(s) from one location to another and leave the object(s) intact in the original location.

— Terms and Notes —

There are many ways to copy
There are many variables that can be changed when copying, for example you can:
- Copy a file using drag and drop while pressing Ctrl.
- Copy a file using copy and paste.
- Copy a file using the Edit menu.
- Copy a file or folder using Send to.
- Undo a Copy.
- Copy a folder and its contents using drag and drop while pressing Ctrl.
- Copy single or multiple objects.
  NOTE: Single objects are used in this exercise, but you can also select multiple objects and then copy them.
- Copy works the same for objects whether they are represented as large icons, small icons, list, or details (any of the view modes).

⌨ STEPS to

Copy objects

—FROM THE EXPLORER—

1 **Select** the object(s) to be copied (see keyboard steps for Exercise 82).
2 **Press** Ctrl + C (Copy)
3 **Select** the object to which you want to copy the cut object(s).
4 **Press** Ctrl + V (Paste)

Copy objects to Floppy (A:) using Send To

—FROM THE EXPLORER—

1 **Select** the object(s) to be copied that are *not* on drive A: *(see keyboard steps for Exercise 82).*
2 **Press** Alt + F (File)
3 **Press** N (Send To)
4 **Press** arrow keys to select Floppy (A:).
5 **Press** ⏎

Undo copy

—FROM THE EXPLORER—

After an object has been copied:

1 **Press** Alt + E (Edit)
2 **Press** U (Undo Copy)

Begin with the desktop displayed and with no tasks on the taskbar.

❶
- **Start** Explorer and **insert** your duplicate data disk into drive A:.
- **Select** Floppy (A:) and **click** ▦ (the List button).
- **Expand** Floppy (A:).

❷ Copy multiple files using drag and drop:
- **Select** both **saveas** and **winfun** (review, Exercise 82).
- **Press** Ctrl while you **drag** the selected files to the folder, My Things (in the right pane), and **drop** them.
  NOTES: As soon as My Things is highlighted you can release the mouse button. When you copy (as opposed to move), a plus sign appears with the pointer.

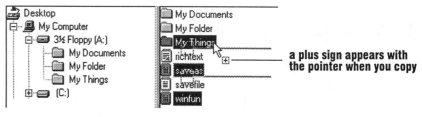

The Copying dialog box appears briefly and shows the files flying into My Things.

- **Select** the My Things folder in the left pane.
  The My Things folder opens, and the copied files in it are displayed in the right pane at the bottom of the list of files.

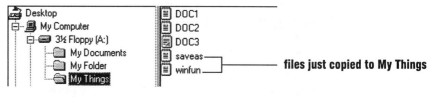

- **Select** Floppy (A:).
  The files remain intact in their original location; in drive A: but not in any folder.

❸ Copy a file by dragging it to an object in the left pane:
- **Press** Ctrl while you **drag** winfun to the folder, My Documents, in the left pane and then **drop** it.

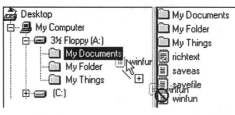

*The Copying dialog box appears briefly and shows **winfun** flying into My Documents.*
***Winfun** remains in the right pane.*

- **Select** My Documents in the left pane.
  ***Winfun** appears at the bottom of the list of files in My Documents.*

My Doc 1
My Doc 2
My Doc 3
winfun

Exercise 86 continued...

4 **Copy a file by using copy and paste:**

- **Select** Floppy (A:).
- **Right-click winfun**, then <u>C</u>opy.
  *Nothing appears to happen, and **winfun** remains in the right pane.*
- **Right-click** My Folder (in either pane), and then **click** <u>P</u>aste.
  The floppy drive makes some noise.
- **Select** My Folder in the left pane.
  ***Winfun** appears at the bottom of the list of files in My Folder.*

5 **Undo a copy:**

- **Right-click** the workspace in the right pane, then **click** <u>U</u>ndo Copy.
  The Confirm Delete dialog box appears.
- **Click** [Yes]
  ***Winfun** disappears from the bottom of the list in the right pane.*
- **Select** Floppy (A:).
  ***Winfun** remains in its original location.*

6 **Copy a folder and its contents:**

NOTE: You can use several methods to perform this action. You can:
  - *drag a folder in the right pane to another folder in the right pane,*
  - *drag a folder in the right pane to a folder in the left pane,*
  - *drag a folder in the left pane to another folder in the left pane, or*
  - *use cut and paste a folder.*
You are instructed to drag the folder from the right pane to the left pane here.

- **Press** [Ctrl] while you **drag** My Things in the *right* pane to
  My Folder in the *left* pane.

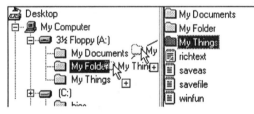

*My Folder appears with a plus sign (+) beside it since it now contains a folder.
My Things remains in the right pane.*

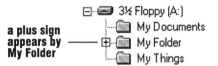

- **Expand** My Folder.
  My Things is displayed under My Folder.
- **Select** the My Things folder that is under My Folder.
  The documents in My Things appear in the right pane.

> DOC1
> DOC2
> DOC3
> saveas
> winfun

- **Select** Floppy (A:)
  The objects in the top level of drive A: are displayed in the right pane.
- **Collapse** Floppy (A:) (review, Exercise 78).

Exercise 86 continued...

— **Terms and Notes** —

*NOTES: When copying, always be sure
to release the mouse button before you
release* [Ctrl].

*If you make a mistake when copying, remember
that you can undo the last action by right-
clicking the workspace and clicking <u>U</u>ndo
(move, copy, or delete).*

7 **Copy a file to a different drive:**

- **Maximize** Explorer.
- **Expand** (C:) if it is not already expanded (review, Exercise 78).
- **Scroll** the left pane, if necessary, until the Windows folder is visible.
- **Select** the Windows folder (review, Exercise 79).
- **Scroll** the right pane, if necessary, until you find 🖉 Cars.

  *NOTE: If you cannot find **Cars**, open any other file with a 🖉 icon.*

- **Scroll** the left pane, if necessary, until Floppy (A:) is visible, but do not select it.
- **Drag** 🖉 Cars in the right pane and **drop** it on Floppy (A:).

  NOTE: Although you must usually press <kbd>Ctrl</kbd> *to **copy** while you drag, you do not need to do so when you transfer a file from one disk to another disk. You cannot **move** files between a floppy drive and a hard drive—when you perform the move action, files are copied instead (in Windows 95).*

  *The Copying dialog box appears briefly while **Cars** is being copied to drive A:.*

- **Select** Floppy (A:).

  ***Cars** appears in the list of files on drive A:.*

Cars is copied to drive A:

8 **Copy a file using Send To:**

- **Select** the Windows folder.
- **Right-click** 🖉 Argyle.

  *NOTE: If you cannot find **Argyle**, open any other file with a 🖉 icon.*

- **Move the pointer on** Send To, then **click** Floppy (A:).

  *The Copying dialog box appears briefly while **Argyle** is being copied to drive A:.*

- **Select** Floppy (A:).

  ***Argyle** appears in the list of files on drive A:.*

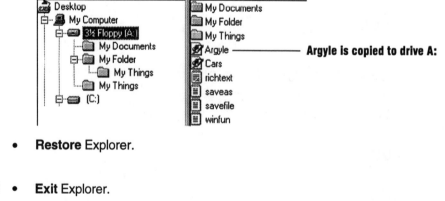

Argyle is copied to drive A:

- **Restore** Explorer.

9
- **Exit** Explorer.
- **Remove** your data disk or go on to the next exercise.

Begin with the desktop displayed and with no tasks on the taskbar.

1 • **Start** Explorer and **insert** your duplicate data disk into drive A:.

• **Select** Floppy (A:) and **click**  (the List button).

• **Expand** Floppy (A:) and then My Folder.

The screen is similar to the illustration at the bottom of the previous page.

2 ## Delete multiple files using the delete key:

• **Select Argyle** and **Cars** (review, Exercise 82).

*NOTE: If you selected files other than **Cars** and **Argyle**, in steps and 7 and 8 on the previous page, select those files.*

• **Press** Del

The Confirm Multiple File Delete dialog box appears.

Confirm Multiple File Delete	✕
Are you sure you want to delete these 2 items?	
Yes	No

• **Click** Yes

The Delete dialog box appears briefly and the two files are deleted.

3 ## Delete a file using the right-click menu:

• **Select** My Documents in the left pane (review, Exercise 79).

• **Right-click winfun**, then **click** Delete.

The Confirm File Delete dialog box appears.

• **Click** Yes

The Delete dialog box appears briefly and the file is deleted.

4 ## Delete a folder and its contents:

• **Right-click** My Things IN THE LEFT PANE under My Folder, then **click** Delete.

The Confirm Folder Delete dialog box appears.

• **Click** Yes

The Delete dialog box appears briefly and the folder and its contents are deleted and My Folder (in the left pane) no longer has a plus sign by it.

5 ## Delete multiple files using the right-click menu:

• **Select** My Things in the left pane (review, Exercise 79).

• **Select saveas** and **winfun** (review, Exercise 82).

• **Right-click** one of the selected files, then **click** Delete.

The Confirm Multiple File Delete dialog box appears.

• **Click** Yes

The Delete dialog box appears briefly and the two files are deleted.

• **Select** Floppy (A:).

A screen similar to the illustration below appears.

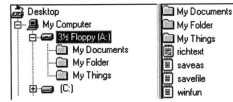

6 • **Exit** Explorer.

• **Remove** your data disk or go on to the next exercise.

EXERCISE 87

Delete Objects

To remove files and folders from a disk.

— Terms and Notes —

NOTE: When you delete objects on a floppy disk drive they do not automatically go into the Recycle Bin as they do when you delete objects on the desktop or on the hard disk (see Exercise 69—Use the Recycle Bin). Because of this, you cannot use the Undo feature to restore deleted files on a floppy disk (see Exercise 68—Undo an Action).

 **STEPS to**

Delete Objects

—FROM THE EXPLORER—

1 **Select** the object(s) to be deleted *(see keyboard steps for Exercise 79 and 82).*

2 **Press** Del

The Delete File (or Folder) dialog box appears.

3 **Press** ↵

EXERCISE 88

Arrange Icons Using Headings

To sort objects by clicking the column headings in the right pane when the objects are in the *details* view mode.

— Terms and Notes —

Sort forward and backward
When you arrange icons using the View menu or the right-click menu you can sort files only from A-Z and 0-9 (forward).
But when you arrange icons using column headings, you can sort files from Z-A and 9-0 (backward) as well as forward.

NOTE: See Exercise 36—Arrange Icons to sort objects using other methods (right-click or View menus).

Begin with the desktop displayed and with no tasks on the taskbar.

1
- **Start** Explorer and **insert** your duplicate data disk into drive A:.
- **Select** Floppy (A:) and **click** ⊞ (the Details button).
- **Maximize** Explorer.
  Your Explorer should be similar to this.

category headings

Name	Size	Type	Modified
🗀 My Documents		File Folder	3/30/95 12:19 PM
🗀 My Folder		File Folder	2/25/95 9:32 AM
🗀 My Things		File Folder	4/26/95 6:38 PM
📄 richtext	1KB	Rich Text Document	5/5/95 12:49 PM
📄 saveas	1KB	Text Document	2/20/95 2:37 AM
📄 savefile	1KB	Text Document	2/20/95 2:35 AM
📄 winfun	1KB	Text Document	2/9/95 7:07 AM

7 object(s)   2.06KB (Disk free space: 1.36MB)

2 Sort files by filenames from Z to A:

- **Click** [Name] two or three times. **Watch** the order of the filenames as you do so, and **stop** when **winfun** is at the top of the list.

the files are sorted by filename - Z to A

Name	Size	Type	Modified
📄 winfun	1KB	Text Document	2/9/95 7:07 AM
📄 savefile	1KB	Text Document	2/20/95 2:35 AM
📄 saveas	1KB	Text Document	2/20/95 2:37 AM
📄 richtext	1KB	Rich Text Document	5/5/95 12:49 PM
🗀 My Things		File Folder	4/26/95 6:38 PM
🗀 My Folder		File Folder	2/25/95 9:32 AM
🗀 My Documents		File Folder	3/30/95 12:19 PM

*NOTE: Remember that **files** are sorted separately from **folders**.*

3 Sort files by date modified from first to last:

- **Click** [Modified] two or three times. **Watch** the order of the modified dated as you do so, and **stop** when the oldest modified date is at the top of the list.

the files are sorted by date modified - first to last

Name	Size	Type	Modified
📄 savefile	1KB	Text Document	6/23/95 9:50 AM
📄 saveas	1KB	Text Document	6/23/95 10:34 AM
📄 winfun	1KB	Text Document	6/23/95 10:47 AM
📄 richtext	1KB	Rich Text Document	6/23/95 11:54 AM
🗀 My Folder		File Folder	6/24/95 9:39 AM
🗀 My Documents		File Folder	6/26/95 10:46 AM
🗀 My Things		File Folder	6/26/95 7:12 PM

Exercise 88 continued...

❹ Sort files by type from A to Z:

- **Click** `Type` two or three times, **watch** the Type column as you do so, and **stop** when the file types are arranged from A-Z.

the files are sorted by type - A to Z

Name	Size	Type	Modified
My Documents		File Folder	3/30/95 12:19 PM
My Folder		File Folder	2/25/95 9:32 AM
My Things		File Folder	4/26/95 6:38 PM
richtext	1KB	Rich Text Document	5/5/95 12:49 PM
saveas	1KB	Text Document	2/20/95 2:37 AM
savefile	1KB	Text Document	2/20/95 2:35 AM
winfun	1KB	Text Document	2/9/95 7:07 AM

❺ Sort files by type from Z to A:

- **Click** `Type` once.

the files are sorted by type - Z to A

Name	Size	Type	Modified
winfun	1KB	Text Document	2/9/95 7:07 AM
savefile	1KB	Text Document	2/20/95 2:35 AM
saveas	1KB	Text Document	2/20/95 2:37 AM
richtext	1KB	Rich Text Document	5/5/95 12:49 PM
My Things		File Folder	4/26/95 6:38 PM
My Folder		File Folder	2/25/95 9:32 AM
My Documents		File Folder	3/30/95 12:19 PM

❻ Resize columns:

- **Move** the pointer on the line between Name and Size in the column headings until the pointer becomes a double-headed arrow.

double-headed arrow

Name	Size

- **Drag** the pointer until the Name column is less than an inch wide.

column is less than 1 inch wide

Name	Size	Type	Modified
My ...		File Folder	3/30/95 12:19 PM
My ...		File Folder	2/25/95 9:32 AM
My ...		File Folder	4/26/95 6:38 PM
richt...	1KB	Rich Text Document	5/5/95 12:49 PM
sav...	1KB	Text Document	2/20/95 2:37 AM
sav...	1KB	Text Document	2/20/95 2:35 AM
winf...	1KB	Text Document	2/9/95 7:07 AM

- **Drag** the line back until the Name column is about its previous size.

The line moves into the Size (or even the Type) column, and that is all right.

Name	Size	Type	Modified
My ...		File Folder	3/30/95 12:19 PM
My F...		File Folder	2/25/95 9:32 AM
My T...		File Folder	4/26/95 6:38 PM
richt...	1KB	Rich Text Document	5/5/95 12:49 PM

❼

- **Exit** Explorer and **remove** your data disk.

EXERCISE 89

Display Hidden Files and Folders

To show files and folders that have hidden attributes and files that have certain filename extensions. The default is to Hide files of these types.

— Terms and Notes —

NOTE: See Topic 21 (page 140).

hidden files
Files and/or folders that have a hidden attribute.

NOTE: You can see if a file or folder has a hidden attribute by choosing to Show all files (in the Options dialog box), then displaying a file's properties, and finally, looking to see if the Hidden attribute has a check mark by it.

attribute
A characteristic (such as read-only, archive, hidden, or system) that changes how a file or folder can be used or displayed.

 **STEPS to**

Display hidden folders and files
—*FROM THE EXPLORER*—

1 Press **Alt** + **V** (View)
2 Press **O** (Options)
3 Press **S** (Show all files)
4 Press **↵**

Hide hidden folders and files
—*FROM THE EXPLORER*—

1 Press **Alt** + **V** (View)
2 Press **O** (Options)
3 Press **T** (Hide files of these types)
4 Press **↵**

162   Lesson Six — The Explorer

Begin with the desktop displayed and with no tasks on the taskbar.

1
- **Start** Explorer by right-clicking My Computer.
- **Click** [≡] (the List button—so your screen will match the illustration below).
- **Expand** drive (C:) and Windows (review, Exercise 78).
- **Select** the Windows folder (it should be at the top of the left pane).
- **Scroll** the right pane to the right (the bottom scroll box left).

A screen similar to the illustration below appears.

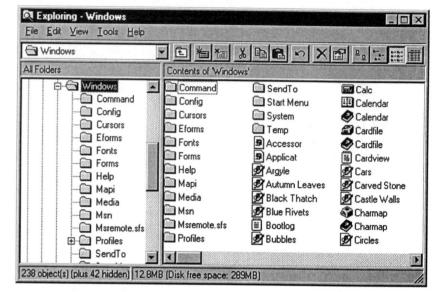

2 Display hidden folders and files:
- **Click** View, then Options.

The Options dialog box opens (see page 142).

- **Click** Show all files unless it already has a check by it, then [OK]

Explorer refreshes and appears with the previously hidden objects now displayed.
You may have to scroll the right pane to see hidden file types.

circled objects were previously hidden

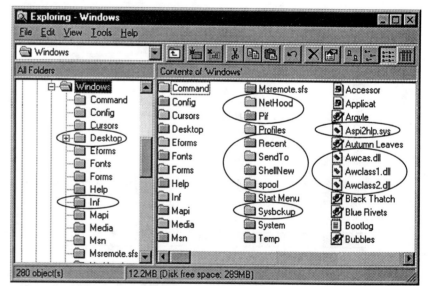

3 Hide hidden folders and files:
- **Click** View, then Options.
- **Click** Hide files of these types, then [OK]

Explorer refreshes and appears without the hidden objects (see top illustration).

- **Exit** Explorer.

Begin with the desktop displayed and with no tasks on the taskbar.

NOTE: These directions assume that the default is currently set.

1 • **Start** Explorer.
   • **Insert** your duplicate data disk into drive A:.
   • **Select** Floppy (A:) (review, Exercise 79).
   • **Click** 🔲 (the List button—so your screen will match the illustration below).
     A screen similar to the illustration below appears.

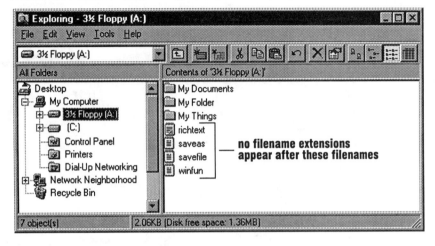

2 **Display MS-DOS file extensions:**

   • **Click** View, then Options.
     The Options dialog box opens (see page 142).
   • **Click** the box by Hide MS-DOS file extensions for file types that are registered to remove the check mark in it.
   • **Click** [OK]
     Explorer refreshes and appears with the previously hidden MS-DOS file extensions now displayed.

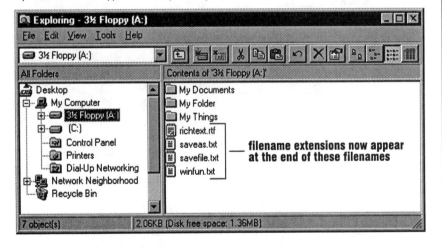

3 **Hide MS-DOS file extensions:**

   • **Click** View, then Options.
   • **Click** the box by Hide MS-DOS file extensions for file types that are registered to place a check mark in it.
   • **Click** [OK]
     Explorer refreshes and appears without MS-DOS file extensions (see top illustration).
   • **Exit** Explorer and remove your disk from drive A:.

EXERCISE 90

Display MS-DOS File Extensions

To display file extensions for registered file types. The default is to Hide MS-DOS file extensions for file types that are registered (but display all other file extensions).

— Terms and Notes —

NOTE: See Topics 11 (page 56) and 22 (page 142).

MS-DOS
(Microsoft Disk Operating System)
The main operating system used before Windows was developed.

 **STEPS to**

Display or hide MS-DOS file extensions

—FROM THE EXPLORER—

1 Press `Alt` + `V` (View)
2 Press `O` (Options)
3 **Display MS-DOS file extensions**
   • Press `E` (Hide MS-DOS file extensions for types that are registered) to remove the check mark from the box.
   or
   Hide MS-DOS file extensions
   • Press `E` (Hide MS-DOS file extensions for types that are registered) to place a check mark in the box.
4 Press `↵`

EXERCISE 91

Display Full MS-DOS Path

To show the entire path to the selected folder in the right pane title. The default is to show only the name of the selected folder in the right pane title.

— Terms and Notes —

path
The route to a folder or file; it consists of the disk drive, all the levels of subfolders that lead to a folder, and the filename itself. For example, C:\WINDOWS\CALC is the path to the Calculator program in the Windows folder. If long filenames are used in a path, the path is enclosed in quotes ("). For example, "A:\My Folder\help2.doc" is the path to the document file, help2 on drive A:.

 **STEPS to**

Display or hide full MS-DOS path

—FROM THE EXPLORER—

1 Press `Alt` + `V` (View)

2 Press `O` (Options)

3 **Display full MS-DOS path**
   • Press `P` (Display the full MS-DOS path in title bar) to place the check mark in the box.

   or

   Hide full MS-DOS path
   • Press `P` (Display the full MS-DOS path in title bar) to remove the check mark from the box.

4 Press `↵`

Begin with the desktop displayed and with no tasks on the taskbar.

NOTE: These directions assume that the default is set; that is, Display the full MS-DOS path in the title bar is NOT selected.

1
• **Start** Explorer by right-clicking the Start button (review, Exercise 76).
• **Click** [List button icon] (the List button—so your screen will match the illustration below).
• **Expand** Programs and Accessories (review, Exercise 78).
• **Select** the Accessories folder (review, Exercise 79).
  A screen similar to the illustration below appears.

title bar for the right pane of Explorer - displays the name of the selected folder

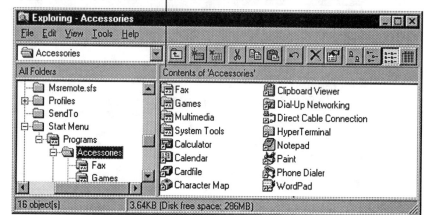

2 Display the full MS-DOS path in the title bar:
• **Click** View, then Options.
  The Options dialog box opens (see page 141).
• **Click** the box by Display the full MS-DOS path in the title bar to place a check mark in it.
• **Click** [OK]
  The full MS-DOS path to the selected folder is now displayed in the title bar.

the title bar displays the full MS-DOS path to the selected folder now

3 Display only the selected folder name in the title bar:
• **Click** View, then Options.
• **Click** the box by Display the full MS-DOS path in the title bar to remove the check mark from it.
• **Click** [OK]
  Only the selected folder name appears in the title bar (see top illustration).
• **Exit** Explorer.

Formatting a Floppy Disk

In this exercise you will format your duplicate data disk. You can use the same procedure to format other disks. Before you format a disk, you need to identify the size and density of that disk. It is easy to visually determine a disk's size—either 3½" or 5¼". It can be more difficult to determine a disk's density (or capacity):

- 3½" disks come in two standard densities:
    HD (high density)—1.44 Mb
    DD (double density)—720 Kb
    Typically, 3½" disks that can be formatted to 1.44 Mb have two holes at the top while those that can be formatted to 720 Kb have only one hole.

- 5¼" disks come in two standard densities:
    HD (high density)—1.2 Mb
    DD (double density)—360 Kb
    Typically, 5¼" disks that can be formatted to 1.2 Mb have plain hub around the inside of the disk while those that can be formatted to 360 Kb have a reinforced hub.

You can format a high density disk to double density, but if you do, you cannot format it back to high density later. You should not format a double density disk to high density. The most common disk size and density used for drive A: in computers today is 3½" HD (1.44 Mb). However, your system may use 3½" DD (720 Kb), 5¼" HD (1.2 Mb) or 5¼" DD (360 Kb) disks.

Begin with the desktop displayed and with no tasks on the taskbar.

1
- **Start** Explorer.
- **Insert** your duplicate data disk into drive A:.
- **Locate**, but do *not* select, Floppy (A:).

2 Choose a format capacity for your disk in drive A:

- **Right-click** Floppy (A:) and **click** Format... .
  The Format - Floppy (A:) dialog box opens.

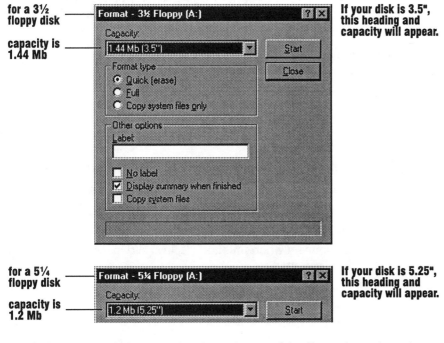

for a 3½ floppy disk

capacity is 1.44 Mb

If your disk is 3.5", this heading and capacity will appear.

for a 5¼ floppy disk

capacity is 1.2 Mb

If your disk is 5.25", this heading and capacity will appear.

- **Skip to** step 3 if the capacity shown in one of the illustrations above is correct (1.44 Mb or 1.2 Mb).

Exercise 92 continued...

— Terms and Notes —

floppy disk density
Density refers to the surface coating on a disk; the closer together the particles on the disk, the higher the disk's capacity.
Typically, 3½" floppy disks come in two densities: DD (double density)—720 Kb and HD (high density)—1.44 Mb.
Typically, 5¼" floppy disks come in two densities; DD (double density)—360 Kb and HD (high density)—1.2 Mb.

⌨ STEPS to

Format a disk
—FROM MY COMPUTER—
1 **Select** the desired floppy disk drive *(see keyboard steps for Exercise 79)*.
2 Press `Alt` + `F` (File)
3 Press `M` (Format)
4 **Select** capacity (only if necessary):
   - Press `Alt` + `P` (Capacity)
   - Press `Alt` + `↓`
   - Press `↓` or `↑` to select the desired capacity.
   - Press `↵`
5 **Select** one format type:
   - Press `Alt` + `Q` (Quick (erase)) or
   - Press `Alt` + `F` (Full) or
   - Press `Alt` + `O` (Copy system files only)
6 Enter a disk label if desired.
   - Press `Alt` + `L` (Label)
   - **Type** the desired label.
7 **Select** Other options as desired:
   - Press `Alt` + `N` (No label)
   - Press `Alt` + `D` (Display summary when finished)
   - Press `Alt` + `Y` (Copy system files)
8 Press `Alt` + `S` (Start)
   The dialog box reports the computer's status and progress.
9 Press `↵` to accept Close.
10 Press `↵` to accept Close, again.

FORMAT A FLOPPY DISK

— Terms and Notes —

startup disk
A disk that contains certain system files that create a system (or bootable) disk. It is a good safeguard to have a startup disk for drive A:—If the hard disk should have a problem, you can boot the computer using this floppy system disk.

bad sectors
Damaged areas on a disk that are marked as unusable when the disk is formatted. A few bad sectors do not necessarily make the entire disk unusable. However, a disk with bad sectors should not be used as a destination disk when copying a disk.

SKIP THIS UNLESS YOU KNOW THAT:
you are using a 3½" <u>DD</u> (720 Mb) disk or a 5½" <u>DD</u> (360 Mb) disk.

NOTE: If your 3½" disk has only one hole at the top, it is probably a 720 Kb disk; if your 5¼" disk has a reinforced hub, it is probably a 360K disk.

- **Click** the Ca<u>p</u>acity drop-down list box.
  The options for capacity drop down.

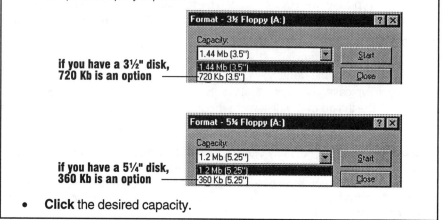

if you have a 3½" disk, 720 Kb is an option

if you have a 5¼" disk, 360 Kb is an option

- **Click** the desired capacity.

3 **Select the format type, "Full":**

There are three Format types; below are explanations of what each does:

1. **<u>Q</u>uick (erase)** quickly removes all the files from a previously formatted disk. You should use a quick format only if you are sure that your disk is not damaged since it does not scan the disk for **bad sectors**.

2. **<u>F</u>ull** prepares a disk that you can store information on. Then it scans the disk for bad sectors. Any files on the disk will be removed.

3. **Copy system files <u>o</u>nly** copies system files to a disk that is already formatted, and does *not* erase the files already on the disk. Use this option to prepare a disk that can be used as a **startup disk** on drive A:.

- **Click** <u>F</u>ull.

Format type ——
Full ——

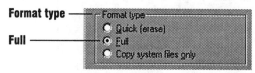

4 **Select the Other option, "Display summary when finished":**

There are three Other options; below are explanations of what each does:

1. **<u>N</u>o label** specifies that you do not want to name the disk.
   IF you do not check this box, you can name your disk in the Label text box.

2. **<u>D</u>isplay** summary **when finished** displays information about the disk after formatting is finished.

3. **Copy s<u>y</u>stem files** copies system files to the disk after it is formatted.

Exercise 92 continued...

- **Click** the Label text box and **type:** MY DISK #1
- **Select** <u>D</u>isplay summary when finished—it may already be selected (it is selected if it has a check mark in the box by it).

  The "Display summary when finished" option should be the only option selected (as illustrated below).

NOTES: You do not need to label your data disk. Many people prefer to select No label.

You can see a disk's label by looking at its properties—right-click Floppy (A:) and click Properties (you can also change the disk's label in the Properties dialog box).

Other options ————

Label text box ————

Display summary when finished ————

⑤ Start the format:

- **Click** [S<u>t</u>art]

  The format process begins; the bottom of the dialog box reports the computer's status and progress.

status ————

progress ————

When the format is complete, the Format Results dialog box appears.

Results for a 3½ HD (1.44 Mb) disk. ————

The bytes of total disk space will be different for disks of different sizes and densities. ————

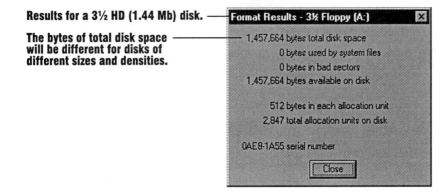

⑥ Close the format:

- **Click** [<u>C</u>lose] (the Close button for the Format Results dialog box).
- **Click** [<u>C</u>lose] (the Close button for the Format Floppy (A:) dialog box).
- **Select** Floppy (A:).
- **Notice** the contents of Floppy (A:) in the right pane.

  Nothing appears in the right pane because all the files on the disk were erased when the disk was formatted.

⑦
- **Exit** Explorer and **remove** your newly formatted data disk.

EXERCISE 93
Practice

Lesson Six
The Explorer

Tasks Reviewed:
- Start Explorer
- Resize Explorer's Panes
- Expand and Collapse Folders
- Select Objects in the Left Pane
- Browse Your Data Disk
- Copy a Disk
- Select Objects in the Right Pane
- Invert Selection
- Select All Objects

Begin with the desktop displayed and with no tasks on the taskbar.

1
- **Start** Explorer by right-clicking the Start menu.
- **Exit** Explorer.
- **Start** Explorer by right-clicking My Computer.
- **Exit** Explorer.
- **Start** Explorer using the Start and Programs menus.
- **Resize** Explorer's panes by making the left pane about 1 inch wide.
- **Resize** Explorer's panes by enlarging the left pane until the scroll bar at the bottom of the left pane disappears (you may have to make several tries).
- **Exit** Explorer.

2
- **Start** Explorer by right-clicking My Computer.
- **Maximize** Explorer.
- **Expand** drive C:.
  NOTE: You may need to scroll to locate objects in this exercise.
- **Expand** the Windows folder.
- **Expand** the Start Menu folder.
- **Expand** the Programs folder.
- **Expand** the Accessories folder.

3
- **View** right pane objects in the *Large icon* mode.
- **Select** objects in the left pane:
  - **Select** My Computer and notice the objects in the right pane.
  - **Select** drive C: and notice the objects in the right pane.
  - **Select** the Windows folder and notice the objects in the right pane.
  - **Select** the Programs folder and notice the objects in the right pane.
  - **Select** the Accessories folder and notice the objects in the right pane.

4
- **Collapse** the Accessories, Programs, Start Menu, and Windows folders.
- **Collapse** drive C:.
- **Collapse** My Computer.
- **Restore** Explorer.
- **Exit** Explorer.

5
- **Start** Explorer using the method you prefer.
- **Insert** your original data disk in drive A:.
- **Select** Floppy (A:) and notice the contents of Floppy (A:) in the right pane.
- **View** right pane objects in the *List* mode.
- **Expand** Floppy (A:).
- **Select** My Documents, then My Folder, then My Things (each in the left pane) and notice the contents of each folder in the right pane.
- **Exit** Explorer.

Exercise 93 continued...

6 • **Start** Explorer using the method you prefer.

• **Copy your original data disk** to the duplicate data disk (the one you formatted in Exercise 92).

• **Exit** Explorer.

7 • **Start** Explorer using the method you prefer.

• **Insert** your duplicate data disk in drive A:.

• **Select** Floppy (A:).

• **View** right pane objects in the *List* mode.

• **Select** objects in the right pane:

  • **Select** the single file, **saveas**.

  • **Select** the connected objects, My Things through **winfun**.

  • **Select** the separate objects, My Documents, **richtext**, and **savefile**.

  • **View** right pane objects in the *Large icon* mode.

  • **Use drag** to select several objects (as desired).

  • **Deselect** the objects.

3 • **View** right pane objects in the *List* mode.

• **Select** the separate objects, **richtext** and **winfun**.

• **Invert** the selection.

• **Select** all objects.

• **Deselect** My Folder and **richtext**.

• **Deselect** the objects.

9 • **Exit** Explorer.

• **Remove** your duplicate data disk or go on to the next exercise.

EXERCISE 94

Practice

Lesson Six
The Explorer

Tasks Reviewed:
- Move Objects
- Copy Objects
- Delete Objects
- Sort Files Using Headings
- Display Hidden Files and Folders
- Display MS-DOS File Extensions
- Display Full MS-DOS Path
- Format a Disk

Begin with the desktop displayed and with no tasks on the taskbar.

1
- **Start** Explorer using the method you prefer.
- **Insert** your duplicate data disk in drive A:.
- **Select** Floppy (A:).
- **Expand** Floppy (A:).
- **View** right pane objects in the *List* mode.

2
- **Move richtext** to My Folder (in the right pane) using drag and drop.
- **Select** My Folder (in the left pane) to view the moved file.
- **Move richtext** to Floppy (A:) using drag and drop.
- **Select** Floppy (A:).

3
- **Move richtext** to My Things using cut and paste.
- **Select** My Things (in the left pane) to view the moved file.
- **Select** Floppy (A:).
- **Undo** the move (in the right pane).

4
- **Move** My Documents to My Things.
- **Expand** My Things.
- **Select** My Things (in the left pane) and notice its contents in the right pane.
- **Select** Floppy (A:).
- **Undo** the move (in the right pane).
- **Arrange** icons by name.

5
- **Select winfun** and **richtext**.
  NOTE: Remember to press Ctrl *when you copy.*
- **Copy** the selected files to My Things (in the right pane) using drag and drop.
- **Select** My Things (in the left pane) to view the copied files.
- **Select** Floppy (A:).

6
- **Copy winfun** to My Documents (in the left pane).
- **Select** My Documents (in the left pane) to view the copied file.
- **Select** Floppy (A:).

7
- **Copy richtext** to My Folder using copy and paste.
- **Select** My Folder (in the left pane) to view the copied file.
- **Select** Floppy (A:).
- **Undo** the copy (in the right pane).

8
- **Copy** My Documents to My Things.
- **Expand** My Things.
- **Select** My Things (in the left pane) and notice its contents in the right pane.
- **Select** Floppy (A:).
- **Collapse** Floppy (A:).

Exercise 94 continued...

9 • **Maximize** Explorer.
 • **Expand** (C:).
 • **Select** Windows.
 • **Copy Autumn Leaves** to Floppy (A:) using drag and drop.
 • **Copy Bubbles** to Floppy (A:) using Send To.
 • **Collapse** (C:).

10 • **Expand** and **select** Floppy (A:).
 • **Select Autumn Leaves** and **Bubbles**.
 • **Delete** the selected files using the [Del] key.
 • **Select** the My Documents folder that is under Floppy (A:) (not the My Documents under My Things).
 • **Delete winfun** using the right-click menu.

11 • **Delete** My Documents <u>under</u> My Things using the right-click menu in the left pane.
 • **Select** My Things (in the left pane).
 • **Select richtext** and **winfun**.
 • **Delete** the selected files using the right-click menu.

12 • **Select** Floppy (A:).
 • **Collapse** Floppy (A:).
 • **View** right pane objects in the Details mode.
 • **Arrange** by filenames from Z to A using the Name column heading.
 • **Arrange** by date modified from oldest to most recent.
 • **Arrange** by date modified from most recent to oldest.
 • **Arrange** by type from A to Z.
 • **Arrange** by type from Z to A.
 • **Arrange** by filenames from A to Z using the Name column heading.
 • **Resize** the Name column to make it one inch wide.
 • **Resize** the Name column to return it to its original size.

13 • **View** right pane objects in the List mode.
 • **Expand** drive C:.
 • **Select** Windows.
 • **Notice** the files and folders.
 • **Display** the hidden files and folders.
 • **Notice** the new files and folders.
 • **Hide** the hidden files and folders.

14 • **Select** Floppy (A:).
 • **Display** the MS-DOS filename extensions.
 • **Notice** the filename extensions that now appear.
 • **Hide** the MS-DOS filename extensions.
 • **Notice** that the filename extensions have disappeared.

Exercise 94 continued...

*NOTE: If you cannot find **Autumn Leaves** and **Bubbles** in step 9, open other files with [icon] icons and then select those files in step 10.*

Exercise 94 (continued)

15 • **Expand** the Windows, Start Menu, and Programs folders.
• **Select** the Accessories folder.
• **Notice** the title for the right pane.
• **Display** the full MS-DOS path.
• **Notice** the title for the right pane.
• **Display** only the folder name in the title bar.
• **Notice** that the title for the right pane has changed back to its original title.
• **Collapse** the Programs, Start Menu, and Windows folders.
• **Collapse** (C:).

16 • **Format** your duplicate data disk using the Full format; label your disk: My Disk #2.
NOTE: Remember not to select Floppy (A:) before you right-click it to start the format.
• **Restore** Explorer.

17 • **Copy your original data disk** to the disk just formatted in step 16.
• **Exit** Explorer and **remove** the duplicate data disk from drive A:.

Lesson Six Worksheets (14 and 15) are in Appendix D

Lesson Seven
Finding Files

Table of Contents

TOPIC 23
Find Files and Folders

Find
A program found in both the Start menu and Explorer's Tools menu that helps you locate files and folders easily by defining search criteria that give hints about the files for which you are looking.

search criteria
The guidelines that you tell Find to follow when it searches for certain files or folders. For example, to find all the files that contain the letters, *doc*, or to find all the files that were created in the last month.

The Find Program

The **Find** program helps you locate files and folders; that is, it finds the folder (including the path to it) where the files and/or folders you are looking for reside. You can access Find from the Start button or from the Explorer's Tools menu. You can also start Find by right-clicking the Start button, My Computer, or any other folder and then clicking <u>F</u>ind. When you access Find from a folder, Find opens with the path to that folder in its Look in box.

You search for files using a **search criteria** (or a combination of several search criteria). You can use criteria to search for files and folders that are based on:

- name (or partial name) and location
- date of creation or last modification
- type, size, or the text contained in a file

Use this tab to enter the criteria for finding files based on name and location.

Use this tab to enter the criteria for finding files based on the date they were created or last modified.

Use this tab to enter the criteria for finding files based on type, size, or the text contained in a file.

Topic 23 continued...

Click the **Browse** button to find the specific folder where you want to begin your search. The Browse dialog box is organized like the left pane of Explorer—you can expand and collapse folders to find the one you want. Selecting a folder and clicking [OK] will put that folder in the Look in box.

— Terms and Notes —

browse
To look at files, folders, disks, printers, programs, documents, and other objects on your computer system.

NOTE: While the Browse window takes a hierarchial form (similar to the left pane of Explorer) when opened from the Find window, it takes a **folder window** *form (more like the right pane of Explorer) when opened in certain other situations.*

Finding a file can be as simple as typing a name (or partial name) in the Named text box and clicking the Find Now button. Or, it can be as complex as using one or more search criteria from each of the Find tabs (shown on the previous page) to locate files. Below is an illustration of the files and folders you would find on your data disk in drive A: if you typed doc in the Named text box.

search criteria

doc
(partial name)

Floppy (A:)
(location)

files and folders found

(all meet the search criteria; that is all contain doc and all are found on Floppy (A:))

Once files and folders have been found, you can perform file management tasks on them such as:

- open
- print
- delete
- sort
- rename

- move
- copy
- change view mode
- create shortcuts
- look at properties

You can save search criteria, or you can save the results of the search and the search criteria.

EXERCISE 95
Start Find

To use the Start button, Explorer, My Computer, or a folder to open the Find feature.

 **STEPS to**

Start Find

—USING THE START MENU—

1 **Press** `Ctrl` + `Esc` (Start menu)
2 **Press** `F` (Find)
3 **Press** `F` (Files or Folders)

—USING THE START BUTTON—

1 **Press** `Ctrl` + `Esc`, `Esc`
2 **Press** `Shift` + `F10`
3 **Press** `F` (Find)

—FROM THE EXPLORER—

1 **Press** `Alt` + `T` (Tools)
2 **Press** `F` (Find)
3 **Press** `F` (Files or Folders)

—USING MY COMPUTER—

1 **Press** `Ctrl` + `Esc`, `Esc`
2 **Press** `Shift` + `Tab`
3 **Press** arrow keys to select My Computer.
4 **Press** `Shift` + `F10`
5 **Press** `F` (Filnd)

—USING A FOLDER—

1 **Select** a folder *(see Steps to select a folder, page 147).*
2 **Press** `Shift` + `F10`
3 **Press** `F` (Find)

Open Find menus

—FROM FIND—

Look at Find menus

• **Press** `Alt` + the first letter of the menu you want to open.

NOTE: Once one menu is opened, you can use right and left arrow keys to move to other menus and up and down arrow keys to move within a menu.

Begin with the desktop displayed and with no tasks on the taskbar.

① Start Find from the Explorer:

• **Click** [🔳 Start], then Programs, then Windows Explorer.
• **Click** Tools, then Find, then Files or Folders.
  The Find: All Files dialog box opens with (C:) in the Look in box.

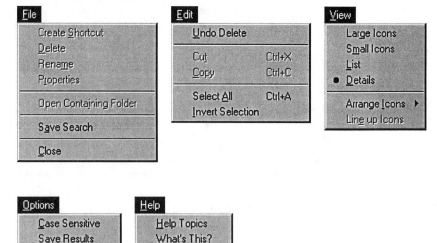

• **Exit** Find.
• **Exit** Explorer.

② Start Find from the Start menu:

• **Click** [🔳 Start]
• **Click** Find, then Files or Folders.
  Again, the Find: All Files dialog box opens with (C:) in the Look in box.

③ Look at Find menus:

• **Click** the File menu and examine the menu.
• **Move** the pointer over the Edit, View, Options, and Help menus examining each menu as it opens.

File	Edit	View
Create Shortcut	Undo Delete	Large Icons
Delete		Small Icons
Rename	Cut Ctrl+X	List
Properties	Copy Ctrl+C	• Details
Open Containing Folder	Select All Ctrl+A	Arrange Icons ▶
Save Search	Invert Selection	Line up Icons
Close		

Options	Help
Case Sensitive	Help Topics
Save Results	What's This?

NOTE: The File menu will have different options available, depending upon the object that is selected in the Find results section (when there is a result section).

④ • **Exit** Find.

Exercise 95 continued...

⑤ Start Find by right-clicking the Start button:

- **Right-click**  , then <u>F</u>ind.

  The Find: All Files dialog box opens with C:\WINDOWS\Start Menu in the Look in box.

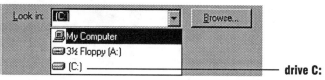

Start Menu folder

NOTE: The last folder (or the drive letter) in the Look in box is where Find will begin looking for files.

⑥ Change the Look in box to drive C:

- **Click** the arrow for the <u>L</u>ook in box.

  The drop-down menu opens.

drive C:

- **Click** 🖴 (C:)

  (C:) now appears in the Look in box.

- **Exit** Find.

⑦ Start Find by right-clicking My Computer:

- **Right-click** My Computer, then <u>F</u>ind.

  The Find: All Files dialog box opens with My Computer in the Look in box.

My Computer folder

- **Exit** Find.

⑧ Start Find by right-clicking a folder:

- **Start** Explorer by right-clicking My Computer.
- **Expand** (C:).
- **Scroll** until you locate the Windows folder.
- **Right-click** the Windows folder, then <u>F</u>ind.

  The Find: All Files dialog box opens with the Windows folder in the Look in box.

Windows folder

NOTE: When you start Find by right-clicking a folder, Find begins its search with that folder (unless you first change it).

- **Exit** Find.
- **Exit** Explorer.

EXERCISE 96

Find Files by Name & Location

To display files that meet search criteria based on filename and location.

— Terms and Notes —

WARNING: You will not be reminded to remove your data disk. Always remove your data disk before you turn your computer off.

 **STEPS to**

Search for files by name and location

—FROM FIND—

Prepare for your search

Choose from the items below:

Enter a name

1 Press **Alt** + **N** (Name)

2 **Type** the desired filename or partial filename.

Change the drive or folder

1 Press **Alt** + **L** (Look in)

2 Press **Alt** + **↓** to open the box.

3 Press **↑** or **↓** to highlight the desired location.

Browse for a folder to search

1 Press **Alt** + **B** (Browse)

2 Press **↑** or **↓** to highlight the desired folder.

• Press **→** to expand a folder.

• Press **←** to collapse a folder.

3 **Continue** until you select the desired folder to search.

4 Press **↵**

Do not search subfolders

• Press **Alt** + **S** (Include subfolders) to deselect the option.

Start a new search (reset to defaults)

1 Press **Alt** + **W** (New Search)

2 Press **↵**

Start the search

• Press **Alt** + **I** (Find Now)

Begin with the desktop displayed and with no tasks on the taskbar.

❶ • **Start** Find by clicking the Start button, then **F**ind, then **F**iles or Folders.

The Find: All Files dialog box opens with the cursor blinking in the Named text box and with (C:) in the Look in box.

❷ Use a filename as a search criteria:

• **Type:** Zig Zag

• **Click** [Find Now]

*The search icon (a magnifier) rotates and displays a page under it as Find examines the folders on drive C: looking for files that have **Zig Zag** in them.*

*The results of your search are displayed at the bottom; Find tells you the folder in which it found **Zig Zag**, its approximate size, its file type, and date last modified.*

Results of your search —

the folder in which Zig Zag was found   file size   file type   modified date

*NOTE: If **Zig Zag** does not appear in the Find results box, go back to the beginning of step 2 and type* Windows Logo *or* Forest, *and continue through the step substituting the new filename for **Zig Zag** throughout the step.*

❸ Change to drive A:

• **Insert** your duplicate data disk in drive A:.

• **Click** the arrow for the **L**ook in box.

The drop-down menu appears with My Computer and Floppy (A:) in it.

Look in: [C:]
  🖥 My Computer
  💾 3½ Floppy (A:) ———————— **floppy (A:)**
  💾 [C:]

• **Click** 💾 3½ Floppy (A:)

❹ Use part of a filename as a search criteria:

• **Click** the **N**amed box.

• **Type:** doc then **press** **↵**

The results of your search are displayed at the bottom of Find.

• **Maximize** Find and examine the results.

The results of your search should match the illustration on page 175.

Exercise 96 continued...

❺ Change the search criteria:

- **Click** the <u>N</u>amed box.
- **Delete** doc , **type:** 2 , **and click** [<u>F</u>ind Now]
  The results are displayed at the bottom; every file contains **2***.*

**every file
contains 2**

Name	In Folder	Size	Type	Modified
My Doc 2	A:\My Documents	1KB	Text Document	6/26/95 10:52 AM
DOC2	A:\My Things	1KB	Text Document	6/26/95 4:05 PM
create2	A:\My Folder	1KB	Rich Text Document	6/23/95 2:31 PM
help2	A:\My Folder	2KB	Rich Text Document	6/25/95 1:43 PM

- **Restore** Find.

❻ Search without including subfolders:

When you start Find, the Include <u>s</u>ubfolders box is selected; that is, it has a check mark in it. Therefore, Find will search the folder or drive in the Look in box and all the folders within that folder or drive.

- **Click** the Include <u>s</u>ubfolders box to deselect it.

**include subfolders
box**

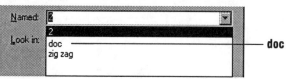

- **Click** the arrow on the right end of the <u>N</u>amed drop-down list box.
  The Named box opens displaying up to the last ten search criteria used.

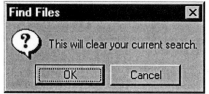 ── **doc**

- **Click** doc, then [<u>F</u>ind Now]
  *Since no subfolders are searched, only one object containing doc is found in drive A:;
  the My Documents folder.*

❼ Browse for a folder to search:

- **Click** [<u>B</u>rowse...]
- **Expand** Floppy (A:), **select** My Documents, then **click** [OK]
  My Documents is displayed in the Look in box.
- **Click** [<u>F</u>ind Now]
  Only My Documents is searched; **My Doc 1***,* **My Doc 2***, and* **My Doc 3** *are displayed.*

❽ Start a new search (reset Find to its defaults):

- **Click** [Ne<u>w</u> Search]
  The Find Files dialog box opens and tells you that this will clear your current search.

  Find Files ☒
  ❓ This will clear your current search.
  [OK] [Cancel]

- **Click** [OK]
  *The Find: All Files dialog box is cleared. It now appears without objects at the bottom, with (C:)
  displayed in the Look in box, and with a check mark by Include subfolders.*

- **Exit** Find.

EXERCISE 97

Find Files by Date Modified

To display files that meet search criteria based on the date the files were created or last modified.

 **STEPS to**

Find files by Date Modified

—FROM FIND—

1 Press **Ctrl** + **Tab** until the Date Modified tab moves to the front.

2 Press **Alt** + **M** (Find all files created or <u>m</u>odified)

3 Choose one option to search by:
   Between (date) and (date)
   - Press **Alt** + **B** (<u>b</u>etween (date) and (date)
   - Press **Tab** to move to the first date entry.
   - **Type** the beginning search date.
   - Press **Tab** to move to the second date entry.
   - **Type** the ending search date.
   During the previous (number) months
   - Press **Alt** + **S** (during the previou<u>s</u> month(s))
   - Press **Tab** to move to number of months spin box.
   - **Type** the number of months; or, press **↑** to increase the number and **↓** to decrease the number.
   During the previous (number) days
   - Press **Alt** + **D** (<u>d</u>uring the previous day(s))
   - Press **Tab** to move to number of months spin box.
   - **Type** the number of days; or, press **↑** to increase the number and **↓** to decrease the number.

4 Press **Alt** + **I** (<u>F</u>ind Now)

Find Files by the Date they were Created or Modified

To locate files that were created or modified within a specific time frame, use the Date Modified tab. First select **Find all files created or <u>m</u>odified:**, then select one of the three ways to search by date:

- **<u>b</u>etween (date) and (date)** searches for files that were created (or modified) between the dates you indicate.
- **during the previou<u>s</u> (number) months(s)** searches for files that were created (or modified) within the number of months you indicate.
- **<u>d</u>uring the previous (number) day(s)** searches for files that were created (or modified) within the number of days you indicate.

Begin with the desktop displayed and with no tasks on the taskbar.

1 • **Start** Find by opening the Start menu.
   • **Click** the Date Modified tab.

2 **Find files modified during the previous month:**
   • **Click** the Find all files created or <u>m</u>odified option button.
   • **Click** the during the previou<u>s</u> month(s) option button.
   • **Click** Find Now

   The results are displayed at the bottom; there are many files that are used by the system included.

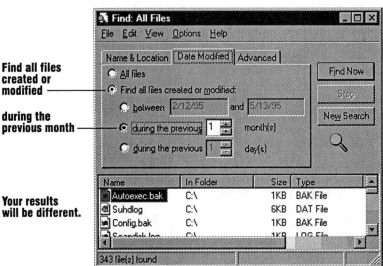

Find all files created or modified

during the previous month

Your results will be different.

3 **Find files modified during the previous two days:**
   • **Click** the <u>d</u>uring the previous day(s) option button.
   • **Click** the up arrow in the spin box to change from 1 to 2 days.

   during the previous **2** *day(s)* — **up arrow in spin box**

   • **Click** Find Now

   The results are displayed at the bottom; many of the files are used by the system.

4 • **Exit** Find.

   NOTE: When you exit Find, the changes you made are reset to their defaults.

Begin with the desktop displayed and with no tasks on the taskbar.

1
- **Start** Find and **make** sure your duplicate data disk is in drive A:.
- **Change** the Look in box to Floppy (A:) (review, Exercise 96, step 3).
- **Click** the Advanced tab.

2 **Find files at most 1 KB in size:**
- **Click** the Size is drop-down box.

  The box opens displaying three options: none, At least, and At most.

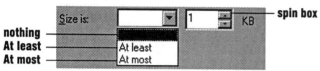

- **Click** At most (this means that every file will be equal to or less than the number of KB shown in the spin box to the right).
- **Click** the up arrow in the spin box to the right so it displays 1.

- **Click** [Find Now]

  Fifteen files are found on drive A: that are At most 1 KB (that is, 1 KB or less).

3 **Sort files by size and look at a file's size in bytes:**
- **Maximize** the Find window.
- **Click** the Size heading to sort the files by size.

  The folders are at the top; the rest of the files all have 1 KB.

  NOTE: The size of files is rounded up to the nearest kilobyte (KB—approximately 1,000 bytes). You can see the exact number of bytes a file occupies by looking at its properties. The files created using this book are relatively small.

- **Right-click winfun** then **click** Properties.

  *The **winfun** Properties opens and shows the Size as about 35 bytes.*

- **Cancel** the **winfun** Properties dialog box.
- **Scroll** to locate **create1** (if necessary).
- **Right-click create1** then **click** Properties.

  *The **create1** Properties opens and shows the Size as about 981 bytes.*

- **Cancel** the **create1** Properties dialog box.

4 **Find files at least 1 KB in size:**
- **Click** the Size is drop-down box, then At least.
- **Click** [Find Now]

  Two files are found on drive A: that are at least 1 KB (that is, 1 KB or more).

Name	In Folder	Size	Type	Modified
help	A:\My Folder	2KB	Rich Text Document	5/13/95 2:21 PM
help2	A:\My Folder	2KB	Rich Text Document	5/13/95 2:21 PM

- **Right-click help** then **click** Properties.

  *The **help** Properties opens and shows the Size as 1,292 bytes (approximately).*

- **Cancel** the **help** Properties dialog box.

5
- **Exit** Find.

— Terms and Notes —

NOTE: Your file sizes may may be different than the results shown in this exercise.

 **STEPS to**

Find files by size

—FROM FIND—

1 **Press** [Ctrl] + [Tab] until the Advanced tab moves to the front.

2 **Press** [Alt] + [S] (Size is)

3 **Press** [Alt] + [↓] to open the box.

4 **Press** [↑] or [↓] to highlight the desired size option:
- none
- At least
- At most

5 **Press** [Tab]

6 **Press** [↑] to increase or [↓] to decrease the number of KB.

  or

  Type the desired number of KB.

7 **Press** [Alt] + [I] (Find Now)

EXERCISE 99

Find Files by File Type

To display files that meet search criteria based on file type.

— Terms and Notes —

NOTE: You can use criteria from one, two, or three of the Find tabs in your search. In fact, you always use the Name & Location section since the Look in box always has an entry that tells Find where to begin its search. The Advance section always defaults to All Files and folders.

Begin with the desktop displayed and with no tasks on the taskbar.

❶
- **Start** Find and **make** sure your duplicate data disk is in drive A:.
- **Change** the Look in box to Floppy (A:) (review, Exercise 96, step 3).
- **Click** the Advanced tab.
  The Of type box displays All Files and Folders.

❷ Find all files and folders:

- **Click** [Find Now]
  The results section displays all the files and folders on your disk—17 file(s) found.
  NOTE: Since folders are just a special kind of file, Windows counts them together.
- **Maximize** Find.
- **Scroll** through the files and folders.
  The files and folders below should all be displayed.

Name	In Folder	Size	Type	Modified
savefile	A:\	1KB	Text Document	6/23/95 9:50 AM
saveas	A:\	1KB	Text Document	6/23/95 10:34 AM
winfun	A:\	1KB	Text Document	6/23/95 10:47 AM
richtext	A:\	1KB	Rich Text Document	6/23/95 11:54 AM
My Documents	A:\		File Folder	6/26/95 10:46 AM
My Things	A:\		File Folder	6/26/95 7:12 PM
My Folder	A:\		File Folder	6/24/95 9:39 AM
My Doc 1	A:\My Documents	1KB	Rich Text Document	6/26/95 10:49 AM
My Doc 2	A:\My Documents	1KB	Text Document	6/26/95 10:52 AM
My Doc 3	A:\My Documents	1KB	Text Document	6/26/95 1:16 PM
DOC3	A:\My Things	1KB	Rich Text Document	6/26/95 4:31 PM
DOC2	A:\My Things	1KB	Text Document	6/26/95 4:05 PM
DOC1	A:\My Things	1KB	Text Document	6/26/95 1:59 PM
create1	A:\My Folder	1KB	Rich Text Document	6/23/95 2:26 PM
create2	A:\My Folder	1KB	Rich Text Document	6/23/95 2:31 PM
help	A:\My Folder	2KB	Rich Text Document	6/25/95 11:34 AM
help2	A:\My Folder	2KB	Rich Text Document	6/25/95 1:43 PM

17 file(s) found

Your results may be different and you will have to scroll to view all the files.

❸ Find one type of file (Rich Text Document):

- **Click** the Of type drop-down box.
  The Of type box drops down.

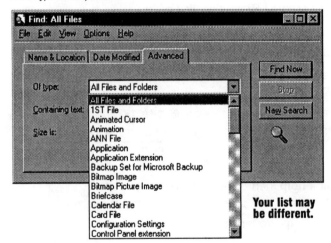

Your list may be different.

 **STEPS to**

Find files by type

—FROM FIND—

1 Press `Ctrl` + `Tab` until the Advanced tab moves to the front.
2 Press `Alt` + `T` (Of type)
3 Press `Alt` + `↓` to open the box.
4 Press `Page Down`, `Page Up`, `↑`, or `↓` to highlight the desired file type.
5 Press `↵`
6 Press `Alt` + `N` (Find Now)

Exercise 99 continued...

- **Scroll** through the list until you find Rich Text Document.
- **Click** Rich Text Document.
- **Click** [Find Now]

All the Rich Text Documents on your disk are listed at the bottom of Find.

Name	In Folder	Size	Type	Modified
richtext	A:\	1KB	Rich Text Document	6/23/95 11:54 AM
My Doc 1	A:\My Documents	1KB	Rich Text Document	6/26/95 10:49 AM
DOC3	A:\My Things	1KB	Rich Text Document	6/26/95 4:31 PM
create1	A:\My Folder	1KB	Rich Text Document	6/23/95 2:26 PM
create2	A:\My Folder	1KB	Rich Text Document	6/23/95 2:31 PM
help	A:\My Folder	2KB	Rich Text Document	6/25/95 11:34 AM
help2	A:\My Folder	2KB	Rich Text Document	6/25/95 1:43 PM

file types are all Rich Text Document

4 Find one type of files (Text Document):

- **Click** the Of type drop-down box.
- **Scroll** through the list until you find Text Document.
- **Click** Text Document.
- **Click** [Find Now]

All the Text Documents on your disk are listed at the bottom of Find.

Name	In Folder	Size	Type	Modified
savefile	A:\	1KB	Text Document	6/23/95 9:50 AM
saveas	A:\	1KB	Text Document	6/23/95 10:34 AM
winfun	A:\	1KB	Text Document	6/23/95 10:47 AM
My Doc 2	A:\My Documents	1KB	Text Document	6/26/95 10:52 AM
My Doc 3	A:\My Documents	1KB	Text Document	6/26/95 1:16 PM
DOC2	A:\My Things	1KB	Text Document	6/26/95 4:05 PM
DOC1	A:\My Things	1KB	Text Document	6/26/95 1:59 PM

file types are all Text Document

5 Find folders:

- **Click** the Of type drop-down box.
- **Scroll** through the list until you find Folder.
- **Click** Folder.
- **Click** [Find Now]

All the folders on your disk are listed at the bottom of Find.

Name	In Folder	Size	Type	Modified
My Documents	A:\		File Folder	6/26/95 10:46 AM
My Things	A:\		File Folder	6/26/95 7:12 PM
My Folder	A:\		File Folder	6/24/95 9:39 AM

types are all File Folder

6
- **Exit** Find.
- **Remove** the duplicate data disk from drive A:.

EXERCISE 100

Find Files by Text in the Files

To display files that meet search criteria based on text that appears within files.

— Terms and Notes —

case sensitive
A command option that tells a program to recognize the difference between upper- and lowercase letters when it is searching for text.

 **STEPS to**

Find files by text in the files
—FROM FIND—

1 **Prepare a non-case-sensitive criteria**
- Press `Ctrl` + `Tab` until the Advanced tab moves to the front.
- Press `Alt` + `O` (Options)
  IF Case Sensitive has a check mark:
  - Press `C` (Case Sensitive)
  IF Case Sensitive has *no* check mark:
  - Press `Alt` to close the menu.
  - Press `Alt` + `C` (Containing text)
  - Type the text to search for without regard to upper- or lowercase.

or

Prepare a case-sensitive criteria
- Press `Ctrl` + `Tab` until the Advanced tab moves to the front.
- Press `Alt` + `O` (Options)
  IF Case Sensitive has a check mark:
  - Press `Alt` to close the menu.
  IF Case Sensitive has *no* check mark:
  - Press `C` (Case Sensitive)
- Press `Alt` + `C` (Containing text)
- Type the text to search for using the exact case for the text for which you are searching.

2 Press `Alt` + `I` (Find Now)

Begin with the desktop displayed and with no tasks on the taskbar.

1
- **Start** Find and **make** sure your duplicate data disk is in drive A:.
- **Change** the Look in box to Floppy (A:) (review, Exercise 96, step 3).
- **Click** the Advanced tab.
- **Click** the Options menu.
  - **IF** Case Sensitive has *no* check mark by it, **close** the Options menu.
  or
  - **IF** Case Sensitive has a check mark by it, **click** Case Sensitive to deselect it.

2 Find files that contain the text, Notepad:
- **Click** the Containing text box.
- **Type:** Notepad
- **Click** [Find Now]
  Two files are found.

Name	In Folder	Size	Type	Mo
savefile	A:\	1KB	Text Document	6/
saveas	A:\	1KB	Text Document	6/

files that contain the text, Notepad

- **Right-click savefile**, then **click** Open.
  *Notepad opens with **savefile**. Notepad is the first word in the document.*
- **Close** Notepad.

3 Find files that contain the text, click:
- **Delete** the text in the Containing text box.
- **Type:** click
- **Click** [Find Now]
  Find searches for all occurrences of click. Six files are found.
- **Size** Find so you can see all the files.

Name	In Folder	Size	Type	Modified
My Doc 3	A:\My Documents	1KB	Text Document	6/26/95 1:16 PM
DOC3	A:\My Things	1KB	Rich Text Document	6/26/95 4:31 PM
create1	A:\My Folder	1KB	Rich Text Document	6/23/95 2:26 PM
create2	A:\My Folder	1KB	Rich Text Document	6/23/95 2:31 PM
help	A:\My Folder	2KB	Rich Text Document	6/25/95 11:34 AM
help2	A:\My Folder	2KB	Rich Text Document	6/25/95 1:43 PM

files that contain the text, click

- **Right-click My Doc 3**, then **click** Open.
  *Notepad opens with **My Doc 3**.*
- **Locate** the word, click.
- **Close** Notepad.

4 Find files that contain the uppercase letters, CLICK:
- **Delete** the text in the Containing text box.
- **Type:** CLICK
- **Click** [Find Now]
  The same six files are displayed that were found in step 3 above.
  *NOTE: Find is still searching for upper- and lowercase instances of **click**.*
- **Click** Options, then Case Sensitive to select it.

Exercise 100 continued...

- **Click** | Find Now |

  Find searches only for instances of uppercase CLICK. Now just two files are found.

Name	In Folder	Size	Type	Modified
create1	A:\My Folder	1KB	Rich Text Document	6/23/95 2:26 PM
create2	A:\My Folder	1KB	Rich Text Document	6/23/95 2:31 PM

  files that contain uppercase instances of the text, CLICK

- **Start** and **maximize** WordPad.

- **Open create1**, a Rich Text Document located in My Folder on drive A: (don't forget to change Files of type to Rich Text Format (*.rtf)).

- **Locate** the uppercase word, CLICK.

- **Restore** and **exit** WordPad.

⑤ Find files that contain the lowercase word, click:

- **Delete** the text in the Containing text box.

- **Type:** click

- **Click** | Find Now |

  Find searches only for instances of lowercase click. Four files are found.

Name	In Folder	Size	Type	Modified
My Doc 3	A:\My Documents	1KB	Text Document	6/26/95 1:16 PM
DOC3	A:\My Things	1KB	Rich Text Document	6/26/95 4:31 PM
help	A:\My Folder	2KB	Rich Text Document	6/25/95 11:34 AM
help2	A:\My Folder	2KB	Rich Text Document	6/25/95 1:43 PM

  files that contain lowercase instances of the text, click

⑥
- **Click** Options, then Case Sensitive to deselect it.

- **Click** | Find Now |

  Find searches for all instances of click. Six files are found.

⑦ Find files that contain the word, friendly:

- **Delete** the text in the Containing text box.

- **Type:** friendly

- **Click** | Find Now |

  One file is found.

Name	In Folder	Size	Type	Modified
winfun	A:\	1KB	Text Document	6/23/95 10:47 AM

- **Right-click winfun**, then **click** Open.

  *Notepad opens with **winfun**; friendly is easy to find.*

- **Close** Notepad.

⑧
- **Exit** Find.

EXERCISE 101

Save Search Criteria

To save a file that contains the search criteria you entered in the Find program.

Begin with the desktop displayed and with no tasks on the taskbar.

①
- **Start** Find and **make** sure your duplicate data disk is in drive A:.
- **Change** the Look in box to Floppy (A:) (review, Exercise 96, step 3).
- **Click** the Advanced tab.
- **Click** the Options menu.
  - **IF** Save Results has *no* check mark by it, **close** the options menu.
  or
  - **IF** Save Results has a check mark by it, **click** Save Results to deselect it.

② **Create a search criteria with several variables:**
- **Maximize** Find.
- **Find** all the files that contain the word, document (review, Exercise 100).
  Eleven files are found that contain the word, document.

Name	In Folder	Size	Type	Modified
savefile	A:\	1KB	Text Document	6/23/95 9:50 AM
saveas	A:\	1KB	Text Document	6/23/95 10:34 AM
richtext	A:\	1KB	Rich Text Document	6/23/95 11:54 AM
My Doc 1	A:\My Documents	1KB	Rich Text Document	6/26/95 10:49 AM
My Doc 2	A:\My Documents	1KB	Text Document	6/26/95 10:52 AM
My Doc 3	A:\My Documents	1KB	Text Document	6/26/95 1:16 PM
DOC3	A:\My Things	1KB	Rich Text Document	6/26/95 4:31 PM
DOC1	A:\My Things	1KB	Text Document	6/26/95 1:59 PM
create1	A:\My Folder	1KB	Rich Text Document	6/23/95 2:26 PM
create2	A:\My Folder	1KB	Rich Text Document	6/23/95 2:31 PM
help	A:\My Folder	2KB	Rich Text Document	6/25/95 11:34 AM

11 file(s) found

- **Find** files Of type, Text Document; keep the word, document, in the Containing text box.
  Five files are found that contain the text, document, and are Text Documents.

Name	In Folder	Size	Type	Modified
savefile	A:\	1KB	Text Document	6/23/95 9:50 AM
saveas	A:\	1KB	Text Document	6/23/95 10:34 AM
My Doc 2	A:\My Documents	1KB	Text Document	6/26/95 10:52 AM
My Doc 3	A:\My Documents	1KB	Text Document	6/26/95 1:16 PM
DOC1	A:\My Things	1KB	Text Document	6/26/95 1:59 PM

STEPS to

Save a search without results

—FROM FIND—

1 **Create** the desired search criteria *(see keyboard steps for Exercises 96, 97, 98, 99, and 100)*.

2 **Press** `Alt` + `O` (Options)

   IF Save Results has a check mark:
   - **Press** `S` (Save Results)

   IF Save Results has *no* check mark:
   - **Press** `Alt` to close the menu.

3 **Press** `Alt` + `F` (File)

4 **Press** `Alt` + `A` (Save Search)

Open a search icon

1 **Press** `Alt` + `F` (File), `C` (Close) to close the Find program.

2 **IF** an icon on the desktop is *not* selected:
   - **Press** `Ctrl` + `Esc`, `Esc`, `Tab`, `Tab`

3 **Press** arrow keys to select the search icon.

4 **Press** `↵` to open Find with the saved criteria.

③ **Save the search criteria:**
- **Click** File, then Save Search
- **Close** Find.
  The icon for the search file is saved in the first available spot on the desktop.

  Files of type
  Text
  Document
  containing text
  document

- **Double-click** (the search icon).
  Find opens with all the criteria you entered previously.
- **Click** the Advance tab.
- **Click** [Find Now]
  The results are the same as the last result in step 2.
- **Go on** to Exercise 102 without stopping.

Go on to Exercise 102

Continue from Exercise 101

EXERCISE 102
Save Search Results

To save a file that contains the results of search criteria you entered in the Find program along with the search criteria.

1 **Save search criteria and its results:**

- **Click** Options, then Save Results.
- **Click** File, then Save Search.
- **Close** Find.

  The icon for the search file is saved in the first available spot on the desktop; it has (2) at the end of its name to differentiate it from the first search file.

  Files of type
  Text Document
  containing text
  document (2) —— **(2) makes this icon different**

- **Right-click** (the search icon that ends with (2)), then **click** Open.

  or

  Double-click (the search icon that ends with (2)).

  Find opens with all the criteria you entered previously and the results this time.

- **Click** the Advance tab.

2 **Print the Find window:**

- **Capture** the Find window () (review, Exercise 23).

- **Print** the Find window (Open WordPad, paste the capture, print, and exit WordPad).

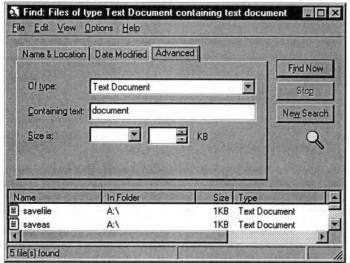

3
- **Click** Options, then Save Results to deselect Save Results.
- **Exit** Find.
- **Put** the two search icons in the Recycle Bin.
- **Empty** the Recycle Bin.

⌨ STEPS to

Save a search and the results

—FROM FIND—

1 **Create** the desired search criteria *(see keyboard steps for Exercises 96, 97, 98, 99, and 100).*

2 **Press** `Alt` + `O` (Options)

   IF Save Results has a check mark:
   - **Press** `Alt` to close the menu.

   IF Save Results has *no* check mark:
   - **Press** `S` (Save Results)

3 **Press** `Alt` + `F` (File)

4 **Press** `Alt` + `A` (Save Search)

Open a search icon

(See Open a search icon on previous page.)

EXERCISE 103

Practice

Lesson Seven
Finding Files

Tasks Reviewed:
- Start Find
- Find Files by Name & Location
- Find Files by Date Modified
- Find Files by File Size

Begin with the desktop displayed and with no tasks on the taskbar.

1
- **Start** Find from the Start menu.
- **Close** Find.
- **Start** Find by right-clicking the Start button.
- **Close** Find.
- **Start** Find by right-clicking My Computer.
- **Close** Find.

2
- **Start** Explorer.
- **Start** Find from Explorer.
- **Close** Find.
- **Expand** (C:).
- **Start** Find by right-clicking any folder.
  When Find opens, the path to the folder you used to open Find is in the Look in box.
- **Close** Find and Explorer.

3
- **Start** Find from the Start menu.
- **Maximize** Find.
- **Find** the file named **Gold Weave**.

Name	In Folder	Size	Type	Mc
Gold Weave	C:\WINDOWS	33KB	Bitmap Image	4/

- **Insert** your duplicate data disk in drive A:.
- **Change** to Floppy A:.
- **Find** files and folders that contain the partial filename, my.

Name	In Folder	Size	Type	Modified
My Documents	A:\		File Folder	6/26/95 10:46 AM
My Things	A:\		File Folder	6/26/95 7:12 PM
My Folder	A:\		File Folder	6/24/95 9:39 AM
My Doc 1	A:\My Documents	1KB	Rich Text Document	6/26/95 10:49 AM
My Doc 2	A:\My Documents	1KB	Text Document	6/26/95 10:52 AM
My Doc 3	A:\My Documents	1KB	Text Document	6/26/95 1:16 PM

4
- **Find** file and folder names that contain the number one (1).

Name	In Folder	Size	Type	Modified
My Doc 1	A:\My Documents	1KB	Rich Text Document	6/26/95 10:49 AM
DOC1	A:\My Things	1KB	Text Document	6/26/95 1:59 PM
create1	A:\My Folder	1KB	Rich Text Document	6/23/95 2:26 PM

3 file(s) found

- **Deselect** Include <u>s</u>ubfolders
- **Open** the <u>N</u>amed drop-down box and **select** my.
- **Find** files and folders that contain the partial filename, my.

Name	In Folder	Size	Type	Modified
My Documents	A:\		File Folder	6/26/95 10:46 AM
My Things	A:\		File Folder	6/26/95 7:12 PM
My Folder	A:\		File Folder	6/24/95 9:39 AM

Exercise 103 continued...

5 • **Browse** folders and select My Documents on Floppy (A:)
- **Find** files and folders that contain the partial filename, my.

Name	In Folder	Size	Type	Modified
My Doc 1	A:\My Documents	1KB	Rich Text Document	6/26/95 10:49 AM
My Doc 2	A:\My Documents	1KB	Text Document	6/26/95 10:52 AM
My Doc 3	A:\My Documents	1KB	Text Document	6/26/95 1:16 PM

- **Start** a new search.
- **Close** Find.

6 • **Start** Find from the Start menu.
- **Access** the Date Modified section.
- **Find** files and folders modified during the previous two months.
  There are probably several hundred files.
- **Find** files and folders modified during the previous three days.
  There are probably around one hundred files and folders.
- **Close** Find.

7 • **Start** Find from the Start menu.
- **Maximize** Find.
- **Access** the Advanced tab.
- **Find** files that are At least 500 KB.
  Find displays around 15 to 80 files. Your results will not match the one below.

Name	In Folder	Size	Type	Modified
Win386	C:\WINDOWS	8,192...	SWP File	6/6/95 11:02 PM
Windows	C:\WINDOWS\HELP	507KB	Help File	4/27/95 12:00 PM
Explorer	C:\WINDOWS\HELP	852KB	Video Clip	4/20/95 5:00 PM
Linking	C:\WINDOWS\HELP	537KB	Video Clip	4/20/95 5:00 PM
Movewin	C:\WINDOWS\HELP	738KB	Video Clip	4/20/95 5:00 PM
Paste	C:\WINDOWS\HELP	988KB	Video Clip	4/20/95 5:00 PM
Scroll	C:\WINDOWS\HELP	1,476...	Video Clip	4/20/95 5:00 PM
Sizewin	C:\WINDOWS\HELP	813KB	Video Clip	4/20/95 5:00 PM
Whatson	C:\WINDOWS\HELP	729KB	Video Clip	4/20/95 5:00 PM
Backup	C:\Program Files\Ac...	799KB	Application	4/27/95 12:00 PM
Disk.img	C:\bios	1,441...	IMG File	3/31/95 3:41 PM

66 file(s) found

- **Scroll** through the files and notice that quite a few of the very large files are Video Clip file types. Video clips use a lot of hard disk memory.
- **Find** files that are At most 1 KB.
  Find probably displays several humdred files and folders.
- **Close** Find.

EXERCISE 104

Practice

Lesson Seven
Finding Files

Tasks Reviewed:
- Find Files by File Type
- Find Files by Text In the Files
- Save Search Criteria
- Save Search Results

Begin with the desktop displayed and with no tasks on the taskbar.

❶
- **Start** Find from the Start menu and **maximize** it.
- **Access** the Advanced tab.
- **Find** the Video Clip file types.

  Find displays several video clip files. Your results may be different.

Name	In Folder	Size	Type	Modified
Closewin	C:\WINDOWS\HELP	401KB	Video Clip	4/20/95 5:00 PM
Dragdrop	C:\WINDOWS\HELP	300KB	Video Clip	4/20/95 5:00 PM
Explorer	C:\WINDOWS\HELP	852KB	Video Clip	4/20/95 5:00 PM
Find	C:\WINDOWS\HELP	478KB	Video Clip	4/20/95 5:00 PM
Linking	C:\WINDOWS\HELP	537KB	Video Clip	4/20/95 5:00 PM
Movewin	C:\WINDOWS\HELP	738KB	Video Clip	4/20/95 5:00 PM
Paste	C:\WINDOWS\HELP	988KB	Video Clip	4/20/95 5:00 PM
Scroll	C:\WINDOWS\HELP	1,476...	Video Clip	4/20/95 5:00 PM
Sizewin	C:\WINDOWS\HELP	813KB	Video Clip	4/20/95 5:00 PM
Taskswch	C:\WINDOWS\HELP	416KB	Video Clip	4/20/95 5:00 PM
Whatson	C:\WINDOWS\HELP	729KB	Video Clip	4/20/95 5:00 PM

`11 file(s) found`

- **Find** the Shortcut file types.

  NOTE: Every shortcut is a very small file that points to an object.
- **Scroll** through the shortcut files.
- **Close** Find.

❷
- **Start** Find and **make sure** your duplicate data disk is in drive A:.
- **Change** the Look in box to Floppy (A:).
- **Access** the Advanced tab.
- **Check** the Options menu and, if Case Sensitive is selected, deselect it.
- **Find** files that contain the text, user.

Name	In Folder	Size	Type	Mo
winfun	A:\	1KB	Text Document	6/

- **Open winfun** and see for yourself that the word, user, is in the file.
- **Exit** Notepad.

❸
- **Find** files that contain the text, enter.

Name	In Folder	Size	Type	Modified
savefile	A:\	1KB	Text Document	6/23/95 9:50 AM
saveas	A:\	1KB	Text Document	6/23/95 10:34 AM
My Doc 1	A:\My Documents	1KB	Rich Text Document	6/26/95 10:49 AM
create1	A:\My Folder	1KB	Rich Text Document	6/23/95 2:26 PM
create2	A:\My Folder	1KB	Rich Text Document	6/23/95 2:31 PM
help2	A:\My Folder	2KB	Rich Text Document	6/25/95 1:43 PM

- **Select** the Case Sensitive option.
- **Click** `Find Now`

  Since Find is searching only for lowercase instances of enter, it finds only two files.

Name	In Folder	Size	Type	Modified
My Doc 1	A:\My Documents	1KB	Rich Text Document	6/26/95 10:49 AM
help2	A:\My Folder	2KB	Rich Text Document	6/25/95 1:43 PM

- **Find** files that contain the initial cap text, Enter.

Name	In Folder	Size	Type	Modified
savefile	A:\	1KB	Text Document	6/23/95 9:50 AM
saveas	A:\	1KB	Text Document	6/23/95 10:34 AM

Exercise 104 continued...

- **Find** files that contain the uppercase text, ENTER.

Name	In Folder	Size	Type	Modified
create1	A:\My Folder	1KB	Rich Text Document	6/23/95 2:26 PM
create2	A:\My Folder	1KB	Rich Text Document	6/23/95 2:31 PM

- **Deselect** the Case Sensitive option.
- **Click** | Find Now |
  Since Find is no longer searching for case sensitive text, it displays all six of the files that contain enter regardless of their case.
- **Close** Find.

4
- **Start** Find.
- **Change** the Look in box to Floppy (A:).
- **Access** the Advanced tab.
- **Check** the Options menu and, if Save Results is selected, deselect it.
- **Select** Rich Text Format file type.
- **Type** Microsoft in the Containing text box.
- **Click** | Find Now |
  Two files meet the criteria.

Name	In Folder	Size	Type	Mc
richtext	A:\	1KB	Rich Text Document	6/
My Doc 1	A:\My Documents	1KB	Rich Text Document	6/

- **Save** the search criteria.
- **Exit** Find.
- **Open** the saved search criteria.

5
- **Click** | Find Now |
- **Select** the Save Results option.
- **Save** the results and search criteria.
- **Close** Find.
- **Open** the results and search criteria.
- **Capture** the screen.
- **Print** the capture and **close** WordPad.

Exercise 104 continued...

6
- **Close** Find.
- **Put** the two search icons in the Recycle Bin.
- **Empty** the Recycle Bin.

Lesson Seven Worksheet (16)
is in Appendix D

Lesson Eight
Other Features

Table of Contents

EXERCISE 105

Use the MS-DOS Prompt

To access the MS-DOS window and prompt, and to use a few MS-DOS commands.

— Terms and Notes —

**MS-DOS
(Microsoft Disk Operating System)**
The main operating system used before Windows was developed.

MS-DOS–based application
A program that is designed to run under the MS-DOS operating system rather than the Windows operating system.

MS-DOS prompt
The signal that MS-DOS is ready for you to tell it what to do. The default MS-DOS prompt displays the path to the current folder followed by the greater than sign (>) and a blinking underline. For example, if you are in Windows, the MS-DOS prompt will look like this: C:\Windows>_

long filename
A filename that is up to 255 characters long and can contain spaces and most symbols. (*See also, page 56.*)

 **STEPS to**

Use the MS-DOS prompt
1 Press [Ctrl] + [Esc] (Start menu)
2 Press [P] (Programs)
3 Press [M] until MS-DOS Prompt is selected.
4 Press [↵]

Switch between MS-DOS window and full screen
1 Press [Alt] + [↵]

Exit the MS-DOS prompt
1 Type: exit
2 Press [↵]

The MS-DOS Prompt

MS-DOS (Microsoft Disk Operating System) is the operating system that was used before Windows was developed. MS-DOS is still needed to bridge the gap between **MS-DOS–based applications** and Windows 95, however. There have been some important changes to MS-DOS to make it blend with Windows 95. One of the most important features is the ability of MS-DOS to recognize **long filenames**. The Windows 95 version of MS-DOS also has improved support for running MS-DOS–based programs, which you may or may not have on your computer.

You do not need to know how to use MS-DOS in order to use Windows 95; but those who are familiar with MS-DOS can still perform most MS-DOS commands—some are no longer available.

Begin with the desktop displayed and with no tasks on the taskbar.

① Open the MS-DOS Prompt window:

*   **Click** [Start]
*   **Move** the pointer on Programs.
*   **Click** [MS-DOS Prompt]
    The MS-DOS window opens with the Windows folder current, as indicated by the prompt.

```
  MS-DOS Prompt                          _ □ ×
 Auto        ▼    □ 🖿 🖺 🔲 🖼 🗗 A

Microsoft(R) Windows 95
   (C)Copyright Microsoft Corp 1981-1995.
C:\WINDOWS>
```
MS-DOS prompt ←

*   **IF** your MS-DOS window does not have borders, **press** [Alt] + [↵]

② Switch the MS-DOS window to a full screen display:

*   **Press** [Alt] + [↵]
    The MS-DOS window becomes a full screen, losing its borders, title bar, and toolbar.

③ Perform the MS-DOS command, CD (Change Directory (folder)):

*   **Type:** CD\ [↵]
    MS-DOS changes to the root directory, i.e., top level folder.
    > C:\>
*   **Type:** CD WINDOWS [↵]
    MS-DOS changes to the Windows folder.
    > C:\WINDOWS>
*   **Type:** CD\ [↵]
    MS-DOS changes back to the top level folder.
    > C:\>

Exercise 105 continued...

- **Type:** CD "PROGRAM FILES\ACCESSORIES" ⏎

  *NOTE: Since the name of the folder, Program Files, is a **long filename**, the path must be enclosed in quotes for MS-DOS to recognize it.*

  DOS changes to the Accessories folder—a subfolder of Program Files.

```
C:\Program Files\Accessories>
```

❹ Perform the MS-DOS command, DIR (Directory):

- **Type:** DIR ⏎

  DOS lists the files in the Accessories folder.

```
C:\Program Files\Accessories>DIR

 Volume in drive C has no label
 Volume Serial Number is 1E34-684F
 Directory of C:\Program Files\Accessories

.              <DIR>          02-03-95  9:18p .
..             <DIR>          02-03-95  9:18p ..
MSPAINT  EXE       306,176    04-27-95 12:00p MSPAINT.EXE
WORDPAD  EXE       183,296    04-27-95 12:00p WORDPAD.EXE
HYPERT~1       <DIR>          02-03-95  9:18p HyperTerminal
BACKUP   EXE       818,176    04-27-95 12:00p BACKUP.EXE
         3 file(s)      1,307,648 bytes
         3 dir(s)     275,267,584 bytes free

C:\Program Files\Accessories>
```

- **Type:** DIR/V ⏎

  DOS lists the files in the Accessories folder showing additional detail (V is for verbose).

```
 Volume in drive C has no label
  Volume Serial Number is 1E34-684F
  Directory of C:\Program Files\Accessories
File Name        Size      Allocated    Modified      Accessed  Attrib

.              <DIR>                   02-03-95  9:18p                D
.
..             <DIR>                   02-03-95  9:18p                D
..
MSPAINT  EXE    306,176     311,296    04-27-95 12:00p  06-07-95     A
MSPAINT.EXE
WORDPAD  EXE    183,296     188,416    04-27-95 12:00p  06-07-95     A
WORDPAD.EXE
HYPERT~1       <DIR>                   02-03-95  9:18p             R  D
HyperTerminal
BACKUP   EXE    818,176     819,200    04-27-95 12:00p  04-21-95     A
BACKUP.EXE
         3 file(s)      1,307,648 bytes
         3 dir(s)       1,318,912 bytes allocated
                      275,267,584 bytes free
                      477,102,080 bytes total disk space,  42% in use

C:\Program Files\Accessories>
```

❺ Switch to the desktop:

- **Press** Alt + Tab

  Windows switches to the desktop.

- **Press** Alt + Tab

- **Type:** CD.. ⏎

  DOS changes to the folder immediately above the current folder, Program Files.

- **Press** Alt + ⏎

  DOS switches back to the window format.

❻ Exit the MS-DOS prompt:

- **Type:** EXIT ⏎

  or

- **Click** the Close button.

  The MS-DOS window is exited and you are returned to the desktop.

EXERCISE 106

Use the Run Command

To use the Run command to start programs and open documents and folders.

— Terms and Notes —

path
The route to a folder or file; it consists of the disk drive, folder, subfolders (if any), and the filename (if the path is to a file). For example, C:\WINDOWS\CALC is the path to the Calculator program. If long folder names or filenames are used in a path, the path must be enclosed in quotes ("). For example, "A:\My Folder\help2.rtf" is the path to the document file, help2 on drive A:.

A full path includes:
• the disk drive (followed by a colon (:) and a backslash (\)),
• all the folders needed to find the document or folder (each followed by a backslash), and
• the filename (including its filename extension) or the final folder.

Example of a path to the Media folder:
        C:\WINDOWS\MEDIA

Example of a path to the skiing.avi in the Media folder:
        C:\WINDOWS\MEDIA\SKIING.AVI

NOTE: The paths have been written here using uppercase letters for clarity. You can also use lowercase letters or mixed upper-and lowercase letters.

A path that includes long filenames must be enclosed in quotes.
Example of a path with a long filename:
`"A:\MY FOLDER\MY DOC 1"`

 **STEPS to**

STEPS to are on the next page.

196   Lesson Eight — Other Features

Begin with the desktop displayed and with no tasks on the taskbar.

❶ Start the Run command:

• **Click** 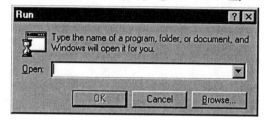 , then   Run...
  The Run command opens.

• **IF** there is something highlighted in the Open box, **press** `Del`

```
Run                                        ? X
   [icon]  Type the name of a program, folder, or document, and
           Windows will open it for you.

   Open: [_____▼]

            [  OK  ]   [ Cancel ]   [ Browse... ]
```

❷ Start programs:

NOTE: Certain programs will start by simply typing their name in the Open box and pressing Enter. In some cases, you need to use the program's filename rather than its standard name.

• **Type:** `notepad` in the Open box and **press** ↵
  Notepad opens.

• **Exit** Notepad.

• **Start** Run, **type:** `paint` in the Open box, and **press** ↵
  A message box appears saying that it cannot find 'paint' (or one of its components).

• **Click** [OK]

• **Type:** `pbrush` in the Open box, and **press** ↵
  Paint opens when you use its actual filename rather than its standard name, Paint.

• **Exit** Paint.

• **Start** Run, **type:** `wordpad` in the Open box and **press** ↵
  WordPad opens.

• **Exit** WordPad.

• **Start** Run, **type:** `winmine` in the Open box and **press** ↵
  Minesweeper opens.

• **Exit** Minesweeper.

• **Start** Run, **type:** `calc` in the Open box and **press** ↵
  Calculator opens.

• **Exit** Calculator.

❸ Use a previous command:

• **Start** Run.

• **Click** the arrow for the Open box.
  A menu appears with up to 26 of the last commands you used.

```
        calc
Run     winmine
        wordpad
        pbrush
        notepad

Open: [calc                              ▼]

            [  OK  ]   [ Cancel ]   [ Browse... ]
```

Exercise 106 continued...

- **Click** notepad, then $\boxed{\text{OK}}$
- **Exit** Notepad.

4 **Use Browse to find a document to open:**

- **Start** Run.
  Run opens with the last command in the Open box.
- **Click** $\boxed{\text{Browse...}}$
  The Browse dialog box opens.

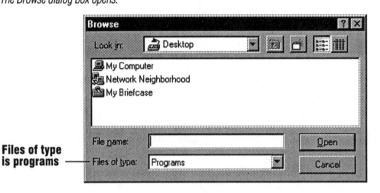

Files of type is programs

- **Click** Files of type, then All files (*.*).
  *NOTE: The Browse window that opens from Run defaults to Files of type, **programs**. Since you are going to open a document, you must change Files of type to **All Files (*.*)**.*
- **Open** My Computer, then (C:), then Windows.
- **Scroll** until you find **Forest**.
- **Click Forest**, then $\boxed{\text{Open}}$
  *The Browse dialog box closes and the path to the document, **Forest** is entered in the Open box. The path is not enclosed in quotes.*

Open: C:\WINDOWS\Forest.bmp ⸺ **path to Forest**

- **Click** $\boxed{\text{OK}}$
  *The document, **Forest** opens in Paint.*
- **Exit** Paint.

5 • **Start** Run and click $\boxed{\text{Browse...}}$
  Since Run already has the path to Windows in its Open box, Browse opens with the Windows folder open.

- **Click** Files of type, then All files (*.*).
- **Scroll** until you find **Metal Links**.
- **Click Metal Links**, then $\boxed{\text{Open}}$
  *The path to the document, **Metal Links** is entered in the Open box surrounded by quotes since there is a long filename in the path.*

Open: "C:\WINDOWS\Metal Links.bmp" **Quotes surround the entire path because one part, Metal Links, is a long filename.**

- **Click** $\boxed{\text{OK}}$
  *The document, **Metal Links** opens in Paint.*
- **Exit** Paint.

Exercise 106 continued...

— **Terms and Notes** —

*NOTE: While the **Browse** window takes a hierarchial form (similar to the left pane of Explorer) when opened from the Find window, it takes a "folder window" form (more like the right pane of Explorer) when opened from the Run window.*

 **STEPS to**

Use the Run command
1. **Press** $\boxed{\text{Ctrl}}$ + $\boxed{\text{Esc}}$
2. **Press** $\boxed{\text{R}}$ (Run)
3. **Type** the program's filename.
   or
   Type the entire path to a program, folder, or document.
4. **Press** ⏎

Use the Browse button to run a file or program
1. **Press** $\boxed{\text{Ctrl}}$ + $\boxed{\text{Esc}}$
2. **Press** $\boxed{\text{R}}$ (Run)
3. **Press** $\boxed{\text{Alt}}$ + $\boxed{\text{B}}$ (Browse)
4. **Use** the actions below, as needed, to select a program or document file:
   Change drives (or other object in the Look in box)
   - **Press** $\boxed{\text{Alt}}$ + $\boxed{\text{I}}$ (Look in)
   - **Press** $\boxed{\downarrow}$ to open the box.
   - **Press** $\boxed{\uparrow}$ or $\boxed{\downarrow}$ to highlight the desired location.
   - **Press** ⏎
   Change Files of type
   - **Press** $\boxed{\text{Alt}}$ + $\boxed{\text{T}}$ (Files of type)
   - **Press** $\boxed{\downarrow}$ to open the box.
   - **Press** $\boxed{\uparrow}$ or $\boxed{\downarrow}$ to select All Files (*.*) or Programs.
   - **Press** ⏎
   Go down one folder level within the Browse box
   - **Press** $\boxed{\text{Tab}}$ until an item in the workspace is selected.
   - **Press** arrow keys to select the desired folder.
   - **Press** ⏎
   Go up one folder level within the Browse box
   - **Press** $\boxed{\text{Backspace}}$
   Select a program or file
   —FROM THE DESIRED FOLDER—
   - **Press** arrow keys to select desired file.
5. **Press** ⏎ or $\boxed{\text{Alt}}$ + $\boxed{\text{O}}$ (Open)
   The program or document (along with its path) are entered in the Open box.
6. **Press** ⏎

6 **Open a document by typing its path in the Open box:**

- **Insert** your duplicate data disk in drive A:.
- **Start** Run.

  NOTE: You can use upper- or lowercase letters or a combination to type the path.

- **Type:** A:\SAVEFILE.TXT and **press** ⏎

  Savefile opens in Notepad.

- **Exit** Notepad.

7
- **Start** Run.
- **Type:** "a:\my things\doc2.txt" and **press** ⏎

  DOC2 opens in Notepad.

- **Exit** Notepad.

8 **Open a folder by typing its path in the Open box:**

- **Start** Run.
- **Type:** C:\WINDOWS and **press** ⏎

  The Windows folder opens.

- **Close** the Windows window.

9
- **Start** Run.
- **Type:** "C:\PROGRAM FILES\ACCESSORIES" and **press** ⏎

  The Accessories folder opens.

- **Close** the Accessories window.

10
- **Start** Run.
- **Type:** "A:\MY DOCUMENTS" and **press** ⏎

  The My Documents folder opens.

  NOTE: Your window may look different; it may have small icons and/or a toolbar.

- **Close** My Documents.

Begin with the desktop displayed and with no tasks on the taskbar.

❶ Open the Startup folder:

- **Right-click** 🏁 **Start**, then **O**pen.
- **Change** to Browse folders by using a single window that changes as you open each folder (review, Exercise 32).
- **Open** Programs, then Startup.
  The Startup folder is empty (unless someone has already put programs in it).

❷ Create a shortcut to Notepad in the Startup folder:

- **Right-click** the workspace, **move** the pointer on Ne**w**, and **click** **S**hortcut.
  The Create Shortcut dialog box opens.
- **Click** Browse... , then **double-click** the Windows folder to open it.
- **Scroll** until you find Notepad.
- **Click** Notepad, then Open .
- **Click** Next > then Finish .
  The Notepad shortcut appears in the Startup window.

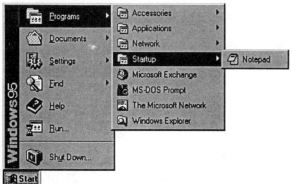

❸ Look at the Startup menu:

- **Exit** the Startup window.
- **Click** 🏁 **Start**, **move** the pointer on **P**rograms, then Startup.
  Startup opens to display Notepad.

- **Click** Notepad.
  Notepad opens.
- **Exit** Notepad.

❹ Use Startup to start programs when Windows opens:

- **Remove** your data disk from drive A:.
- **Click** 🏁 **Start**, Shut Down, then **R**estart the computer, then **Y**es.
- **Log on** as you normally do.
  When Windows opens, Notepad is opened also.
- **Exit** Notepad.

Exercise 107 continued...

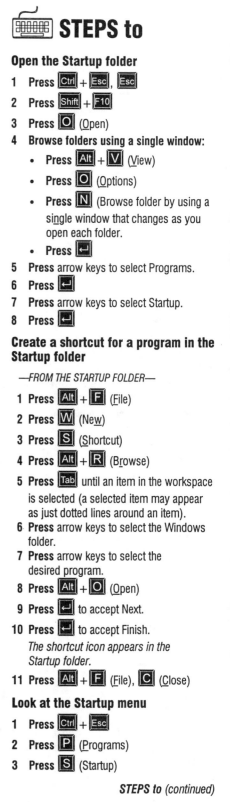

EXERCISE 107
Use Startup

To put shortcuts to programs in the Startup menu so they start when you turn on the computer.

⌨ STEPS to

Open the Startup folder

1 Press **Ctrl** + **Esc**, **Esc**
2 Press **Shift** + **F10**
3 Press **O** (**O**pen)
4 **Browse folders using a single window:**
   - Press **Alt** + **V** (**V**iew)
   - Press **O** (**O**ptions)
   - Press **N** (Browse folder by using a single window that changes as you open each folder.
   - Press **↵**
5 **Press** arrow keys to select Programs.
6 **Press** **↵**
7 **Press** arrow keys to select Startup.
8 **Press** **↵**

Create a shortcut for a program in the Startup folder

   —FROM THE STARTUP FOLDER—

1 **Press** **Alt** + **F** (**F**ile)
2 **Press** **W** (Ne**w**)
3 **Press** **S** (**S**hortcut)
4 **Press** **Alt** + **R** (B**r**owse)
5 **Press** **Tab** until an item in the workspace is selected (a selected item may appear as just dotted lines around an item).
6 **Press** arrow keys to select the Windows folder.
7 **Press** arrow keys to select the desired program.
8 **Press** **Alt** + **O** (**O**pen)
9 **Press** **↵** to accept Next.
10 **Press** **↵** to accept Finish.
   The shortcut icon appears in the Startup folder.
11 **Press** **Alt** + **F** (**F**ile), **C** (**C**lose)

Look at the Startup menu

1 **Press** **Ctrl** + **Esc**
2 **Press** **P** (**P**rograms)
3 **Press** **S** (**S**tartup)

STEPS to (continued)

Exercise 107 (continued)
USE STARTUP

— Terms and Notes —

NOTE: *It is very handy to have Windows 95 open with several of your most frequently used programs appearing as buttons on the taskbar.*

 **STEPS to**

Change shortcuts so they open minimized

—*FROM THE STARTUP FOLDER WITH SHORTCUTS*—

1 **Select** the shortcut icon to change.
2 **Press** Shift + F10
3 **Press** R (Properties)
4 **Press** Ctrl + Tab to change to the Shortcut tab.
5 **Press** Alt + R (Run)
6 **Press** ↓ or ↑ until Minimized appears in the box.
7 **Press** ↵
8 **Close** the folder window.

Start programs with Startup

1 **Press** Ctrl + Esc
2 **Press** U (Shut Down)
3 **Press** R (Restart the computer?)
4 **Press** ↵
5 **Log on** as usual.
   The program(s) in the Startup menu open automatically—they open minimized if you changed them to do so.

Exercise 107 (continued)

⑤ Create a shortcut to Calculator in the Startup folder:
NOTE: These directions use a different method to create a shortcut than those in step 2.
- **Start** Explorer by right-clicking the Start button, then **E**xplore.
  Explorer opens with the Start Menu in the title bar and its contents in the right pane.
- **Expand** Programs and **locate** the Startup folder in the left pane (you will use it later).
- **Scroll** up (in the left pane) to find the Windows folder, and **select** it.
- **Right-click** Calc, then Create **S**hortcut.
  Shortcut to Calc appears, selected, at the end of the files in the right pane.
- **Scroll** the left pane until the Startup folder is visible.
- **Drag** Shortcut to Calc to the Startup folder.
- **Close** Explorer.

⑥ Change the shortcuts so the programs open minimized:
- **Right-click** [Start], then **O**pen.
- **Open** Programs, then Startup.
  The Startup folder opens with the shortcuts to Notepad and Calculator in it.

  | Startup   _ □ × |
  | File Edit View Help |
  | Notepad   Shortcut to Calc |
  | 2 object(s)   540 byt |

- **Right-click** Shortcut to Calc, then **P**roperties.
  The Shortcut to Calc Properties dialog box opens.
- **Click** the Shortcut tab, then the arrow for the **R**un box.
  The Run drop-down box opens.

  Run: Normal window ▼
  Minimized ———— Normal window / Minimized / Maximized

- **Click** Minimized, then [OK]

⑦
- **Repeat** the instructions in step 6 so Notepad will open minimized.
- **Close** the Startup window.

⑧ Use Startup to start programs minimized:
- **Click** [Start], Sh**u**t Down, then **R**estart the computer, then **Y**es.
- **Log on** as you normally do.
  When Windows opens, Notepad and Calculator are buttons on the taskbar.
- **Click** the Notepad task button, then **close** Notepad.
- **Click** the Calculator task button, then **close** Calculator

⑨ Remove the programs from the Startup folder:
- **Right-click** [Start], then **O**pen.
- **Open** Programs, then Startup.
- **Delete** the Notepad and Calculator shortcuts.
- **Exit** the Startup folder.
- **Empty** the Recycle Bin.

The Media Player

Media Player is a **multimedia** program. It permits your computer to show video and animation without additional special hardware. There are several animated Help files that you can play using the Media Player. Media Player will play sound if you have speakers. If you have a CD-ROM disk and speakers, you can use CD Player to play audio compact disks (CDs) and Sound Recorder to play or record sounds.

Begin with the desktop displayed and with no tasks on the taskbar.

① Start Media Player:

- **Click** 📶 **Start** and **move** the pointer on Programs, then Accessories, then Multimedia.

- **Click** 🎬 Media Player

  Media Player opens.

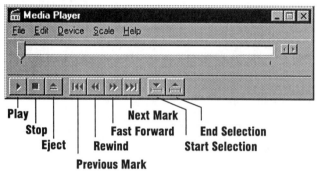

Play
Stop
Eject
Rewind
Previous Mark
Fast Forward
Next Mark
Start Selection
End Selection

② Open a Video for Windows (*.avi) file:

- **Click** File, then Open.

- **Click** 🔼

- **Double-click** the Help folder.

- **Click** the Files of type box, then Video for Windows (*.avi).
  Several video files appear in the Help folder workspace.

- **Click Sizewin**, then [Open]
  The video clip appears below Media Player, and a scale (marked in 2 second intervals) appears in Media Player that tells you that the video clip is 18.8 seconds long.

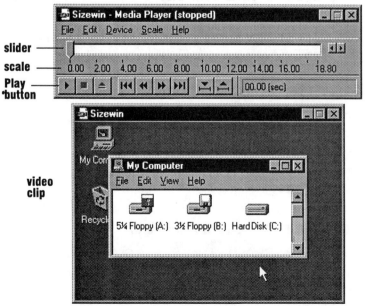

slider
scale
Play button
video clip

Exercise 108 continued...

EXERCISE 108

View Animation Files

To start Media Player and to open and play files that are animated, and to play animated files without using Media Player.

— Terms and Notes —

multimedia
The combination of many various communication methods, including text, graphics, sound, animation, and video.

③ Play a video clip:

- **Click** ▶

  *The **Sizewin** video clip plays its animation of sizing a window and the slider moves along the scale as the video clip plays.*

  NOTE: The Play button is replaced by the Pause button.

④ Stop a video clip:

- **Click** ▶, then when the slider moves to about 8.00 on the scale, **click** ■

  *The **Sizewin** video clip stops with the slider about half way through the scale.*

⑤ Rewind a video clip:

- **Click and hold** ◀◀ until the slider is at the beginning of the scale.

  The slider returns to the beginning of the scale.

⑥ Pause a video clip:

- **Click** ▶, then when the slider moves to about 8.00 on the scale, **click** ❙❙

  *The **Sizewin** video clip pauses.*

- **Click** ▶ and let the video clip play to the end.

  *The **Sizewin** video clip continues playing.*

⑦ Drag the slider:

- **Drag** the slider back and forth and notice how the **Sizewin** animation changes as you drag the slider.

- **Drag** the slider fast, then slow.

  *The **Sizewin** animation moves faster or slower in accordance with the mouse pointer.*

⑧ Simplify Media Player's controls:

- **Double-click** Media Player's title bar.

  *Media Player disappears and some simple controls appear at the bottom of **Sizewin**.*

  ▶ ■ ┃━━━━━━━━━━━━━━━┃   **simple controls at the bottom of Sizewin**

- **Click** ▶

  *The **Sizewin** animation plays.*

- **Double-click** Sizewin's title bar.

  Media Player reappears.

- **Close** Media Player.

  *Both Media Player and **Sizewin** close.*

⑨ Play other Help animations from Find:

- **Find** the Video Clip type of files on drive C: (review, Exercise 99).

  (Start Find using the Start menu, then click the Advanced tab, Of type, Video Clip, and finally, Find Now)

Exercise 108 continued...

- **Maximize** Find.

Name	In Folder	Size	Type	Modified
Closewin	C:\WINDOWS\HELP	401KB	Video Clip	4/20/95 5:00 PM
Dragdrop	C:\WINDOWS\HELP	300KB	Video Clip	4/20/95 5:00 PM
Explorer	C:\WINDOWS\HELP	852KB	Video Clip	4/20/95 5:00 PM
Find	C:\WINDOWS\HELP	478KB	Video Clip	4/20/95 5:00 PM
Linking	C:\WINDOWS\HELP	537KB	Video Clip	4/20/95 5:00 PM
Movewin	C:\WINDOWS\HELP	738KB	Video Clip	4/20/95 5:00 PM
Paste	C:\WINDOWS\HELP	988KB	Video Clip	4/20/95 5:00 PM
Scroll	C:\WINDOWS\HELP	1,476...	Video Clip	4/20/95 5:00 PM
Sizewin	C:\WINDOWS\HELP	813KB	Video Clip	4/20/95 5:00 PM
Taskswch	C:\WINDOWS\HELP	416KB	Video Clip	4/20/95 5:00 PM
Whatson	C:\WINDOWS\HELP	729KB	Video Clip	4/20/95 5:00 PM

11 file(s) found		

- **Double-click Closewin**.
  Closewin opens, plays its animation, and then closes.
- **Double-click Dragdrop**, and while it is still playing, **click** ■
- **Click** ▶
- **Close Dragdrop**.
- **Play** the other animated Help files as desired.
- **Exit** Find.

⑪ Open the Skiing video file:

*NOTE: If you cannot find **Skiing**, skip this page and go on to the Exercise 109.*

- **Start** Media Player (review, step 1).
- **Click** File, then Open.
- **Click** the Files of type box, then Video for Windows (*.avi).
  Skiing is probably the only file in the workspace.
- **IF** you do not have **Skiing**, skip to Exercise 109.
- **Click Skiing**, then [Open]
  Skiing is opened.

⑫ Play the Skiing video file:

- **IF** you have speakers and would like to hear the video, **turn** the speakers on.
- **Click** ▶
- **Exit** Media Player.

EXERCISE 109

Use the Control Panel

To access dialog boxes and programs that let you change settings in Windows 95.

— Terms and Notes —

Control Panel
A folder that combines all command, control and configuration functions for Windows 95 in one place.

NOTE: Since many of the controls and configurations are sensitive, you are instructed to simply look at some of the features and then cancel out of them without making any changes.

 **STEPS to**

Open the Control Panel
1 Press `Ctrl` + `Esc`
2 Press `S` (Settings)
3 Press `C` (Control Panel)

Open a Control Panel object
1 **Press** arrow keys to select the desired object.
2 **Press** `↵` to open the object. Begin with the desktop displayed and with no tasks on the taskbar.

---

❶ **Open the Control Panel:**

- **Click** 🏁 Start
- **Move** the pointer on Settings.
- **Click** 🖳 Control Panel
  The Control Panel opens.

You may not have some of these objects, and you may have some objects not found here.

❷ **Look at the New Hardware Wizard:**

- **Double-click** 📇 Add New Hardware
  The Add New Hardware Wizard opens.

- **Click** Cancel to close without making any changes.

Exercise 109 continued...

❸ Look at Add/Remove Software Properties:

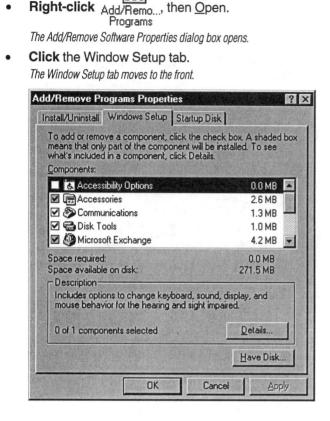

- **Right-click** Add/Remo..., then Open.
  Programs
  The Add/Remove Software Properties dialog box opens.

- **Click** the Window Setup tab.
  The Window Setup tab moves to the front.

- **Click** Cancel to close without making any changes.

❹ Look at Date/Time Properties:

- **Double-click**
  Date/Time
  The Date/Time Properties dialog box opens.

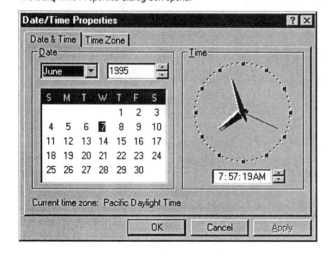

- **Click** Cancel to close without making any changes.

Exercise 109 continued...

— Terms and Notes —

BELOW ARE MOST OF THE CONTROL PANEL
OBJECTS AND A SHORT DESCRIPTION OF
WHAT THEY DO:

Accessibility Options
Changes accessibility options for your system.

Add New Hardware
Adds new hardware to your system.
Add/Remove Programs
Sets up programs and creates shortcuts.

Date/Time
Changes date, time and time zone information.

Display
Changes settings for your display.

Fonts
Views, adds and removes fonts on your computer.

Joysticks
Changes settings for joystick devices.

Keyboard
Changes settings for your keyboard.

Mail and Fax
Microsoft Exchange Profiles.

Microsoft Mail Postoffice
Administers a Microsoft Workgroup Postoffice.

Modems
Installs a new modem and changes modem
properties.

Mouse
Changes settings for your mouse.

Multimedia
Changes settings for multimedia devices.

Network
Configures network hardware and software.

Passwords
Changes passwords and sets security options.

Printers
Adds, removes and changes settings for printers.

Regional Settings
Changes how numbers, currencies, dates and times
are displayed.

Sounds
Changes system and program sounds.

System
Provides system information and changes advanced
settings.

⑤ Look at Regional Settings Properties:

• **Double-click** Regional
Settings

The Regional Settings Properties dialog box opens.

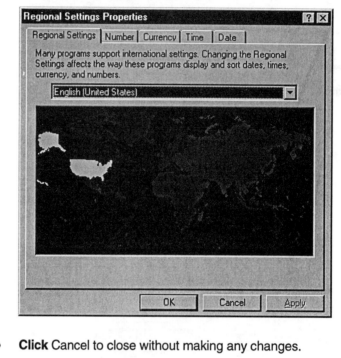

• **Click** Cancel to close without making any changes.

⑥ Look at System Properties:

• **Double-click** System

The System Properties dialog box opens.

• **Click** Cancel to close without making any changes.

⑦ • **Close** the Control Panel.

Begin with the desktop displayed and with no tasks on the taskbar.

❶ Open the Display Properties:

- **Open** the Control Panel (review, Exercise 109, step 1).

- **Double-click**
  Display

  The Display Properties opens.

- **Click** the Appearance tab.
  The Appearance tab moves to the front.

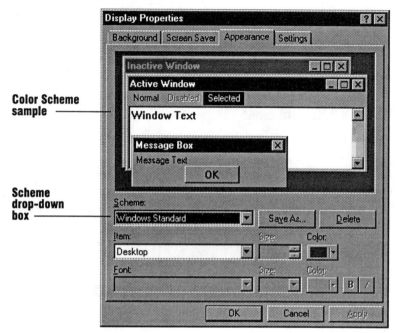

Color Scheme sample ⟶

Scheme drop-down box ⟶

❷ View color schemes:

- **Click** the Scheme drop-down list box.
- **Press** [Page Up] until you reach the top scheme, Brick.

  *The sample color scheme changes to the **Brick** color scheme.*

- **Press** [↓]

  *The sample color scheme displays the **Desert** color scheme.*

  NOTE: There is a chance that your top color scheme may be Blue and Black, and that the next one may be Blues 256.

- **Press** [↓] until you scroll through the entire list and **notice** the sample color scheme change as you move through the various color schemes.

❸ Change the color scheme:

- **Press** [↑] and [↓] until you select a color scheme you like and **press** [↵]

  or

  Click the scroll bar until you see a color scheme you like and **click** it.

- **Click** [Apply]

  The screen changes to the new color scheme.

Exercise 110 continued...

EXERCISE 110

Change Screen Colors

To access the Appearance tab in the Display Properties box and make changes to the screen display.

⌨ STEPS to

View Color Schemes

1 **Open** the Control Panel *(see Exercise 109).*
2 **Open** the Display Properties *(see Exercise 109).*
3 **Press** [Ctrl] + [Tab] until the Appearance tab moves to the front.
4 **Press** [Alt] + [S] (Scheme)
5 **Press** [Alt] + [↓] to open the box.
6 **Press** [↓] and watch as the color schemes change in the sample area.
7 **Continue pressing** [↓] and watch as the color schemes change each time you press the down arrow.

Change Color Schemes

—FROM THE SCHEME DROP-DOWN BOX—

1 **Press** [↓] and [↑] until the desired color scheme is selected.
2 **Press** [↵]
3 **Press** [Alt] + [A] (Apply)

Change to the Windows Standard color scheme

- **Follow** the directions above selecting Windows Standard in step 1 above.

Design a Color Scheme

—FROM THE APPEARANCE TAB OF DISPLAY PROPERTIES—

Change the following items as desired:

NOTE: If a control is dimmed, it cannot be used in the current situation.

Change window items

1 **Press** [Alt] + [I] (Item)
2 **Press** [Alt] + [↓] to open the box.
3 **Press** arrow keys to select the desired item.
4 **Press** [↵]

STEPS to continued on page 209

— **Terms and Notes** —

COLOR SCHEMES
Brick
Desert
Eggplant
High Contrast Black
High Contrast Black (extra large)
High Contrast Black (large)
High Contrast White
High Contrast White (extra large)
High Contrast White (large)
Lilac
Lilac (large)
Maple
Marine (high color)
Plum (high color)
Pumpkin (large)
Rainy Day
Red, White, and Blue (VGA)
Rose
Rose (large)
Slate
Spruce
Starts and Stripes (VGA)
Storm (VGA)
Teal (VGA)
Wheat
Windows Standard
Windows Standard (extra large)
Windows Standard (large)

WINDOW ITEMS
3D Objects
Active Title Bar
Active Window Border
Application Background
Caption Buttons
Desktop
Icon
Icon Spacing (Horizontal)
Icon Spacing (Vertical)
Inactive Title Bar
Inactive Window Border
Menu
Message Box
Palette Title
Scrollbar
Selected Items
Tool Tip
Window

NOTE: Some items are not shown in the sample color scheme area.

④ Change the color scheme to Windows Standard:

WITH THE APPEARANCE TAB OF DISPLAY PROPERTIES STILL OPEN:

- **Click** the Scheme drop-down list box.
- **Scroll** to the bottom of the list.
- **Click** the Windows Standard color scheme.
- **Click** | Apply |

  *NOTE: If you previously chose a **large** or **extra large** color scheme, you may not be able to see the Apply button now.*

- **IF** you cannot see the Apply button, **press** [Alt]+[A] (Apply).

- **IF** the taskbar has increased in size to a double line, **move** the pointer on the top line until it becomes a double-headed arrow and **drag** the taskbar to a single line.

⑤ Design a color scheme:

Window Items

NOTE: Some items are named in the sample itself, for example, Message Box.

WITH THE APPEARANCE TAB OF DISPLAY PROPERTIES STILL OPEN:

- **Click** the Item drop-down list box.
- **Scroll** until you find Active Title Bar and **click** it.
- **Notice** that the Size is 18 and the Color is dark blue.
- **Click** the Item Size spin box up arrow until the size is 30 and **notice** that the title bars in the sample area increase in size every time you click the up arrow.
- **Click** the Item Color box (not the Font Color box).
  The color box opens with 20 colors.

- **Click** the desired color.
  The two active title bars in the sample area change to the selected color.

⑥ Change the font:

WITH THE APPEARANCE TAB OF DISPLAY PROPERTIES STILL OPEN AND WITH ACTIVE TITLE BAR STILL IN THE ITEM BOX:

- **Click** the arrow at the end of the Font box.

Exercise 110 continued...

The Font box opens.

- **Click** MS Serif.
  The Font style changes on the title bars and the title bars return to their original size.

❼ Change the font size:

- **Click** the arrow by the Font Size box.
  The Size box opens with 8 highlighted.
- **Press** ⬇️ (to 10) and **notice** that the size of font in the title bars increases.
- **Press** ⬇️ four more times and **notice** the size of font in the title bars gets larger with each press.
- **Click** 14.

❽ Change the font color:

- **Click** the arrow by the Font Color box (*not* the Item Color box).
  The font color box opens.
- **Click** a color other than the title bar color.
  The active title bar font color changes from white to the color you chose.

❾ Change the font type:

- **Click** [B] (the bold button).
  The title bar font becomes smaller since it loses its bold attribute.
- **Click** [/] (the italic button).
  The title bar font becomes italic (slanted).
- **Click** [B] (the bold button).
  The title bar font becomes bold.
- **Click** [/] (the italic button).
  The active title bar font becomes straight since it loses its italic attribute.

❿ Change the color scheme to Windows Standard:

WITH THE APPEARANCE TAB OF DISPLAY PROPERTIES STILL OPEN:

- **Click** the Scheme drop-down list box and **scroll** to the bottom.
- **Click** the Windows Standard color scheme.
- **Click** [Apply]
- **Close** Display Properties.
- **Close** the Control Panel.

⌨ STEPS to

(continued from page 207)

Change window item size

1 **Press** [Alt] + [Z] (Size)
2 **Press** ⬆️ to increase the size.
   or
   Press ⬇️ to decrease the size.

Change window item color

1 **Press** [Alt] + [L] (Color)
2 **Press** [Ctrl] + [Space]
3 **Press** [Alt] + [O] (Other)
   The current Basic color is selected.
4 **Press** arrow keys to select the desired color from the Basic colors section.
   A faint dotted outline indicates movement to a new color.
5 **Press** [Space] to choose the color.
6 **Press** [↵] to return to the Appearance tab.
   The selected color is displayed in the sample area.

Change the font

1 **Press** [Alt] + [I] (Item)
2 **Press** [Alt] + ⬇️ to open the box.
3 **Press** arrow keys to select the desired item.
4 **Press** [↵]

Change the font size

1 **Press** [Alt] + [E] (Size)
2 **Press** [Alt] + ⬇️ to open the box.
3 **Press** ⬆️ or ⬇️ to select the desired size.
4 **Press** [↵]

Change the font color

1 **Press** [Alt] + [R] (Color)
2 **Follow** steps 2-6 for Changing window item color (above)

Change font type
Bold:

1 **Press** [Tab] to move forward or [Shift] + [Tab] to move backward until a faint dotted box appears on the Bold button.
2 **Press** [Space] to toggle between selecting and deselecting the button.

Italic:

1 **Press** [Tab] to move forward or [Shift] + [Tab] to move backward until a faint dotted box appears on the Bold button.
2 **Press** [Space] to toggle between selecting and deselecting the button.

EXERCISE 111

Change Mouse Settings

To access the Mouse Properties dialog box and change or look at the various mouse controls.

 STEPS to

Open the Mouse Properties

1   **Open** the Control Panel *(see Exercise 109).*
2   **Open** the Mouse Properties *(see Exercise 109).*
3   **Press** |Ctrl| + |Tab| until the desired tab moves to the front.

Change the button configuration

—FROM THE BUTTONS TAB—

*   **Press** |Alt| + |R| (Right-handed) mouse
    or
    Press |Alt| + |L| (Left-handed) mouse

Look at the pointers

—FROM THE POINTERS TAB—

With Schemes selected (as it is when you first select the Pointers tab):

1   **Press** |Tab| two (or three) times (until OK is selected but without dotted lines within it).
2   **Press** |↑|, |↓|, |Page Up| or |Page Down| to scroll through the pointers.

Change pointer size

—FROM THE POINTERS TAB—

1   **Press** |Alt| + |S| (Scheme)
2   **Press** |Alt| + |↓| to open the box.
3   **Press** |↑| or |↓| to select an item.
    normal size:
    • **Select** Windows Standard.
    large size:
    • **Select** Windows Standard (large).
    extra large size:
    • **Select** Windows Standard (extra large).

Toggle pointer trails

—FROM THE MOTION TAB—

*   **Press** |Alt| + |O| (Show pointer trails)

Begin with the desktop displayed and with no tasks on the taskbar.

❶ Open the Mouse Properties:

*   **Open** the Control Panel (review, Exercise 109, step 1).

*   **Double-click** 🖱 Mouse
    The Mouse Properties opens.

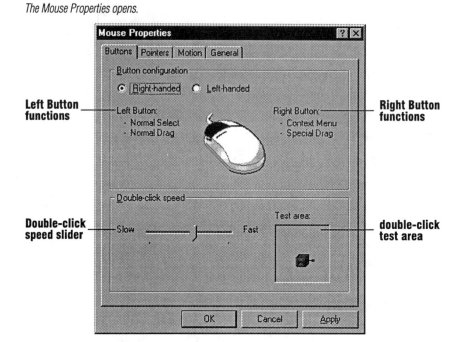

❷ Change the button configuration:

*   **Notice** the Left Button and Right Button functions.
*   **Click** Left handed.
    The Left Button and Right Button functions switch.
*   **Click** Right handed.
    The Left Button and Right Button functions switch back.

❸ Change and test the double-click speed:

*   **Double-click** the box in the Test area. Try until the box opens.
    A jack-in-the-box pops up.

 jack-in-the-box

*   **Drag** the slider toward the Slow end.
*   **Double-click** the Test area. Is it easy to open (or close) the box?
*   **Drag** the slider closer to the Fast end.
*   **Double-click** the Test area. Is it hard to open (or close) the box?
*   **Drag** the slider as far right as possible.
*   **Double-click** the Test area. Can you open (or close) the box?
*   **Drag** the slider to about the middle the scale.
*   **Double-click** the box in the Test area until it is closed.

Exercise 111 continued...

4 **Look at the pointers:**

- **Click** Pointers tab.
  The Pointers tab moves to the front.
- **Scroll** through the mouse pointers.
- **Click** the Normal Select pointer (at the top of the list).
  The Normal Select pointer shape appears in the box above the list of pointers and to the right.

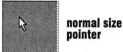 **normal size pointer**

5 **Change the pointer size:**

- **Click** the S̲cheme box, then Windows Standard (large).
  The pointers become larger.

 **large size pointer**

- **Click** the S̲cheme box, then Windows Standard (extra large).
  The pointers become even larger.

 extra large size pointer

- **Click** the S̲cheme box, then (None).
  The pointers return to their original sizes.

6 **Look at pointer trails:**

- **Click** the Motion tab.
  The Motion tab moves to the front.

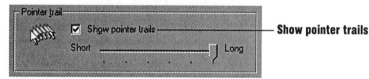 **Show pointer trails**

- **Click** Sh̲ow Pointer Trails to select it.
- **Move** the mouse around and watch the pointer trails that follow the pointer.
- **Drag** the slider toward the short end.
- **Move** the mouse around and watch the pointer trails that follow the pointer.
- **Drag** the slider all the way to the long end.
- **Click** Sh̲ow Pointer Trails to deselect it.

7
- **Close** Mouse Properties.
- **Close** the Control Panel.

— Terms and Notes —

Pointer Shapes

NAME	SHAPE
Normal Select	⬉
Help Select	⬉?
Working In Background	⬉⧗
Busy	⧗
Precision Select	+
Text Select	I
Handwriting	✎
Unavailable	⊘
Vertical Resize	↕
Horizontal Resize	↔
Diagonal Resize 1	↖
Diagonal Resize 2	↗
Move	✥
Alternate Select	↑

EXERCISE 112

Look at Fonts

To access the Fonts folder and view the fonts that are available on your system.

— Terms and Notes —

Panose
A type of Font-mapping information that is stored with a font to describe its traits:
    serif
    san serif
    normal
    bold
    italic
If a font has no Panose information it is displayed at the bottom of the list when viewing files by their similarity to another font.

serif
A font design that has small cross strokes at the top and bottom of the characters.

For example: **T**

san serif
A font design that has no cross strokes at the top and bottom of the characters; it is straight.

For example: **T**

TrueType font 🗛
Scalable fonts that are shipped with Windows; Arial, Courier New, Lucida Console, Symbol, Times New Roman, and Wingdings.

Begin with the desktop displayed and with no tasks on the taskbar.

❶ Open the Fonts folder:

- **Open** the Control Panel (review, Exercise 109, step 1).
- **Double-click** 🗛 Fonts
  The Fonts folder opens.
- **Right-click** the workspace and **click** <u>V</u>iew, then <u>L</u>ist.
  The Fonts are displayed in the List view; some of your fonts may be different.

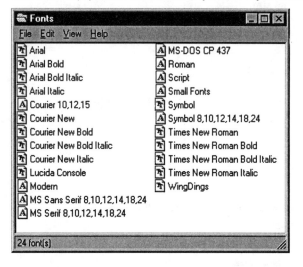

❷ View fonts by similarity:

*NOTE: You can compare all the fonts to any font that has **panose** information.*

- **Click** <u>V</u>iew, then List Fonts By <u>S</u>imilarity.
  The Fonts folder format changes.

font that the other fonts are compared to

- **Click** the <u>L</u>ist fonts by similarity to box.
- **Scroll** until you find Times New Roman, and **click** it.
  The order of the fonts changes with the most similar fonts at the top and the least similar fonts (or fonts with no panose information available) at the bottom.
- **Click** the <u>L</u>ist fonts by similarity to box.
- **Scroll** until you find Arial, and **click** it.
- **Click** <u>V</u>iew, then <u>L</u>ist.

❸ Hide font variations:

- **Click** <u>V</u>iew, <u>H</u>ide Variations (Bold, Italic, etc.) to select it.
  All the duplicate font names (those which represent variations of a font) disappear.
- **Click** <u>V</u>iew, <u>H</u>ide Variations (Bold, Italic, etc.) to deselect it.

 **STEPS to**

STEPS to are on the next page.

Exercise 112 continued...

4 **View a font:**

- **Double-click** Arial.

  or

  Right-click Arial, then <u>O</u>pen.
  The Arial (TrueType) dialog box opens.

- **Scroll** through the document to examine it.

5 **Print a font:**

- **Click** [Print] , then [OK]
  *The **Arial** font description and example is printed.*

Arial (TrueType)

Typeface name: Arial
File size: 64 KB
Version: MS core font:V2.00

Typeface © The Monotype Corporation plc. Data © The Monotype Co

---

abcdefghijklmnopqrstuvwxyz
ABCDEFGHIJKLMNOPQRSTUVWXYZ
1234567890.:,;("*!?')

---

12 The quick brown fox jumps over the lazy dog. 1234567890

18 The quick brown fox jumps over the lazy dog. 12345678⁹

24 The quick brown fox jumps over the lazy d

36 The quick brown fox jumps ⎜

48 The quick brown fox j

60 The quick brown

72 The quick bro⎜

- **Click** [Done]
  The Arial dialog box is closed.

Exercise 112 continued...

STEPS to

Open the Fonts folder

1 **Open** the Control Panel
   (see Exercise 109).

2 **Open** the Fonts icon
   (see Exercise 109).

—FROM THE FONTS FOLDER—

View fonts by similarity

1 **Press** [Alt] + [V] (<u>V</u>iew)

2 **Press** [S] (List Fonts By <u>S</u>imilarity)

View fonts in the List view

1 **Press** [Alt] + [V] (<u>V</u>iew)

2 **Press** [L] (<u>L</u>ist)

Hide font variations
Toggle Hide Variations:

1 **Press** [Alt] + [V] (<u>V</u>iew)

2 **Press** [H] (<u>H</u>ide Variations
   (Bold, Italic, etc.))

View and print a font

1 **Press** arrow keys to select the
   desired font.

2 **Press** [↵]

   To print the font:

   - **Make** sure your printer is ready to
     receive data.

   - **Press** [Alt] + [P] (<u>P</u>rint)
     The Print dialog box opens.

   - **Press** [↵]
     The font prints.

3 **Press** [Alt] + [D] (<u>D</u>one).

   or

   Press [Alt] + [F4]

6 • **Open** the Wingdings font (review, step 4).

NOTE: When the Wingdings font is selected, typing the keyboard letters produces a simple picture.

• **Print** the Wingdings font (review, step 5).

*The **Wingdings** font description and example is printed.*

Wingdings (TrueType)

Typeface name: Wingdings
File size: 70 KB
Version: Version 2.00; 20 September, 1994

Copyright © 1992-1994 Microsoft Corp. All Rights Reserved. © 19

• **Close** the Wingdings dialog box.
• **Close** the Fonts folder.
• **Close** the Control Panel if it is still open.

Begin with the desktop displayed and with no tasks on the taskbar.

1 • **Start** the MS-DOS Prompt window.
 • **Switch** the MS-DOS window to a full screen.
 • **Switch** to the desktop.
 • **Switch** back to the MS-DOS prompt.
 • **Switch** the MS-DOS full screen to a window.
 • **Exit** the MS-DOS window.

2 • **Start** the Run command.
 • **Start** Notepad using the Run command.
 • **Exit** Notepad.
 • **Start** Calculator using the Run command (its filename is Calc).
 • **Exit** Calculator.

3 • **Start** the Run command.
 • **Use** a previous command to open Notepad.
 • **Exit** Notepad.

4 • **Start** the Run command.
 • **Use** Browse to locate and open the file, **Windows Logo** in the Windows folder (remember to change Files of type to All Files (*.*)).
 • **Exit** Paint.

5 • **Start** the Run command.
 • **Make** sure your duplicate data disk is in drive A:.
 • **Type** the path to **winfun.txt** (it is not in a folder).
 • **Open** winfun.
 • **Close** Notepad.

6 • **Start** the Run command.
 • **Make** sure your duplicate data disk is in drive A:.
 • **Type** the path to **My Doc 2.txt** in the My Documents folder (remember the quotes).
 • **Open My Doc 2**.
 • **Close** Notepad.

7 • **Start** the Run command.
 • **Type** the path to the Windows folder.
 • **Open** the Windows folder.
 • **Close** the Windows folder.

EXERCISE 113

Practice

**Lesson Eight
Other Features**

Tasks Reviewed:
• Use the MS-DOS Prompt
• Use the Run Command
• Use Startup
• View Animated Files

Exercise 113 continued...

8
- **Open** the Startup folder.
- **Create** a shortcut to Notepad in the Startup folder.
- **Change** the Notepad shortcut so it opens minimized.
- **Close** the Startup folder window.
- **Look** at the Startup menu. Is Notepad in it?
- **Close** menus.
- **Shut Down** Windows 95 using the Restart the Computer option.
- **Log on** to Windows 95 as usual. Is Notepad on the taskbar?
- **Click** Notepad to open it, then **close** Notepad.
- **Open** the Startup folder, **delete** the Notepad shortcut, and **close** the Startup folder window.
- **Empty** the Recycle Bin.

9
- **Start** Media Player.
- **Open Paste** in the Windows\Help folder (remember to change Files of type to Video for Windows (*.avi)).
- **Play** the **Paste** video clip.
- **Play** the **Paste** video clip again, and stop half way through it.
- **Rewind** the **Paste** video clip.
- **Play** the **Paste** video clip and pause half way through it, then finish playing it.
- **Drag** the slider.
- **Simplify** Media Player's controls.
- **Play** the **Paste** video clip.
- **Switch** back to the standard Media Player's controls.
- **Exit** Media Player.

10
- **Find** all the Video Clip file types (use the Find program).
- **Play** the Video Clips as desired.
- **Exit** Find.

11
- **Play** the **Skiing** video clip if you have it, and close it when you are through.

Begin with the desktop displayed and with no tasks on the taskbar.

1
- **Open** the Control Panel.
- **Open** the Date/Time properties.
- **Cancel** the Date/Time properties without making changes.
- **Open** the Printers folder.
- **Close** the Printers folder.
- **Close** the Control Panel.

    NOTE: If folder windows are set to Browse using a single window, the Control Panel is not open so you need not close it.

2
- **Open** the Control Panel.
- **Open** the Display Properties.
- **Change** to a color scheme of your choice.
- **Apply** the change.
- **Change** to the Windows Standard color scheme.
- **Apply** the change.

3
- **Choose** Menu from the Item list.
- **Change** the size of the Menu bar.
- **Change** the color of the Menu bar.
- **Change** the Menu bar font to MS Serif.
- **Change** the Menu bar font size to 12.
- **Change** the Menu bar font color.
- **Change** the Menu bar font type to bold and italic.
- **Change** to the Windows Standard color scheme.
- **Apply** the change.
- **Exit** the Display Properties.
- **Exit** the Control Panel.

4
- **Open** the Control Panel.
- **Open** the Mouse Properties.
- **Test** the double-click speed.
- **Increase** the mouse double-click speed.
- **Test** the double-click speed.
- **Decrease** the mouse double-click speed.
- **Test** the double-click speed.
- **Change** the mouse double-click speed to a medium speed (the middle of the scale).

5
- **Look** at the Mouse Pointers.
- **Change** the pointer size to Windows Standard (extra large).
- **Change** the pointer size to Windows Standard.
- **Turn on** pointer trails.
- **Drag** the mouse around and look at the trails.
- **Turn off** pointer trails.
- **Close** the Mouse Properties.
- **Exit** the Control Panel.

Exercise 114 continued...

EXERCISE 114
Practice
**Lesson Eight
Other Features**

Tasks Reviewed:
- Use the Control Panel
- Change Screen Colors
- Change the Mouse
- Look at Fonts

6
- **Open** the Control Panel.
- **Open** the Fonts folder.
- **View** fonts in the List mode.
- **View** fonts in the Similarity mode.
- **View** fonts in the List mode.
- **Hide** font variations.
- **View** all font variations.

7
- **Look** at the Times New Roman font (open it).
- **Print** the Times New Roman font.

Times New Roman (TrueType)

Typeface name: Times New Roman
File size: 84 KB
Version: MS core font:V2.00

Typeface © The Monotype Corporation plc. Data © The Monotype Co

---

abcdefghijklmnopqrstuvwxyz
ABCDEFGHIJKLMNOPQRSTUVWXYZ
1234567890.:,;("*!?')

12 The quick brown fox jumps over the lazy dog. 1234567890

18 The quick brown fox jumps over the lazy dog. 1234567890

24 The quick brown fox jumps over the lazy dog.

36 The quick brown fox jumps ov

48 The quick brown fox ju

60 The quick brown f

72 The quick brow

- **Close** the Times New Roman font.
- **Close** the Fonts folder and the Control Panel (if it is open).

Lesson Eight Worksheet (17) is in Appendix D

Appendices

Table of Contents

APPENDIX A
Upgrading to Windows 95

Where are the familiar Windows features?

Start a program? *(See Exercise 3)*

Switch between windows? *(See Exercise 8)*

Program groups? *(See Topics 12 and 13)*

File Manager? *(See Exercise 37 and Lesson Six)*

Control Panel? *(See Exercises 109, 110, 111, and 112)*

MS-DOS Prompt? *(See Exercise 105)*

Run command? *(See Exercise 106)*

Help? 🄵🄱 as usual *(See Lesson 4)*

Find them in the illustrations below.

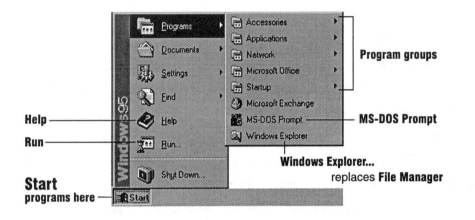

Help — Run —

Program groups

MS-DOS Prompt

Windows Explorer...
replaces **File Manager**

Start
programs here —

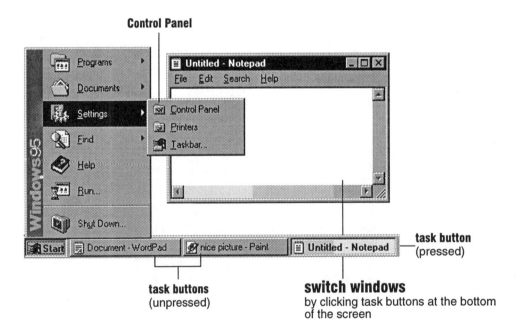

Control Panel

task button
(pressed)

task buttons
(unpressed)

switch windows
by clicking task buttons at the bottom
of the screen

What's new in Windows 95

Start button (See Exercises 2 and 3)
Click it to open the Start menu from which you can open other menus and launch programs.

Taskbar (See Exercises 8, 23, 24, 25, 26, and 27)
Lets you quickly switch between tasks. You can still use [Alt]+[Tab] to switch between windows.

My Computer (See Lesson Three)
The quick route to folders, files, and other objects on your computer.

Windows Explorer (See Lesson Six)
Lets you examine your entire computer system.

Network Neighborhood
A quick way to browse your network.

Long filenames (See Topic 11 and Exercise 59)
A filename that is up to 255 characters and can contain spaces and most symbols.

The desktop (See Lesson Five)
The Windows 95 opening screen; it contains a few objects, the Start menu, and the taskbar. It is the heart of Windows 95—your control center.

Properties (See Topic 10 and Exercise 15)
A characteristic of an object; properties for an object are grouped together in easy-to-access properties dialog boxes, also called Property Sheets.

Folders
The new name for directories.

Shortcuts (See Topic 17)
An icon that contains a direct route to a specific object. Identify them by a small jump arrow in the lower left corner. While not totally new, they are used much more extensively in Windows 95 than before.

Shortcut menus (See Exercise 34)
Also called right-click menus, they are easy-to-use menus that appear when you right-click an object or area.

Close, Minimize, and Maximize buttons
See Exercises 4, 5, 6, and 7
The Close button [X] has been added to the Maximize and Minimize button in windows, so now there are three buttons in the top right corner of windows.

What's This? (See Exercise 48)
A dialog box help feature that offers information about dialog box options.

Find command (See Lesson Seven)
A comprehensive search program that locates files and folders using search criteria you enter that give hints about the files you are looking for.

Documents menu (See Topic 18 and Exercise 58 and 71)
A menu located in the Start menu that holds up to 15 of your most recently used documents; use it to quickly open a recently used document.

Quick View (See Exercise 42)
A simple program that lets you take a look at a document without opening it or the program it was created in.

Wizards (See Exercise 58)
Features found throughout Windows 95 in which step-by-step instructions walk a user through unfamiliar procedures.

User Profiles (See Appendix B)
A feature that lets more than one person use the same computer and retain his/her personal desktop settings.

New programs and accessories
WordPad, Paint, Microsoft Exchange, Microsoft Fax, Phone Dialer, HyperTerminal, CD Player, Volume Control, MS-DOS Prompt, File Transfer, Disk Defragmenter, ScanDisk, DriveSpace, and Backup.

Plug and Play
An industry-wide feature available in Windows 95 in which new hardware devices are automatically detected and configured.

Faster Printing
Windows prints "in the background" so you can get back to work quickly.

Improved system performance
Windows works "behind the scenes" to make sure it is running at the optimal performance level.

Improved networking
Windows 95 provides a well-integrated, high-performance, 32 bit network architecture that is easy to manage and control.

Accessibility options for people with disabilities
Windows 95 has provided many features to assist users who have movement, sight, or hearing disabilities.

Microsoft Network
Microsoft's new online service provides Electronic mail (including Internet Mail), bulletin boards, and the latest headline news.

APPENDIX B

User Profiles

To access User Profile tab of the Passwords Properties and choose the level of personal desktop settings you allow different users of the same computer to access.

— Terms and Notes —

user profile
A feature that lets more than one person use the same computer and retain their own personal desktop colors, icons, and program groups.

User Profiles

Multiple users can use one computer system without enabling **user profiles**. However, if users want to have personalized desktop settings, you must enable User Profiles. Lesson Five in this book has students work with files and folders on the desktop. If you have a setting where more than one user is using one computer, Lesson Five has the potential to cause conflicts. You may want to create user profiles.

Begin with the desktop displayed and with no tasks on the taskbar.

① Open the Control Panel:

- **Click** 🏁 Start
- **Move** the pointer on Settings.
- **Click** 🖳 Control Panel
  The Control Panel opens.

② Open the Passwords Properties dialog box:

- **Double-click** 🔑 Passwords
  The Passwords Properties dialog box opens.

customize personal settings

User Profile Settings

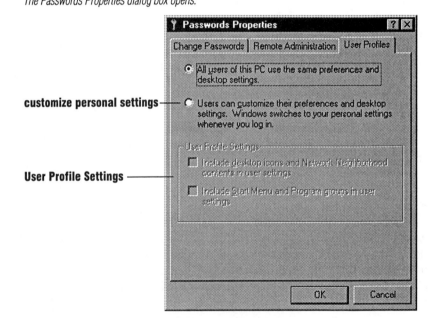

③ Enable users to personalize desktop settings:

- **Click** Users can customize their preferences and desktop settings.
  The User Profile Settings become now available to select from.

Appendix B continued...

④ Choose User Profile Settings:

- **Select** Include <u>d</u>esktop icons and Network Neighborhood content in user settings (sets up separate Desktop, NetHood, and Recent folders).
  and/or
- **Select** Include <u>S</u>tart Menu and Program groups in user settings (sets up separate Start Menu folder and subfolders).

  NOTE: Most instructional settings will do fine with just the first option, Include desktop icons, etc. The second option, Include Start Menu and Program groups, takes up more disk space and creates a separate set of all the Start menu folders and subfolders which probably are not necessary.

- **Click** [OK]
- **Close** the Control Panel.

⑤ Add new users:

- **Close** any programs and folders that are open.
- **Click** [🏁 Start], then Sh<u>u</u>t Down, then <u>C</u>lose all programs and log on as a different user?

  A log on screen appears.

- **Press** [Alt]+[U] (<u>U</u>ser name).
- **Type** a new user name, for example, student1.
- **Press** [Alt]+[P] (<u>P</u>assword).
- **Type** a password (use a password that you will remember because it will not appear again).

  The password appears as small x's for every letter you type.

- **Click** [OK]

  NETWORK USERS ONLY:
  A dialog box appears saying that you have not logged on at this computer before, and asking is you would like the computer to retain your individual settings for use when you log on here in the future?

  - **Click** [<u>Y</u>es]

  The Set Windows Password dialog box appears asking you to confirm new password.

Set Windows Password	? ☒
Please confirm the password you entered. This will be used as your Windows password.	[OK] [Cancel]
<u>N</u>ew password: [xxxxx]	
<u>C</u>onfirm new password: [ ]	

- **Type** the password you typed eariler.

  Again, the password appears as small x's for every letter you type.

- **Click** [OK]

  A new user has been defined and has accessed the desktop.

- **Repeat** this step to add more new users.

Appendix B continued...

⑥ Look at the profiles

- **Right-click** 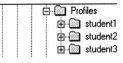, then **E**xplore.
  The Explorer opens with the Start Menu folder open; the Profiles folder appears a few folders above the Start Menu folder.

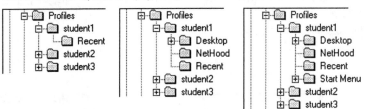

- **Expand** Profiles (click the plus (+) beside Profiles.
  The Profiles folder expands to display the user name folders. It would look like this if you added three new users named student1, student2, and student3.

```
└─🗁 Profiles
      ⊞─🗁 student1
      ⊞─🗁 student2
      ⊞─🗁 student3
```

- **Expand** student1.
  The student1 folder expands to display the folders within it. Below are some possible results.

```
└─🗁 Profiles            └─🗁 Profiles            └─🗁 Profiles
    └─🗁 student1             └─🗁 student1             └─🗁 student1
        └─🗁 Recent               ⊞─🗁 Desktop             ⊞─🗁 Desktop
    ⊞─🗁 student2                  └─🗁 NetHood             └─🗁 NetHood
    ⊞─🗁 student3                  └─🗁 Recent              └─🗁 Recent
                              ⊞─🗁 student2             ⊞─🗁 Start Menu
                              ⊞─🗁 student3             ⊞─🗁 student2
                                                       ⊞─🗁 student3
```

NOTE: The folders that appear within a user folder depends upon which options you chose in step 4 and whether or not you are on a network. And, even though there is a Desktop folder, it may not appear if the Hide files of this type option is selected.

⑦ Change to all users use the same settings:

NOTE: You can add users in both this mode and the "personalize settings" mode.

- **Open** the Control Panel and the Passwords dialog box.
- **Click** User Profiles, then All **u**sers of this PC use the same preferences and desktop settings.
- **Close** the Passwords dialog box and the Control Panel.

⑧ Change the current user's password:

- **Open** the Contol Panel and the Passwords dialog box.
- **Click** [Change Windows Password...]
- **Type** the old password in the **O**ld password box.
- **Type** the new password in the **N**ew password box.
- **Type** the new password again in the Con**f**irm new password box.
- **Click** [OK]
  A dialog box announces that your password has been successfully changed.
- **Close** the Passwords dialog box and the Control Panel.

APPENDIX C
Check-off List for Exercises, Printouts, and Worksheets.

LESSON ONE - Windows Basics
Exercise

_____ 1 — Start Windows
_____ 2 — Open and Close Menus
_____ 3 — Start a Program
_____ 4 — Exit a Program
_____ 5 — Maximize a Window
_____ 6 — Restore a Window
_____ 7 — Minimize a Window
_____ 8 — Switch Tasks
_____ 9 — Move a Window
_____ 10 — Size a Window
_____ 11 — Scroll Through a Window
_____ 12 — Exit Windows
_____ 13 — Practice
_____ Worksheet 1, page 228
_____ Worksheet 2, page 229
_____ Worksheet 3, page 230
_____ Worksheet 4, page 231
_____ Worksheet 5, page 232
_____ Worksheet 6, page 233

LESSON TWO - Beyond Basics
Exercise

_____ 14 — Use a Dialog Box
_____ 15 — Use a Property Sheet
_____ 16 — Use a Program
_____ 17 — Save a Document
_____ 18 — Start a New Document
_____ 19 — Open a Document
_____ 20 — Print a Document
_____ Print **saveas**, step 2
_____ Print **saveas**, step 3
_____ 21 — Page Setup
_____ 22 — Arrange Windows
_____ 23 — Move the Taskbar
_____ 24 — Size the Taskbar
_____ 25 — Hide the Taskbar
_____ 26 — Access the Desktop
_____ 27 — Control Programs from the Taskbar
_____ 28 — Use Rich Text Format with WordPad
_____ Print **richtext**, step 8
_____ 29 — Practice
_____ Print **create2**, step 5
_____ Print **savefile**, step 6
_____ Worksheet 7, page 234
_____ Worksheet 8, page 235

LESSON THREE - My Computer
Exercise

_____ 30 — Use My Computer
_____ 31 — Browse Folders Using Separate Windows
_____ 32 — Browse Folders Using a Single Window
_____ 33 — My Computer Menus
_____ 34 — My Computer Right-Click Menus
_____ 35 — Change Disk Drives with My Computer
_____ 36 — Arrange Icons
_____ 37 — Start Explorer from My Computer
_____ 38 — Start a Program from a Folder
_____ 39 — Open a Document from a Folder
_____ 40 — Create and Delete Folders
_____ 41 — Move Files into a Folder
_____ 42 — Use Quick View
_____ 43 — Print from a Folder
_____ Print **saveas**, step 3
_____ 44 — Practice
_____ 45 — Practice
_____ Print **winfun**, step 13
_____ Worksheet 9, page 236
_____ Worksheet 10, page 237
_____ Worksheet 11, page 238

LESSON FOUR - Help
Exercise

_____ 46 — Identify Button Names
_____ 47 — Identify Menu Information
_____ 48 — Use Dialog Box Help
_____ 49 — Use Help Topics, Contents
_____ 50 — Use Help Topics, Index
_____ 51 — Use Help Topics, Find
_____ 52 — Print Help Topics
_____ Print a help topic, step 2
_____ Print a book, step 3
_____ 53 — Copy Help Topics
_____ Print **help**, step 6
_____ 54 — Annotate Help Topics
_____ 55 — Keep Help on Top
_____ 56 — Practice
_____ 57 — Practice
_____ Print a help topic, step 1
_____ Print **help2**, step 7
_____ Worksheet 12, page 239

This page may be copied.

LESSON FIVE - The Desktop
Exercise
_____ 58 — Clear the Document Menu
_____ 59 — Save a Document on the Desktop
_____   Print **My Doc 1**, step 4
_____ 60 — Create a Document on the Desktop
_____ 61 — Create a Shortcut
_____ 62 — Look at a Shortcut's Property Sheet
_____ 63 — Use Drag-and-Drop to Print
_____   Print **My Doc 2**, step 1
_____   Print **savefile**, step 2
_____ 64 — Create a Folder on the Desktop
_____ 65 — Arrange the Desktop
_____ 66 — Capture the Screen
_____   Print the screen image, step 3
_____ 67 — Capture a Window
_____   Print the window image, step 4
_____ 68 — Undo an Action
_____ 69 — Use the Recycle Bin
_____ 70 — Organize the Desktop
_____ 71 — Use the Documents Menu
_____   Print **My Doc 3**, step 2
_____ 72 — Open a File Menu Document
_____ 73 — Wrap Up Lesson Five
_____ 74 — Practice
_____   Print **DOC 1**, step 5
_____   Print **DOC 3**, step 7
_____   Print the screen image, step 9
_____ 75 — Practice
_____   Print the window image, step 1
_____   Print **DOC 2**, step 9
_____   Worksheet 13, page 240

LESSON SIX - The Explorer
Exercise
_____ 76 — Start Explorer
_____ 77 — Resize Explorer's Panes
_____ 78 — Expand and Collapse Folders
_____ 79 — Select Objects in the Left Pane
_____ 80 — Browse Your Data Disk
_____ 81 — Copy a Disk
_____ 82 — Select Objects in the Right Pane
_____ 83 — Invert Selection
_____ 84 — Select All Objects
_____ 85 — Move Objects
_____ 86 — Copy Objects
_____ 87 — Delete Objects
_____ 88 — Arrange Icons Using Headings
_____ 89 — Display Hidden Files and Folders
_____ 90 — Display MS-DOS File Extensions
_____ 91 — Display Full MS-DOS Path
_____ 92 — Format a Floppy Disk
_____ 93 — Practice
_____ 94 — Practice
_____   Worksheet 14, page 241
_____   Worksheet 15, page 242

LESSON SEVEN - Finding Files
Exercise
_____ 95 — Start Find
_____ 96 — Find Files by Name & Location
_____ 97 — Find Files by Date Modified
_____ 98 — Find Files by File Size
_____ 99 — Find Files by File Type
_____ 100 — Find Files by Text In the Files
_____ 101 — Save Search Criteria
_____ 102 — Save Search Results
_____   Print the Find window, step 2
_____ 103 — Practice
_____ 104 — Practice
_____   Print the Find window, step 5
_____   Worksheet 16, page 243

LESSON EIGHT - Other Features
Exercise
_____ 105 — Use the MS-DOS Prompt
_____ 106 — Use the Run Command
_____ 107 — Use Startup
_____ 108 — View Animation Files
_____ 109 — Use the Control Panel
_____ 110 — Change the Screen Colors
_____ 111 — Change Mouse Settings
_____ 112 — Look at Fonts
_____   Print the Arial font, step 5
_____   Print the Wingdings font, step 6
_____ 113 — Practice
_____ 114 — Practice
_____   Print the Times New Roman font, step 7
_____   Worksheet 17, page 244

APPENDIX D
Lesson Worksheets

Table of Contents

WORKSHEET 1

NAME _____ SCORE _____

LESSON ONE—Topics 1 and 2

DIRECTIONS: Use the following terms to fill in the blanks below:

monitor	computer	disk drive	read only memory (ROM)
printer	software	floppy disk	application software (program)
hardware	firmware	system software	memory (RAM-random access memory)
keyboard	hard disk	operating system	processor (CPU-central processing unit)

1. A chip that holds information that cannot be changed.
   1. _____

2. An electronic device that performs complex tasks at high speed and with great accuracy; it has two main parts—the *processor* and the *memory*.
   2. _____

3. The group of parts that make up the computer system; it can be seen and touched.
   3. _____

4. The area of the computer that holds the instructions (programs) and information you give it. When you turn the computer off, data in it disappears.
   4. _____

5. A device used to enter data and issue commands to the computer.
   5. _____

6. A kind of *system software*—instructions that are built into the computer system on ROM chips.
   6. _____

7. Software that does a specific task, such as word processing.
   7. _____

8. A large capacity storage area that offers fast access to store and retrieve information.
   8. _____

9. A magnetically coated disk on which information can be stored and retrieved.
   9. _____

10. A mechanical device that you use to transfer information back and forth between the computer's memory and a disk.
    10. _____

11. A device that makes a hard copy of data in the computer.
    11. _____

12. Instructions that tell your computer how to perform a task. It is stored on disks in program files. It cannot be seen or touched. There are two main kinds: application and system.
    12. _____

13. Software that acts as a link between you, application software (programs), and hardware.
    13. _____

14. Software that runs the computer.
    14. _____

15. The part of the computer that processes the instructions in the memory (RAM).
    15. _____

16. A screen that displays the information in the computer.
    16. _____

This page may be copied.

WORKSHEET 2

NAME _____ SCORE_____

LESSON ONE—Topics 3, 4, and 5

1. The bar on the desktop that lets you quickly start programs and easily switch between tasks.

    1. _____

2. A phrase that is commonly used to describe Microsoft Windows and other similar programs that use *pictures* to help you *communicate* with the computer.

    2. _____

3. The button located at the left end of the taskbar that is labeled *Start.* You click it to open the Start menu from which you can open other menus and launch programs.

    3. _____

4. Two or more computers that are linked together to share programs, data, and certain hardware components, for example, a printer.

    4. _____

5. A set of instructions that your computer carries out to perform a specific task, such as word processing.

    5. _____

6. An operating system that uses a graphics environment to connect you to the computer system's hardware and software in an easy-to-understand, intuitive way; it also offers many useful programs.

    6. _____

7. One of the many *things* that you use when working with the computer system—items such as: files, Control Panel tools, programs, My Computer, folders, Network Neighborhood, shortcuts, the Recycle Bin, disk drives, and My Briefcase.

    7. _____

8. An icon containing a direct route to a specific object and displaying a small jump-arrow in the lower-left corner. Double-click it to open the file or program it represents quickly.

    8. _____

9. The operator (or user) of the computer system (its hardware and software).

    9. _____

10. Remote access through a modem or fax/modem which allows you to: communicate with bulletin board services, transfer files, and send and receive faxes.

    10. _____

11. The combination of many various communication methods, including text, graphics, sound, animation, and video.

    11. _____

12. The ability of an operating system to run more than one program at one time.

    12. _____

13. The simple opening screen in Windows 95 that contains a few objects, the Start menu, and a taskbar.

    13. _____

WORKSHEET 3

NAME _____ SCORE_____

LESSON ONE—Topics 6, 7, and 8

DIRECTIONS: Use the following terms to fill in the blanks below:

mouse	title bar	window title	Restore button ⧉
window	workspace	Close button ☒	Maximize button ▢
commands	accessories	keyboard shortcuts	Minimize button ▬
keyboard	Control menu	Control menu button	pointer (mouse pointer)
menu bar			

---

1. A small, hand-held device used to control the pointer on the screen.

2. A menu with items that you use to manipulate a program window (Restore, Move, Size, Minimize, Maximize, and Close).

3. Key combinations that are used to activate certain commands instead of using the mouse.

4. A button located at the right end of the title bar that you click to exit a window.

5. A button located at the right side of the title bar that you can click to reduce a window to a task button on the taskbar.

6. The rectangular work area for a task, folder, program, or document.

7. The horizontal bar at the top of a window that holds the window's name.

8. The bar located under the title bar that lists the available menus.

9. The arrow-shaped cursor on the screen that moves with the mouse as you slide it over a flat surface. Its shape changes depending on the job it is doing.

10. The button in the middle of three buttons located at the right end of the title bar on a Maximized window; it returns a maximized window to its previous size.

11. The button in the middle of the three buttons located at the right end of the title bar; it enlarges a window to its greatest possible size.

12. The name of a window, located just to the right of the Control menu button. A document name, if any, is listed first followed by the program name.

13. Instructions that cause an action to be carried out.

14. Different kinds of programs (applications) that come with Windows.

15. An icon at the left side of the title bar that opens the Control menu. It matches the icon for the program that it is in.

16. A device used to enter data and issue commands to the computer.

17. The inner part of the window where the work in a program or document is carried out.

1. _____

2. _____

3. _____

4. _____

5. _____

6. _____

7. _____

8. _____

9. _____

10. _____

11. _____

12. _____

13. _____

14. _____

15. _____

16. _____

17. _____

WORKSHEET 4

NAME _____ SCORE _____

LESSON ONE—Exercises 1, 2, 3, and 4

DIRECTIONS: Use the following terms to fill in the blanks below:

menu	menu item	Close button	Control menu button
Exit	user name	Control menu	program (application)
Close	dialog box	cascading menu	launch (start a program)
password	application		

---

1. A menu with items that you use to manipulate a program window (Restore, Move, Size, Minimize, Maximize, and Close).

   1. _____

2. A button located at the right end of the title bar that you click to exit a window.

   2. _____

3. A command that lets you leave a Windows program (application). It is usually found on the Control menu.

   3. _____

4. Means the same thing as *program*. While the term is used a lot in Windows, this book uses the term *program* more often.

   4. _____

5. A list of items from which you may choose one.

   5. _____

6. A name given to a person using Windows. By using different names and passwords for different people, each person's work can be kept secure.

   6. _____

7. Another term that is sometimes used to mean starting a program (*or application*).

   7. _____

8. An icon at the left side of the title bar that opens the Control menu. It matches the icon for the program that it is in.

   8. _____

9. A combination of characters that you type, when prompted, in order to access Windows (or some Windows feature). The characters appear as small x's when you type them. This is a security feature that prevents access to Windows (or a Windows network) without the correct combination of characters.

   9. _____

10. A menu that opens when you choose a menu item that is followed by a right-pointing triangle (▸).

    10. _____

11. One of the choices on a menu.

    11. _____

12. A set of instructions that your computer carries out to perform a specific task, such as word processing.

    12. _____

13. A command that lets you leave a Windows program (application). It is usually found on the File menu.

    13. _____

14. A special kind of window that offers different controls for you to manipulate.

    14. _____

This page may be copied.

WORKSHEET 5

NAME _____ SCORE_____

LESSON ONE—Exercises 5, 6, 7, and 8

DIRECTIONS: Use the following terms to fill in the blanks below:

task	unpressed	Restore button ⬕	Minimize button ▫
pressed	task button	dimmed command	active task button
taskbar	active window	Maximize button ⬛	inactive task button
desktop			

1. A task button located on the taskbar that is unpressed, thus indicating the task it represents is open, but not active.

   1. _____

2. The button in the middle of the three buttons located at the right end of the title bar; it enlarges a window to its greatest possible size.

   2. _____

3. A task button located on the taskbar that appears to be pressed, thus indicating that the task it represents is active.

   3. _____

4. An open (but not necessarily active) program.

   4. _____

5. The button in the middle of three buttons located at the right end of the title bar on a Maximized window; it returns a maximized window to its previous size.

   5. _____

6. The simple opening screen in Windows 95 that contains a few objects, the Start menu, and a taskbar.

   6. _____

7. A 3-D effect in which a button (or other item) appears sunken, indicating it is selected (or active).

   7. _____

8. A window whose title bar is highlighted, indicating that it is currently being used.

   8. _____

9. The bar on the desktop that lets you quickly start programs and easily switch between tasks.

   9. _____

10. A command that cannot be used in the current situation; it is displayed in gray instead of black.

    10. _____

11. A button located at the right side of the title bar that you can click to eliminate a window from the desktop while allowing the program to remain open on the taskbar.

    11. _____

12. A button located on the taskbar that represents an open program; each one displays the program's icon and its name.

    12. _____

13. A 3-D effect in which a button (or other item) appears raised, indicating it is deselected (or inactive).

    13. _____

This page may be copied.

WORKSHEET 6

LESSON ONE—Exercises 9, 10, 11, and 12

DIRECTIONS: Use the following terms to fill in the blanks below:

title bar	scroll box	scroll arrows	double-headed arrow
warm boot	scroll bar	sizing handle	drag (mouse action)

---

1. The process of restarting the computer by pressing [Ctrl]+[Alt]+[Del]

    1. _____

2. A bar that appears at the right and/or bottom edge of a window whose contents are not completely visible. It contains two scroll arrows and a proportional scroll box (when data is present).

    2. _____

3. The shape the pointer takes when it is used to size a window or the taskbar.

    3. _____

4. To move the pointer on an item, hold down the left button, slide the pointer to a new location, and release the button.

    4. _____

5. The box in a scroll bar; it shows two things: 1) the *position* of the information displayed in relation to the entire document, and 2) the *size* of the entire document in relation to the screen size.

    5. _____

6. The horizontal bar at the top of a window that holds the window's name.

    6. _____

7. The arrows at each end of a scroll bar, used to scroll through the contents of a window.

    7. _____

8. An area in the bottom right corner of windows that can be sized; it is used to size windows.

    8. _____

This page may be copied.

WORKSHEET 7

NAME _____ SCORE_____

LESSON TWO—Topics 9 and 10; and Exercises 14, 15, 16, and 17

DIRECTIONS: Use the following terms to fill in the blanks below:

file	controls	dialog box	associated file
Save	Save As	right-click	common dialog boxes
object	workspace	program file	document (data file)
default	data disk	property sheet	data file (document)

---

1. A special kind of window that offers different controls for you to manipulate.

   1. _____

2. Dialog boxes, such as Open, Save, and Print, that are basically the same in different programs. They make it easier for you to learn new programs.

   2. _____

3. A file that holds a set of instructions that performs a task, such as word processing.

   3. _____

4. The inner part of the window where the work in a program or document is carried out.

   4. _____

5. A special kind of dialog box that groups the settings for an object's properties.

   5. _____

6. A file that consists of data that has been created in a program, such as a letter typed in WordPad or a picture drawn in Paint.

   6. _____

7. A file type that has been identified as belonging to a certain program, such as .TXT with Notepad, .BMP with Paint, or .DOC with Word 6. When you open one, the program related to it opens automatically.

   7. _____

8. Any data you create with a program, for example, a report or a picture.

   8. _____

9. Different kinds of elements in dialog boxes that allow you to manipulate a program's appearance and function.

   9. _____

10. An automatic setting in a program.

   10. _____

11. One of the many *things* that you use when working with the computer system—items such as: files, Control Panel tools, programs, My Computer, folders, Network Neighborhood, shortcuts, the Recycle Bin, and disk drives.

   11. _____

12. The command that saves changes to a previously named document on which you are working.

   12. _____

13. A set of data or program instructions that is saved on a disk as a named unit.

   13. _____

14. A floppy disk on which you can save data files.

   14. _____

15. Quickly press and release the *right* mouse button.

   15. _____

16. A command that opens a dialog box that lets you save a new document or rename a previously saved document.

   16. _____

This page may be copied.

WORKSHEET 8

LESSON TWO—Exercises 18, 19, 21, 22, 26, 27, and 28

DIRECTIONS: Use the following terms to fill in the blanks below:

taskbar	landscape	document type	tile vertically
toolbar	changed file	unchanged file	Word for Windows
cascade	Control menu	file type icon	tile horizontally
portrait	active window	common commands	Rich Text Format
shortcut			

---

1. A menu with items that you use to manipulate a program window (Restore, Move, Size, Minimize, Maximize, and Close).

1. _____

2. An icon containing a direct route to a specific object and displaying a small jump-arrow in the lower-left corner. Double-click it to open the file or program it represents quickly.

2. _____

3. A file (or workspace) that has had some kind of modification—either the file is new or the file has been edited in some way since it was last saved.

3. _____

4. The bar on the desktop that lets you quickly start programs and easily switch between tasks.

4. _____

5. A row of buttons that provide quick access to frequently used commands.

5. _____

6. Commands such as New and Save that work the same in all Windows programs.

6. _____

7. To resize and arrange the windows on the desktop *one on top of the other* so that each window displays part of its workspace.

7. _____

8. A window whose title bar is highlighted, indicating that it is currently being used.

8. _____

9. A file that has not been modified (edited) since it was last saved.

9. _____

10. A paper orientation in which the paper is wider than it is tall.

10. _____

11. A paper orientation in which the paper is taller than it is wide.

11. _____

12. To resize and layer windows on the desktop so that the title bar of each window is visible.

12. _____

13. To resize and arrange the windows on the desktop *side by side* so that each window displays part of its workspace.

13. _____

14. A file format that is commonly used by programmers. Windows 95 Help files use this type of file.

14. _____

15. A sophisticated and commonly used word processing program made by Microsoft but not shipped with the Windows 95 program.

15. _____

16. The icon that is connected with a particular file type, such as Word 6 documents or text documents.

16. _____

17. Different kinds of documents that are defined by the programs that create them.

17. _____

This page may be copied.

WORKSHEET 9

LESSON THREE—Topic 11

> DIRECTIONS: Use the following terms to fill in the blanks below:
>
> | | | |
> |---|---|---|
> | file | program file | associated file |
> | filename | long filename | filename extension |
> | file types | short filename | data file (document) |

1. Different kinds of files that are defined by the programs that create the files.

    1. _____

2. A file type that has been identified as belonging to a certain program, such as .TXT with Notepad, .BMP with Paint, or .DOC with Word 6. When you open one, the program related to it opens automatically.

    2. _____

3. A file that consists of data that has been created in a program, such as a letter typed in WordPad or a picture drawn in Paint.

    3. _____

4. A set of data or program instructions that is saved on a disk as a named unit.

    4. _____

5. A file that holds a set of instructions that perform a task, such as word processing.

    5. _____

6. A filename that is no longer that eight characters, can contain a filename extension, and *cannot* contain spaces and certain symbols.

    6. _____

7. The name assigned to a collection of data that is stored on a disk.

    7. _____

8. The optional *period and up to three characters* at the end of a filename.

    8. _____

9. A filename that is up to 255 characters long and *can* contain spaces and most symbols.

    9. _____

WORKSHEET 10

NAME _____ SCORE _____

LESSON THREE—Topic 12

DIRECTIONS: Use the following terms to fill in the blanks below:

disk   disk drive   CD-ROM drive
folder   subfolder   hard disk drive
hierarchy   group folder   floppy disk drive

---

1. A folder that is within another folder, or below another folder in the folder structure.

                                                   1. _____

2. A built-in storage device that has a non-removable disk (a fixed disk) with a large capacity. It provides fast retrieval and storage of files.

                                                   2. _____

3. A mechanical device that you use to transfer information back and forth between the computer's memory and a disk.

                                                   3. _____

4. A read-only optical disk that can store relatively large amounts of data.

                                                   4. _____

5. Media on which information is stored and retrieved in named units called *files*.

                                                   5. _____

6. A storage device that retrieves and stores files on a removable media called *floppy diskettes*.

                                                   6. _____

7. A system of things (or people) ranked one above the other. On computers, it describes the multilevel structure of folders and subfolders on a disk; or, in the case of Windows 95, it describes a multilevel structure of objects on the entire computer system.

                                                   7. _____

8. A folder within the Start Menu folder that holds groups of program shortcuts and other folders; they represent menus within the Start menu.

                                                   8. _____

9. A structure that holds files and/or other folders that are stored on a disk. It can also hold other objects, such as printers and disk drives.

                                                   9. _____

WORKSHEET 11

NAME _____ SCORE_____

LESSON THREE—Topics 13 and 14; and Exercises 30, 34, 39, and 42

DIRECTIONS: Use the following terms to fill in the blanks below:

browse	desktop	My Computer	data file (document)
toolbar	folder window	My Briefcase	document (data file)
workspace	shortcut menu	right-click menu	Network Neighborhood
Quick View			

---

1. Any data you create with a program, for example, a report or a picture.

   1. _____

2. An object that appears on the desktop (if you have a networked system) that lets you browse through other computers on your network.

   2. _____

3. A file that consists of data that has been created in a program, such as a letter typed in WordPad or a picture drawn in Paint.

   3. _____

4. A row of buttons that provide quick access to frequently used commands.

   4. _____

5. An object that appears on the desktop (if you have a modem) and lets you keep files on one computer up-to-date from a remote location by using a second computer and modems.

   5. _____

6. The simple opening screen in Windows 95 that contains a few objects, the Start menu, and a taskbar.

   6. _____

7. An easy-to-use menu that opens whenever you right-click an object or area, except in a dialog box (*see shortcut menu*).

   7. _____

8. A simple program that displays the contents of the selected item; it will appear on the menu only if there is a *viewer* available for the type of file you select and if it has been installed.

   8. _____

9. The obvious, quick, easy-to-use route to the folders, files, and other objects on your computer system.

   9. _____

10. A window that displays the contents of a folder (or certain other objects, such as disk drives). It offers many of the same folder managing features as the Explorer.

    10. _____

11. To look at files, folders, disks, printers, programs, documents, and other objects on your computer system.

    11. _____

12. The inner part of the window where the work in a program or document is carried out.

    12. _____

13. Another name for right-click menu (an easy-to-use menu that opens whenever you right-click and object or area).

    13. _____

This page may be copied.

WORKSHEET 12

NAME _____ SCORE _____

LESSON FOUR—Topic 15; and Exercises 47, 49, 50, and 51

DIRECTIONS: Use the following terms to fill in the blanks below:

Find	status bar	Options button	Related Topics button
Index	Back button	Help Topics button	Click here button 🔳
Contents	Help topics	Help Topics program	Wizard

---

1. A shortcut box you can click to start the program or open the window related to the current Help topic.

1. _____

2. A button at the top of a Help topic that returns you to the Help Topics program.

2. _____

3. The bar at the bottom of a program; it displays information about the program, and it can be turned on and off from the View menu.

3. _____

4. A button at the top of a Help topic that returns you to the previous Help topic. Use this button to backtrack through the topics you have viewed so far.

4. _____

5. An area of the Help Topics program that displays organized categories (books) that you look through to find and then choose the Help topic you want.

5. _____

6. The Windows 95 Help program; it has three sections to help you locate find Help topics: Contents, Index, and Find.

6. _____

7. A shortcut box you click to go to a Help topic related to the one you are currently viewing.

7. _____

8. A button at the top of a Help topic that lets you work with the Help topic. You can Annotate, Copy, Print, change Font, Keep Help on Top, or Use System Colors for the current Help topic.

8. _____

9. Information about a Windows subject; they usually begin with a title and contain information about a particular task, command, or dialog box.

9. _____

10. An area of the Help program that lets you search for the actual words contained in all the Help topics for a given program. When you use it for the first time, Windows must create its list of words.

10. _____

11. An area of the Help Topics program that displays a list of words and phrases that you can search to find a related Help topic.

11. _____

12. A feature found throughout Windows in which step-by-step instructions walk a user through unfamiliar procedures.

12. _____

This page may be copied.

WORKSHEET 13

NAME _____ SCORE_____

LESSON FIVE—Topics 16, 17, and 18; and Exercises 59, 61, 62, and 63

DIRECTIONS: Use the following terms to fill in the blanks below:

path	property	drag and drop	document-centric
target	command line	property sheet	document (data file)
desktop	long filename	jump-arrow ↗	right-drag (mouse action)
shortcut			

1. The route to a folder or file; it consists of the disk drive, folder, subfolders (if any), and the filename (if the route is to a file).

1. _____

2. A small arrow that appears in the lower-left corner of *shortcut* icons thereby distinguishing them from other icons.

2. _____

3. A place where you enter the path to a file.

3. _____

4. Any data you create with a program, for example, a report or a picture. A document and a data file are the same thing.

4. _____

5. The name of the object that a shortcut is pointing to (the name includes the path to the object).

5. _____

6. The simple opening screen in Windows 95 that contains a few objects, the Start menu, and a taskbar.

6. _____

7. A filename that is up to 255 characters long and can contain spaces and most symbols.

7. _____

8. A procedure in which you move a document and release it on an object so the object can do something useful to the document, for example, move, copy, delete, or print it.

8. _____

9. An icon containing a direct route to a specific object and displaying a small jump-arrow in the lower-left corner. Double-click it to quickly open the file or program it represents.

9. _____

10. A characteristic of an object; many of them can be changed by using a control in a Properties dialog box.

10. _____

11. A special kind of dialog box that groups the settings for an object's properties.

11. _____

12. A system that focuses on documents and their contents rather than the programs used to create the documents.

12. _____

13. Move the pointer on an item, hold down the *right* mouse button, slide the pointer to a new location, and release the mouse button.

13. _____

WORKSHEET 14

NAME _____ SCORE _____

LESSON SIX—Topics 19 and 20

DIRECTIONS: Use the following terms to fill in the blanks below:

file	object	collapse	folder 🗀
tree	expand	Explorer	folder window
shell	browse	hierarchy	Explorer's left pane

1. To hide the folders that are displayed in an object in the left pane of Explorer that has a minus sign (-) beside it.

1. _____

2. A structure that holds files and/or other folders that are stored on a disk. It can also hold other objects, such as printers and disk drives.

2. _____

3. To display unseen folders in an object in the left pane of Explorer that has a plus sign (+) beside it.

3. _____

4. To look at files, folders, disks, printers, programs, documents, and other objects on your computer system.

4. _____

5. A set of data or program instructions that is saved on a disk as a named unit.

5. _____

6. The Windows 95 program that you can use to examine your computer system (including remote computers if your system is networked).

6. _____

7. The part of the Explorer that displays the hierarchical structure on your computer system (including remote computers if your system is networked).

7. _____

8. A representation of the hierarchy (structure) on a computer system; especially a horizontal representation.

8. _____

9. A window that displays the contents of a folder (or certain other objects, such as disk drives). It offers many of the same features as the Explorer.

9. _____

10. A program, such as Explorer, that lets you control your system.

10. _____

11. A system of things (or people) ranked one above the other. On computers, the term *hierarchy* describes the multilevel structure of folders and subfolders on a disk; or, in the case of Windows 95, it describes a multilevel structure of objects on the entire computer system.

11. _____

12. One of the many *things* that you use when working with the computer system—items such as: files, Control Panel tools, programs, My Computer, folders, Network Neighborhood, shortcuts, The Recycle Bin, disk drives, and My Briefcase.

12. _____

WORKSHEET 15

NAME _____ SCORE _____

LESSON SIX—Topic 22; and Exercises 78, 81, 89, 90, 91, and 92

DIRECTIONS: Use the following terms to fill in the blanks below:

path	hidden files	associated file	Hide files of these types
attribute	startup disk	floppy disk size	MS-DOS (Microsoft Disk Operating System)
bad sectors	Show all files	floppy disk density	

---

1. A file type that has been identified as belonging to a certain program, such as .TXT with Notepad, .BMP with Paint, or .DOC with Word 6. When you open one, the program related to the file opens automatically.

1. _____

2. Files and/or folders that have a hidden attribute.

2. _____

3. A characteristic (such as read-only, archive, hidden, or system) that changes how a file or folder can be used or displayed.

3. _____

4. An option that specifies that all files and folders should be displayed (including hidden and system files and folders).

4. _____

5. An option that specifies that certain files and folders should not be displayed (including hidden files and folders and files with certain extensions).

5. _____

6. The physical dimensions of floppy disks; typically they come in two sizes, 5¼" and 3½".

6. _____

7. Density refers to the surface coating on a disk; the closer together the particles on the disk, the higher the disk's capacity.

7. _____

8. The main operating system used before Windows was developed.

8. _____

9. The route to a folder or file; it consists of the disk drive, folder, subfolders (if any), and the filename (if the route is to a file).

9. _____

10. A disk that contains certain system files that create a system (or bootable) disk. It is a good safeguard to have one for drive A:—if the hard disk should have a problem, you can boot the computer using this floppy system disk.

10. _____

11. Damaged areas on a disk that are marked as unusable when the disk is formatted.

11. _____

This page may be copied.

WORKSHEET 16

NAME _____ SCORE _____

LESSON SEVEN—Topic 23; and Exercise 100

DIRECTIONS: Use the following terms to fill in the blanks below:

Find   browse   search criteria   case sensitive

1. A command option that tells a program to recognition of the difference between upper- and lowercase letters when it is searching for text.

    1. _____

2. To look at files, folders, disks, printers, programs, documents, and other objects on your computer system.

    2. _____

3. A program found in both the Start menu and Explorer's Tools menu that helps you locate files and folders easily by defining search criteria that give hints about the files you are looking for.

    3. _____

4. The guidelines that you tell Find to follow when it searches for certain files or folders.

    4. _____

This page may be copied.

WORKSHEET 17

NAME _____ SCORE _____

LESSON EIGHT—Topic 22; and Exercises 78, 81, 89, 90, 91, and 92

DIRECTIONS: Use the following terms to fill in the blanks below:

path	multimedia	long filename	MS-DOS–based application
serif	san serif	Control Panel	MS-DOS (Microsoft Disk Operating system)
Panose	MS-DOS prompt	TrueType font 🔠	

1. Scalable fonts that are shipped with Windows; Arial, Courier New, Lucida Console, Symbol, Times New Roman, and Wingdings.

   1. _____

2. A program that is designed to run under the MS-DOS operating system, rather than the Windows operating system.

   2. _____

3. The signal that MS-DOS is ready for you to tell it what to do.

   3. _____

4. The combination of many various communication methods, including text, graphics, sound, animation, and video.

   4. _____

5. The route to a folder or file; it consists of the disk drive, folder, subfolders (if any), and the filename (if the route is to a file).

   5. _____

6. A type of Font-mapping information that is stored with a font to describe its traits: serif, san serif, normal, bold, and italic.

   6. _____

7. A folder that combines all commands, control and configuration functions for Windows 95 in one place.

   7. _____

8. A filename that is up to 255 characters long and can contain spaces and most symbols.

   8. _____

9. A font design that has small cross strokes at the top and bottom of the characters.

   For example: **T**

   9. _____

10. A font design that has no cross strokes at the top and bottom of the characters; it is straight.

   For example: **T**

   10. _____

11. The main operating system used before Windows was developed.

   11. _____

This page may be copied.

WORKSHEET 1
LESSON ONE
1. read only memory (ROM)
2. computer
3. hardware
4. memory (RAM-random access memory)
5. keyboard
6. firmware
7. application software (program)
8. hard disk
9. floppy disk
10. disk drive
11. printer
12. software
13. operating system
14. system software
15. processor (CPU-central processing unit)
16. monitor

Missed	Score
0.	100
1.	94
2.	88
3.	82
4.	75
5.	69
6.	63
7.	57
8.	50
9.	44
10.	38
11.	32
12.	25
13.	19
14.	13
15.	7
16.	0

WORKSHEET 2
LESSON ONE
1. taskbar
2. graphical user interface (GUI)
3. Start button
4. networking
5. program (application)
6. Microsoft Windows 95
7. object
8. shortcut
9. you
10. telecommunication
11. multimedia
12. multitasking
13. desktop

Missed	Score
0.	100
1.	93
2.	85
3.	77
4.	70
5.	62
6.	55
7.	47
8.	40
9.	32
10.	24
11.	17
12.	9
13.	0

WORKSHEET 3
LESSON ONE
1. mouse
2. Control menu
3. keyboard shortcuts
4. Close button
5. Minimize button
6. window
7. title bar
8. menu bar
9. pointer (mouse pointer)
10. Restore button
11. Maximize button
12. window title
13. commands
14. accessories
15. Control menu button
16. keyboard
17. workspace

Missed	Score
0.	100
1.	94
2.	89
3.	83
4.	77
5.	71
6.	65
7.	59
8.	53
9.	48
10.	42
11.	36
12.	30
13.	24
14.	18
15.	12
16.	6
17.	0

WORKSHEET 4
LESSON ONE
1. Control menu
2. Close button
3. Close
4. application
5. menu
6. user name
7. launch
8. Control menu button
9. password
10. cascading menu
11. menu item
12. program (application)
13. Exit
14. dialog box

Missed	Score
0.	100
1.	93
2.	86
3.	79
4.	72
5.	65
6.	58
7.	51
8.	44
9.	37
10.	30
11.	23
12.	16
13.	9
14.	0

WORKSHEET 5
LESSON ONE
1. inactive task button
2. Maximize button
3. active task button
4. task
5. Restore button
6. desktop
7. pressed
8. active window
9. taskbar
10. dimmed command
11. Minimize button
12. task button
13. unpressed

Missed	Score
0.	100
1.	93
2.	85
3.	77
4.	70
5.	62
6.	55
7.	47
8.	40
9.	32
10.	24
11.	17
12.	9
13.	0

WORKSHEET 6
LESSON ONE
1. warm boot
2. scroll bar
3. double-headed arrow
4. drag (mouse action)
5. scroll box
6. title bar
7. scroll arrows
8. sizing handle

Missed	Score
0.	100
1.	88
2.	75
3.	63
4.	50
5.	68
6.	25
7.	13
8.	0

WORKSHEET 7
LESSON TWO
1. dialog box
2. common dialog boxes
3. program file
4. workspace
5. property sheet
6. data file (document)
7. associated file
8. document (data file)
9. controls
10. default
11. object
12. Save
13. file
14. data disk
15. right-click
16. Save As

Missed	Score
0.	100
1.	94
2.	88
3.	82
4.	75
5.	69
6.	63
7.	57
8.	50
9.	44
10.	38
11.	32
12.	25
13.	19
14.	13
15.	7
16.	0

WORKSHEET 8
LESSON TWO
1. Control menu
2. shortcut
3. changed file
4. taskbar
5. toolbar
6. common commands
7. tile horizontally
8. active window
9. unchanged file
10. landscape
11. portrait
12. cascade
13. tile vertically
14. Rich Text Format
15. Word for Windows
16. file type icon
17. document type

Missed	Score
0.	100
1.	94
2.	89
3.	83
4.	77
5.	71
6.	65
7.	59
8.	53
9.	48
10.	42
11.	36
12.	30
13.	24
14.	18
15.	12
16.	6
17.	0

NOTE: Worksheet solutions are on back to back pages so they can be removed from the book (for classroom use) without losing other appendices.

WORKSHEET 9
LESSON THREE
1. file types
2. associated file
3. data file (document)
4. file
5. program file
6. short filename
7. filename
8. filename extension
9. long filename

Missed	Score
0.	100
1.	89
2.	78
3.	67
4.	56
5.	45
6.	34
7.	23
8.	12
9.	0

WORKSHEET 10
LESSON THREE
1. subfolder
2. hard disk drive
3. disk drive
4. CD-ROM drive
5. disk
6. floppy disk drive
7. hierarchy
8. group folder
9. folder

Missed	Score
0.	100
1.	89
2.	78
3.	67
4.	56
5.	45
6.	34
7.	23
8.	12
9.	0

WORKSHEET 11
LESSON THREE
1. document (data file)
2. Network Neighborhood
3. data file (document)
4. toolbar
5. My Briefcase
6. desktop
7. right-click menu
8. Quick View
9. My Computer
10. folder window
11. browse
12. workspace
13. shortcut menu

Missed	Score
0.	100
1.	93
2.	85
3.	77
4.	70
5.	62
6.	55
7.	47
8.	40
9.	32
10.	24
11.	17
12.	9
13.	0

WORKSHEET 12
LESSON FOUR
1. Click here button
2. Help Topics button
3. status bar
4. Back button
5. Contents
6. Help Topics program
7. Related Topics button
8. Options button
9. Help topics
10. Find
11. Index

Missed	Score
0.	100
1.	92
2.	84
3.	76
4.	68
5.	60
6.	52
7.	44
8.	36
9.	28
10.	20
11.	12
12.	0

WORKSHEET 13
LESSON FIVE
1. path
2. jump-arrow
3. command line
4. document (data file)
5. target
6. desktop
7. long filename
8. drag and drop
9. shortcut
10. property
11. property sheet
12. document-centric
13. right-drag (mouse action)

Missed	Score
0.	100
1.	93
2.	85
3.	77
4.	70
5.	62
6.	55
7.	47
8.	40
9.	32
10.	24
11.	17
12.	9
13.	0

WORKSHEET 14
LESSON SIX
1. collapse
2. folder
3. expand
4. browse
5. file
6. Explorer
7. Explorer's left pane
8. tree
9. folder window
10. shell
11. hierarchy
12. object

Missed	Score
0.	100
1.	92
2.	84
3.	76
4.	68
5.	60
6.	52
7.	44
8.	36
9.	28
10.	20
11.	12
12.	0

WORKSHEET 15
LESSON SIX
1. associated file
2. hidden files
3. attribute
4. Show all files
5. Hide files of these types
6. floppy disk size
7. floppy disk density
8. MS-DOS (Microsoft Disk Operating System)
9. path
10. startup disk
11. bad sectors

Missed	Score
0.	100
1.	91
2.	82
3.	73
4.	61
5.	55
6.	46
7.	37
8.	28
9.	19
10.	10
11.	0

WORKSHEET 16
LESSON SEVEN
1. case sensitive
2. browse
3. Find
4. search criteria

Missed	Score
0.	100
1.	75
2.	50
3.	25
4.	0

WORKSHEET 17
LESSON EIGHT
1. TrueType font
2. MS-DOS–based application
3. MS-DOS prompt
4. multimedia
5. path
6. panose
7. Control Panel
8. long filename
9. serif
10. san serif
11. MS-DOS (Microsoft Disk Operating System)

Missed	Score
0.	100
1.	91
2.	82
3.	73
4.	61
5.	55
6.	46
7.	37
8.	28
9.	19
10.	10
11.	0

These fourteen file and three folders should be on your data disk when you start Lesson Six. You can follow the directions below to create this disk if necessary (if the previous lessons were performed correctly, your data disk should be accurate without doing this). You can purchase this disk from DDC publishing (800-528-3897) if you prefer.

1	**savefile**			MY DOCUMENTS (folder)
2	**saveas**		9	**My Doc 1**
3	**winfun**		10	**My Doc 2**
4	**richtext**		11	**My Doc 3**
	MY FOLDER (folder)			MY THINGS (folder)
5	**create1**		12	**DOC1**
6	**create2**		13	**DOC2**
7	**help**		14	**DOC3**
8	**help2**			

DIRECTIONS: Start with an blank, formatted disk that fits in drive A:

1. savefile

- Open Notepad, type the following text pressing Enter at the end of every line and twice between paragraphs.

```
Notepad is a program (also called an application) that is used
to create and edit unformatted text files.  An unformatted text
file is a file that contains only ASCII text characters (letters,
numbers, and symbols) and a few codes such as a carriage return.

WordPad is a simple word processor.  WordPad has automatic
word wrap, so you do not have to press Enter at the end of each
line (as you do in Notepad).  You press Enter only at the end
of short lines and paragraphs in WordPad.

The Save command either resaves a previously named document or
opens the Save As dialog box so you can name and save a new
document.
```

- Save the document on drive A:; name it **savefile**.
- Do not exit Notepad and do not clear the screen.

2. saveas

- Press ⌨ twice and type only the last paragraph in this document; type it at the end of the previous document.

```
Notepad is a program (also called an application) that is used
to create and edit unformatted text files.  An unformatted text
file is a file that contains only ASCII text characters (letters,
numbers, and symbols) and a few codes such as a carriage return.

WordPad is a simple word processor.  WordPad has automatic
word wrap, so you do not have to press Enter at the end of each
line (as you do in Notepad).  You press Enter only at the end
of short lines and paragraphs in WordPad.

The Save command either resaves a previously named document or
opens the Save As dialog box so you can name and save a new
document.
```
type -->
```
The Save As... command opens a dialog box to let you either name
and save a new document or rename and save a previously named
document.
```

- Use Save As to save the document on drive A:; name it **saveas**.
- Clear the screen (start a new document), but do not exit Notepad.

3. **winfun**
    *   Type the following text in Notepad.

    ```
    Windows is a user-friendly program.
    ```

    *   Save the document on drive A:; name it **winfun**.
    *   Exit Notepad.

4. **richtext**
    *   Open WordPad.
    *   Start a new Rich Text Document; make sure Word wrap "wraps to ruler."
    *   Type the following text in WordPad.

    > WordPad can work with documents in three different formats: Word for Windows 6.0, Rich Text Format, and Text Document. This book instructs you to use Rich Text Format most of the time, Text Document once, and Word for Windows 6.0 twice.
    >
    > The icons associated with Word for Windows documents is different depending on whether or not you have Word for Windows on your system. Word for Windows is a word processor made by Microsoft.

    *   Save the document on drive A:; name it **richtext**.

    *   FOLDER: Create a folder on drive A:; name it My Folder (you can do it in the Save As dialog box as you save the next document).

5. **create1**
    *   Start a new Rich Text Document.
    *   Type the following text in WordPad.

    > When WordPad is started, the cursor (a blinking vertical line) is displayed in the top left corner of the workspace. The cursor is called an "insertion point" because it shows where the next character you type will be "inserted."
    >
    > You create a document by typing. Press the ENTER key only at the end of short lines and paragraphs or to insert blank lines. WordPad will automatically move a word to the next line when the word is too long to fit on the present line.
    >
    > You can move the "insertion point" by using the arrow keys or the mouse. The mouse pointer shape appears as an "I-Beam" in the WordPad workspace. To move the cursor with the mouse, you can move the "I-Beam" to the desired location AND CLICK THE MOUSE BUTTON.

    *   Save the document in My Folder on drive A:; name it **create1**.
    *   Do not clear the screen.

6. **create2**
    *   Do not type the text below, but use Save As to save the text in the box above in My Folder on drive A:; name it **create2**.

    > When WordPad is started, the cursor (a blinking vertical line) is displayed in the top left corner of the workspace. The cursor is called an "insertion point" because it shows where the next character you type will be "inserted."
    >
    > You create a document by typing. Press the ENTER key only at the end of short lines and paragraphs or to insert blank lines. WordPad will automatically move a word to the next line when the word is too long to fit on the present line.
    >
    > You can move the "insertion point" by using the arrow keys or the mouse. The mouse pointer shape appears as an "I-Beam" in the WordPad workspace. To move the cursor with the mouse, you can move the "I-Beam" to the desired location AND CLICK THE MOUSE BUTTON.

7. **help**

- Start a new Rich Text Document.
- Follow the directions in Exercise 53 (page 97) to create the document below, or type the following text in WordPad.

To copy information from a Help topic

1   In the Help topic window, click the Edit menu or the Options button, and then click Copy.
           You can also use the right mouse button to click inside the topic or pop-up window.
2   In the document where you want the information to appear, click the place where you want to put
the information.
3   On the Edit menu, click Paste.

Tip

        If you want to copy only part of a topic, select the part you want to copy before you click the
Copy command.

Tips

You can print a group of related topics by clicking a book in the Help Contents and then clicking Print.
        To print the Help in a pop-up window, use your right mouse button to click inside the pop-up
window, and then click Print Topic.

CONTENTS
Displays Help topics organized by category. Double-click a book icon to see what topics are in that
category. To see a topic, double-click it.
You can close a book by double-clicking it.

- Save the document in My Folder on drive A: using Rich Text Format; name it **help**.

8. **help2**

- Start a new Rich Text Document.
- Follow the directions in Exercise 57, steps 2-6 (page 103) to create the document below or type the following text in WordPad.

Disk Space Troubleshooter

This troubleshooter helps you solve problems you may encounter if you run out of disk space. To free up
disk space, just click a method you want to try, and then carry out the suggested steps.

   ◇   Empty the Recycle Bin
   ◇   Use ScanDisk to check for errors that may be using up disk space
   ◇   Back up unneeded files and remove them from your hard disk
   ◇   Remove Windows components that you don't use
   ◇   Create more disk space by using DriveSpace disk compression

   ◇   See more ways to free up disk space

Windows Startup Troubleshooter

If you have trouble starting Windows, you can use several methods to start your computer with or without
starting Windows or the network. After you identify and resolve the problem, you can restart your computer
as you usually do.

Lists the alignments available for the selected paragraph.

      Left: Aligns text at the left indent.

      Right: Aligns text at the right indent.
      Center: Centers the text between margins.

- Save the document in My Folder on drive A: using Rich Text Format; name it **help2**.
- Exit Windows Help (if you used page 103 to create the document) but do not exit WordPad.

- FOLDER: Create a folder on drive A:; name it My Documents.

9. **My Doc 1**

   - Start a new Rich Text Document.

   - Type the following text in WordPad.

   > Most of what you do on your computer system is centered around producing documents of one kind or another. Microsoft designed Windows 95 to be document-centric, that is, centered around documents rather than the programs used to create documents.

   - Save the document in My Documents on drive A: using Rich Text Format; name it **My Doc 1**.

   - Exit WordPad.

10. **My Doc 2**

    - Open Notepad.

    - Type the following text in Notepad.

    ```
    The idea behind the Windows 95 desktop is that you can use it
    pretty much the way you use your personal desktop.  You can put
    your computer, clock, phone, folders, and documents on the
    Windows 95 desktop.  You can decorate it to fit your mood, and
    even scan your favorite picture and put it on the desktop.
    ```

    - Save the document in My Documents on drive A:; name it **My Doc 2**.

11. **My Doc 3**

    - Start a new document.

    - Type the following text in Notepad.

    ```
    You can create a new folder when you save a document.  When you
    are in the Save As dialog box, simply right-click the workspace,
    and then click New, then Folder.
    ```

    - Save the document in My Documents on drive A:; name it **My Doc 3**.

    - FOLDER: Create a folder on drive A:; name it My Things.

12. **DOC1**

    - Start a new document.

    - Type the following text in Notepad.

    ```
    On the Start menu, Documents are listed before Programs (as you
    move up).  When you open the Documents menu, you will find a
    list of up to 15 of the most recently used documents.
    ```

    - Save the document in My Things on drive A:; name it **DOC1**.

13. **DOC2**

     - Start a new document.

     - Type the following text in Notepad.

     > Shortcuts are powerful because they let you have quick access to
     > all the objects you need. Meanwhile, Windows does all the work
     > of keeping track of what you are doing.

   - Save the document in My things on drive A:; name it **DOC2**.
   - Exit Notepad.

14. **DOC3**

     - Open WordPad

     - Start a new Rich Text Document.

     - Type the following text in WordPad.

     > When you start WordPad (and many other programs), you can easily open one of the last documents you
     > used. Simply click File, then click the desired document.

   - Save the document in My Things on drive A: using Rich Text Format; name it **DOC3**.
   - Exit Wordpad.

APPENDIX G

Log of Keyboard Steps to Perform Windows 95 Tasks

APPENDIX H
Index of Keyboard Steps to Perform Windows 95 Tasks

APPENDIX I

Keyboard Shortcuts and Procedures

General

Get help .... `F1`

Open the Start menu .... `Ctrl`+`Esc`

   or, if no task is selected, ... `Alt`+`S`

Open an accessories
   program .... `Ctrl`+`Esc`, `P`, `→`, `↑` or `↓`, `↵`

Exit a program or folder .... `Alt`+`F4`

   or .... `Alt`+`Space`, `C`

Open program's Control menu .... `Alt`+`Space`

Open program's Control menu on the taskbar
...... `Ctrl`+`Esc`, `Esc`, `Tab`, `←` / `→` (to select task button), `Shift`+`F10`

Switch to previous window .... `Alt`+`Tab`

Cycle through open windows.. Hold `Alt` and repeatedly press `Tab`

Maximize an open window .... `Alt`+`Space`, `X`

Restore a maximized window .... `Alt`+`Space`, `R`

Minimize an open window .... `Alt`+`Space`, `N`

Cascade windows .... `Ctrl`+`Esc`, `Esc`, `Tab`, `Shift`+`F10`, `C`

Tile windows horizontally.. `Ctrl`+`Esc`, `Esc`, `Tab`, `Shift`+`F10`, `H`

Tile windows vertically ...... `Ctrl`+`Esc`, `Esc`, `Tab`, `Shift`+`F10`, `V`

Undo cascade or tile .... `Ctrl`+`Esc`, `Esc`, `Tab`, `Shift`+`F10`, `U`

Clear the Document menu .. `Ctrl`+`Esc`, `S`, `T`, `Ctrl`+`Tab`, `C`

Show small/large icons in
   Start menu (toggle) .... `Ctrl`+`Esc`, `S`, `T`, `S`

Add item to Start menu .... `Ctrl`+`Esc`, `S`, `T`, `Ctrl`+`Tab`, `A`

Remove item from
   Start Menu .... `Ctrl`+`Esc`, `S`, `T`, `Ctrl`+`Tab`, `R`

Find the desktop (or minimize
   all windows) .... `Ctrl`+`Esc`, `Esc`, `Tab`, `Shift`+`F10`, `M`

Move to an item on the desktop or in a folder, list, or menu
.... press the item's first letter, repeatedly if necessary

Menu Bars

Access or cancel the menu bar .... `Alt` or `F10`

Move through menus .... `→`, `←`

Open a menu from the menu bar .... `↓`

Open a menu .... `Alt` + underlined letter

Move through menu items .... `↓`, `↑`

Open the selected menu item .... `↵`

Close a menu .... `Esc`

Toggle toolbar on/off .... `Alt`+`V`, `T`

Dialog Boxes

Move forward through dialog box options .... `Tab`

Move backward through dialog box options .... `Shift`+`Tab`

Move forward through tabs .... `Ctrl`+`Tab`

Move backward through tabs .... `Shift`+`Ctrl`+`Tab`

Move to an item .... `Alt` + its underlined letter

Open selected list box .... `Alt`+`↓`

Open list box (if only one) .... `F4`

Go to the top of a list box .... `Ctrl`+`Home`

Go to the bottom of a list box .... `Ctrl`+`End`

Go to a specific item in a list box .... press its first letter

Select or deselect items in a check box .... `Space`

Activate dialog box commands .... `↵`

Open and Save As dialog boxes

Open the Look in or Save in list box .... `F4`

Refresh dialog box .... `F5`

Move one level up (if a folder is selected) .... `Backspace`

Desktop

Find the desktop (or
   minimize all windows) ... `Ctrl`+`Esc`, `Esc`, `Tab`, `Shift`+`F10`, `M`

Select an item
   (on the desktop) .... `Ctrl`+`Esc`, `Esc`, `Tab`, `Tab`, arrow keys

Create a folder on
   the desktop.... `Ctrl`+`Esc`, `Esc`, `Tab`, `Tab`, `Shift`+`F10`, `W`, `F`

Create a shortcut on
   the desktop.... `Ctrl`+`Esc`, `Esc`, `Tab`, `Tab`, `Shift`+`F10`, `W`, `S`

Use the desktop right-click menu:

First, select the desktop
   right-click menu .... `Ctrl`+`Esc`, `Esc`, `Tab`, `Tab`, `Shift`+`F10`

Then choose from the options below:

   Arrange icons by name .... `I`, `N`

   Arrange icons by type .... `I`, `T`

   Arrange icons by size .... `I`, `Z`

   Arrange icons by modification date .... `I`, `D`

   Align icons .... `E`

   Toggle Auto Arrange on/off (default is off) .... `I`, `A`

   Change the display .... `I`, `R`

The Taskbar

Open Taskbar Properties..........................`Ctrl`+`Esc`, `S`, `T`

Open taskbar shortcut menu .. `Ctrl`+`Esc`, `Esc`, `Tab`, `Shift`+`F10`

Hide/display the taskbar (toggle) ....`Ctrl`+`Esc`, `S`, `T`, `U`

Hide/display the clock (toggle) ....`Ctrl`+`Esc`, `S`, `T`,`C`

Open Date/Time
Properties..................... `Ctrl`+`Esc`, `Esc`, `Tab`, `Shift`+`F10`, `A`

Shut down the computer........................... `Ctrl`+`Esc`, `U`, `↵`

Desktop, My Computer, folder windows, and Explorer

Find a file or folder.. `F3`

Rename the selected item .... `F2`

Open selected item .... `↵`

Open selected item's properties .... `Alt`+`↵`

Open selected item's shortcut menu .... `Shift`+`F10`

Cut selected item .... `Ctrl`+`X`

Copy selected item.. `Ctrl`+`C`

Paste selected item... `Ctrl`+`V`

Delete selected item... `Del`

Delete selected item without ability to undo............ `Shift`+`Del`

Undo action .... `Ctrl`+`Z`

Undo multiple actions................................. `Ctrl`+`Z` repeatedly

Select all .... `Ctrl`+`A`

Create a shortcut for selected item.................. `Shift`+`F10`, `S`

My Computer, folder windows, and Explorer

View items as large icons................................ `Alt`+`V`, `G`

View items as small icons .... `Alt`+`V`, `M`

View items in a list.. `Alt`+`V`, `L`

View items showing details .... `Alt`+`V`, `D`

Arrange icons by name .... `Alt`+`V`, `I`, `N`
   (except My Computer)

Arrange icons by type .... `Alt`+`V`, `I`, `T`

Arrange icons by size................................. `Alt`+`V`, `I`, `S`
   (except Explorer, which is `Z`)

My Computer, folder windows, and Explorer (continued)

Arrange icons by modification date .... `Alt`+`V`, `I`, `D`
   (except My Computer)

Align icons..`Alt`+`V`, `E`

Toggle Auto Arrange (default is off) .... `Alt`+`V`, `I`, `A`

Refresh a window .... `F5`

Move one folder level up .... `Backspace`

Create a subfolder for selected folder .... `Alt`+`F`, `W`, `F`

Close current folder and all
   its parent folders............................... `Alt`+`Space`, `Shift`+`C`

Explorer only

Go to folder (by typing its path) .... `Ctrl`+`G`

Switch between panes (and toolbar, if open).......... `F6` or `Tab`

Expand all levels of subfolders...............`*` (on numeric keypad)

Collapse a series of parent folders.............. `←`, `←` repeatedly

Expand selected folder with
   plus (+) by it.............................`+` (on numeric keypad) or `→`

Collapse selected folder with
   minus (-) by it........................... `-` (on numeric keypad) or `←`

Arrange icons by size .... `Alt`+`V`, `I`, `Z`

My Computer only

Arrange icons by drive letter....................... `Alt`+`V`, `I`, `D`

Arrange icons by free space........................ `Alt`+`V`, `I`, `F`

GLOSSARY

A

accessories Different kinds of programs (applications) that come with Windows.

active task button A task button located on the taskbar that appears to be pressed, thus indicating that the task it represents is active. *See pressed.*

active window The window whose title bar is highlighted, indicating that it is currently being used.

application (program) Means the same thing as *program*. While the term *application* is used a lot in Windows, this book uses the term *program* more often. *See program.*

application software (program) Software that does a specific task, such as word processing. *See software.*

associated file A file type that has been identified as belonging to a certain program, such as .TXT with Notepad, .BMP with Paint, or .DOC with Word 6. When you open an associated file, the program related to the file opens automatically.

attribute A characteristic (such as read-only, archive, hidden, or system) that changes how a file or folder can be used or displayed. *See file type.*

B

Back button A button at the top of a Help topic that returns you to the previous Help topic. Use this button to backtrack through the topics you have viewed so far.

bad sectors Damaged areas on a disk that are marked as unusable when the disk is formatted. A few bad sectors do not necessarily make the entire disk unusable. However, a disk with bad sectors should not be used as a destination disk when copying a disk.

browse To look at files, folders, disks, printers, programs, documents, and other objects on your computer system.

button, active task *See active task button.*
button, Back *See Back button.*
button, Click here *See Click here button.*
button, Close *See Close button.*
button, Control menu *See Control menu button.*
button, Help Topics *See Help topics button.*
button, inactive task *See inactive task button.*
button, Maximize *See Maximize button.*
button, Minimize *See Minimize button.*
button, Options *See Options button.*
button, Related Topics *See Related Topics button.*
button, Restore *See Restore button.*
button, Start *See Start button.*
button, task *See task button.*

byte (b) A unit of memory that holds one character.

C

cascade To resize and layer windows on the desktop so that the title bar of each window is visible. *See tile horizontally and tile vertically.*

cascading menu A menu that opens when you choose a menu item that is followed by a right-pointing triangle (➢).

case sensitive A command option that tells a program to recognition of the difference between upper- and lowercase letters when it is searching for text.

CD-ROM drive (Compact Disk Read Only Memory drive) A read-only optical disk that can store relatively large amounts of data.

changed file A file (or workspace) that has had some kind of modification—either the file is new or the file has been edited in some way since it was last saved.

Click here button A shortcut box you can click to start the program or open the window related to the current Help topic.

Close A command that lets you leave a Windows program (application). It is usually found on the Control menu.

Close button A button located at the right end of the title bar that you click to close a window.

collapse To hide the folders that are displayed in an object that is in the left pane of Explorer. Objects that can be collapsed have a minus sign (-) beside them. *See expand.*

command line A place where you enter the path to a file. *See path.*

commands Instructions that cause an action to be carried out.

common commands Commands such as New and Save that work the same in most Windows programs.

common dialog boxes Dialog boxes, such as Open, Save, and Print, that are basically the same in different programs. Common dialog boxes make it easier for you to learn new programs.

computer An electronic device that performs complex tasks at high speed and with great accuracy. There are two main parts of a computer—the *processor* and the *memory*.

Contents An area of the Help Topics program that displays organized categories (books) that you look through to find and then choose the Help topic you want. *See Help topics program.*

Control menu A menu with items that you use to manipulate a program window (Restore, Move, Size, Minimize, Maximize, and Close). It is opened by clicking the Control button or by right-clicking the task button for the program.

Control menu button An icon at the left side of the title bar that opens the Control menu. The Control button icon matches the icon for the document type that is open.

Control Panel A folder that combines all commands, control and configuration functions for Windows 95 in one place.

controls Different kinds of elements in dialog boxes that allow you to manipulate a program's appearance and function. *See dialog box.*

CPU (central processing unit) *See processor.*

D

data disk A floppy disk on which you can save data files.

data file (document) A file that consists of data that has been created in a program, such as a letter typed in WordPad or a picture drawn in Paint.

default An automatic setting in a program.

desktop The simple opening screen in Windows 95 that contains a few objects, the Start button, and a taskbar.

dialog box A special kind of window that offers different controls for you to manipulate. *See controls.*

dimmed command A command that cannot be used in the current situation; it is displayed in gray instead of black.

disk Media on which information is stored and retrieved in named units called *files.*

disk drive A mechanical device that you use to transfer information back and forth between the computer's memory and a disk.

document (data file) Any data you create with a program, for example, a report or a picture. A document and a data file are the same thing.

document type Different kinds of documents that are defined by the programs that create them. While some programs create only one type of document, WordPad can create three different types of document: Word for Windows 6.0 (file extension is .DOC), Rich Text Format (file extension is .RTF), and Text Only (file extension is .TXT)

document-centric A system that focuses on documents and their contents rather than the programs used to create the documents.

DOS *See MS-DOS and operating system.*

double-headed arrow The shape the pointer takes when it is used to size a window or the taskbar.

drag (mouse action) Move the pointer on an item, hold down the left button, slide the pointer to a new location, and release the button.

drag and drop A procedure in which you drag a document and drop it on an object so the object can do something useful to the document, for example, move, copy, delete, or print it.

E

Exit A command that lets you leave a Windows program (application). It is usually found on the File menu.

expand To display unseen folders in an object displayed in the left pane of Explorer. Objects that can be expanded have a plus sign (+) beside them. *See collapse.*

Explorer The Windows 95 program that you can use to explore your computer system (including remote computers if your system is networked). *See shell.*

Explorer's left pane The part of the Explorer that displays the hierarchical structure on your computer system (including remote computers if your system is networked).

F

file A set of data or program instructions that is saved on a disk as a named unit. *See data file and program file.*

file, associated *See associated file.*
file, changed *See changed file.*
file, data *See data file.*
file, program *See program file.*
file, unchanged *See unchanged file.*

file type icon The icon that is connected with a particular file type, such as Word 6 documents or text documents. File type icons for a particular file type may differ depending upon: 1) the program the file type is associated with (not the program they are created in) and 2) the icon that is designated for its association.

file types Different kinds of files that are defined by the programs that create the files. Every file has a file type icon connected with it. *See file type icon.*

filename The name assigned to a collection of data that is stored on a disk.

filename extension The optional *period and up to three characters* at the end of a filename.

GLOSSARY

files, hidden *See hidden files.*
files, Show all See show all files.

Find (a search program) A program found in both the Start menu and Explorer's Tools menu that helps you locate files and folders easily by defining search criteria that give hints about the files you are looking for. See search criteria.

Find (in Help) An area of the Help program that lets you search for the actual words contained in all the Help topics for a given program. When you use Find for the first time, Windows must create the list of words. *See Help topics program.*

firmware A kind of *sytems software*—instructions that are built into the comuter system on ROM chips. *See read only memory.*

floppy disk A magnetically coated disk on which information can be stored and retrieved.

floppy disk density Density refers to the surface coating on a disk; the closer together the particles on the disk, the higher the disk's capacity. Typically, 3½" floppy disks come in two densities: DD (double density)—720 Kb and HD (high density)—1.44 Mb. Typically 5¼" floppy disks come in two densities: DD (double density)—360 Kb and HD (high density)—1.2 Mb.

floppy disk drive 🖫 A storage device that retrieves and stores files on a removable media called *floppy diskettes.*

floppy disk size The physical size of floppy disks; typically they come in two sizes, 5¼" and 3½".

folder 📁 A structure that holds files and/or other folders that are stored on a disk. A folder can also hold other objects, such as printers and disk drives. (Folders have traditionally been called *directories.*)

folder window A window that displays the contents of a folder (or certain other objects, such as disk drives). Folder windows offer many of the same folder managing features as the Explorer. Double-click a folder to open its window and see what is in it.

G

graphical user interface (GUI) A phrase that is commonly used to describe Microsoft Windows and other similar programs that use *pictures* to help you *communicate* with the computer.

group folder 📁 A folder within the Start Menu folder that holds groups of program shortcuts and other folders; they represent menus within the Start menu.

H

hard disk A large capacity storage area that offers fast access to store and retrieve information.

hard disk drive 🖴 A built-in storage device that has a non-removable disk (a fixed disk) with a large capacity. Hard disks provide fast retrieval and storage of files.

hardware The group of parts that make up the computer system. Hardware can be seen and touched.

Help, Contents *See Contents.*
Help, Find *See Find (in Help).*
Help, Index *See Index.*

Help topics Information about a Windows subject. A Help topic usually begins with a title and contains information about a particular task, command, or dialog box.

Help Topics button A button at the top of a Help topic that returns you to the Help Topics program.

Help Topics program The Windows 95 Help program; it has three sections to help you locate Help topics: Contents, Index, and Find. There is a main Help Topics program for Windows in general, and there are smaller Help Topics programs for Windows Accessory programs such as WordPad and Paint. *See Contents, Index, and Find (in Help).*

hidden files Files and/or folders that have a hidden attribute. *See attribute.*

Hide files of these types An option that specifies that certain files and folders should not be displayed (including hidden files and folders and files with certain extensions that are listed in a box below the option). *See hidden files and Show all files.*

hierarchy A system of things (or people) ranked one above the other. On computers, the term *hierarchy* describes the multilevel structure of folders and subfolders on a disk; or, in the case of Windows 95, it describes a multilevel structure of objects on the entire computer system. The structure is also referred to as a *tree.*

I

inactive task button A task button located on the taskbar that is unpressed, thus indicating the task it represents is open, but not active. *See unpressed.*

Index An area of the Help Topics program that displays a list of words and phrases that you can search to find a related Help topic. *See Help topics program.*

J

jump-arrow 🔲 A small arrow that appears in the lower-left corner of *shortcut* icons thereby distinguishing them from other icons.

K

keyboard A device used to enter data and issue commands to the computer.

kilobyte (Kb) A unit of memory that holds about 1,000 characters.

keyboard shortcuts Key combinations that are used to activate certain commands instead of using the mouse.

L

landscape A paper orientation in which the paper is wider than it is tall, as are typical landscapes. *See portrait.*

launch A term that is sometimes used to mean start a program (*or application*).

long filename A filename that is up to 255 characters long and can contain spaces and most symbols. *See short filename.*

M

Maximize button 🔲 The button in the middle of the three buttons located at the right end of the title bar; it enlarges a window to its greatest possible size. When you maximize a window, the Maximize button is replaced by the Restore button. *See Restore button.*

megabyte (Mb) A unit of memory that holds about 1,000,000 characters.

memory (RAM-random access memory) The area of the computer that holds the instructions (programs) and information you give it. When you turn the computer off, everything in RAM disappears.

menu A list of items from which you may choose one.

menu bar The bar located under the title bar that lists the available menus.

menu item One of the choices on a menu.

Microsoft Windows 95 An operating system that uses a graphics environment to connect you to the computer system's hardware and software in an easy-to-understand, intuitive way. Microsoft Windows also offers many useful programs.

Minimize button 🔲 A button located at the right side of the title bar that you can click to reduce a window to a task button on the taskbar.

monitor A screen that displays the information in the computer.

mouse A small, hand-held device used to control the pointer on the screen.

MS-DOS (Microsoft Disk Operating System) The main operating system used before Windows was developed. *See operating system.*

MS-DOS prompt The signal that MS-DOS is ready for you to tell it what to do. The default MS-DOS prompt displays the path to the current folder followed by the greater than sign (>) and a blinking underline. For example, if you are in Windows, the MS-DOS prompt will look like this: C:\Windows>_

MS-DOS–based application A program that is designed to run under the MS-DOS operating system rather than the Windows operating system.

multimedia The combination of many various communication methods, including text, graphics, sound, animation, and video.

multitasking The ability of an operating system to run more than one program at one time.

My Briefcase 💼 An object that may appear on the desktop; it lets you keep files on one computer up-to-date from a remote location by using a second computer and modems.

My Computer 🖥 My Computer is the obvious, quick, easy-to-use route to the folders, files, and other objects on your computer system.

N

Network Neighborhood 🖧 An object that may appear on the desktop; it lets you browse through other computers on your network or a remote network.

networking Two or more computers that are linked together to share programs, data, and certain hardware components, for example, a printer.

O

object One of the many *things* that you use when working with the computer system—items such as: files, Control Panel tools, programs, My Computer, folders, Network Neighborhood, shortcuts, the Recycle Bin, disk drives, and My Briefcase. *NOTE: As used here,* object *is really just another catch-all term for an item, element, thing, whatcha-ma-call-it, or thing-a-ma-jig. The terms* object *and* object-oriented *have a more formal computer-related meaning that is not used in this book.*

operating system Software that acts as a link between you, application software (programs), and hardware.

Options button A button at the top of a Help topic that lets you work with the Help topic. You can Annotate, Copy, Print, change Font, Keep Help on Top, or Use System Colors for the current Help topic.

GLOSSARY

P

Panose A type of Font-mapping information that is stored with a font to describe its traits: serif, san serif, normal, bold, and italic. If a font has no Panose information it is displayed at the bottom of the list when viewing fonts by their similarity to another font.

password A combination of characters that you type, when prompted, in order to access Windows (or some Windows feature). The characters appear as small x's when you type them. The password feature is a security feature that prevents access to a Windows network (or other feature) without the correct combination of characters.

path The route to a folder or file; it consists of the disk drive, folder, subfolders (if any), and the filename (if the path is to a file). For example, C:\WINDOWS\CALC is the path to the Calculator program. If long folder names or filenames are used in a path, the path must be enclosed in quotes ("). For example, "A:\My Folder\help2.rtf" is the path to the document file, **help2** on drive A:. *See command line.*

Plug and Play The ability of Windows 95 to automatically detect and configure new hardware devices. Plug and Play is an industry-wide venture with specifications set by the Plug and Play association. If a device is not recognized, Windows 95 walks you through improved manual device installation procedures.

pointer (mouse pointer) The arrow-shaped cursor on the screen that moves with the mouse as you slide it over a flat surface. The pointer's shape changes depending on the job it is doing.

portrait A paper orientation in which the paper is taller than it is wide, as are typical portraits. *See landscape.*

pressed A 3-D effect in which a button (or other item) appears sunken, indicating it is selected (or active). *See unpressed.*

printer A device that makes a hard copy of data in the computer.

processor (CPU-central processing unit) The part of the computer that processes the instructions in the memory.

program (application) A set of instructions that your computer carries out to perform a specific task, such as word processing.

program file A file that holds a set of instructions that performs a task, such as word processing.

property A characteristic of an object; many properties can be changed by using a control in a Properties dialog box.

property sheet A special kind of dialog box that groups the settings for an object's properties. *See property.*

Q

Quick View A simple program that displays the contents of the selected item; it will appear on the menu only if there is a *viewer* available for the type of file you select and if it has been installed (the typical install does not install Quick View).

R

RAM (random access memory) *See memory.*

read only memory (ROM) A chip that holds information that cannot be changed.

Related Topics button ☐ A shortcut box you click to go to a Help topic related to the one you are currently viewing.

Restore button ☐ The button in the middle of three buttons located at the right end of the title bar on a maximized window; it returns a maximized window to its previous size. When you restore a maximized window, the Restore button is replaced by the Maximize button. *See Maximize button.*

Rich Text Format A file format that is commonly used by programmers. Windows 95 Help files use Rich Text Format.

right-click Quickly press and release the *right* mouse button.

right-click menu An easy-to-use menu that opens whenever you right-click an object or area, except in a dialog box. *See shortcut menu.*

right-drag (mouse action) Move the pointer on an item, hold down the *right* mouse button, slide the pointer to a new location, and release the mouse button.

ROM (read only memory) *See read only memory.*

S

san serif A font design that has no cross strokes at the top and bottom of the characters; it is straight.
For example: **T** *See Serif.*

Save The command that saves changes to a previously named document on which you are working.

Save As A command that opens a dialog box that lets you save a new document or rename a previously saved document.

scroll arrows The arrows at each end of a scroll bar, used to scroll through the contents of a window.

scroll bar A bar that appears at the right and/or bottom edge of a window whose contents are not completely visible. Each scroll bar contains two scroll arrows and a proportional scroll box (when data is present).

scroll box The box in a scroll bar; it shows two things: 1) the *position* of the information displayed in relation to the entire document (for example, if the scroll box is in the center of the scroll bar, you are looking at the center of the document), and 2) the *size* of the entire document in relation to the screen size (for example, if the scroll box takes up a large part of the scroll bar, you can see most of the entire document; but, if the scroll box takes up just a little part of the scroll bar, you can see only a small portion of the entire document).

search criteria The guidelines that you tell Find to follow when it searches for certain files or folders. For example, to find all the files that contain the letters, *doc*, or to find all the files that were created in the last month. *See Find (a search program).*

serif A font design that has small cross strokes at the top and bottom of the characters.
For example: **T**   *See san serif.*

shell A program, such as Explorer, that lets you control your system. *See Explorer.*

short filename A filename that is no longer that eight characters, can contain a filename extension, and *cannot* contain spaces and certain symbols. *See long filename.*

shortcut An icon containing a direct route to a specific object and displaying a small jump-arrow in the lower-left corner. Double-click a shortcut to quickly open the file or program it represents. You can customize your desktop by creating shortcuts for the programs you use most often.

shortcut menu Another name for right-click menu (an easy-to-use menu that opens whenever you right-click an object or area). This book calls shortcut menus *right-click menus* because the term seems more specific and less confusing than *shortcut menu*. *See right-click menu.*

Show all files An option that specifies that all files and folders should be displayed (including hidden and system files and folders). *See Hide files of these types.*

sizing handle An area in the bottom right corner of windows that can be sized; it is used to size windows. (You can size a window using any of its corners. However, because the bottom right corner's sizing handle is a large sizing area, the pointer changes to a diagonal arrow easier than it does in the other window corners.)

software Instructions that tell your computer how to perform a task. Software is stored on disks in program files. Software cannot be seen or touched. There are two main kinds of software: application software and system software. *See application software and system software.*

Start button The button located at the left end of the taskbar that is labeled *Start*. You click the Start button to open the Start menu from which you can open other menus and launch programs.

startup disk A disk that contains certain system files that create a system (or bootable) disk. It is a good safeguard to have a startup disk for drive A:—if the hard disk should have a problem, you can boot the computer using this floppy system disk.

status bar The bar at the bottom of a program; it displays information about the program, and it can be turned on and off from the View menu.

subfolder A folder that is within another folder, or below another folder in the folder structure.

system software Software that runs the computer system. *See software.*

T

target The name of the object to which a shortcut is pointing (the name includes the path to the object). *See path.*

task An open (but not necessarily active) program.

task button A button located on the taskbar that represents an open program; each task button displays the program's icon and its name.

taskbar The bar on the desktop that lets you quickly start programs and easily switch between tasks.

telecommunication Remote access through a modem or fax/modem which allows you to: Communicate with bulletin board services, transfer files, and send and receive faxes.

tile horizontally To resize and arrange the windows on the desktop *one on top of the other* so that each window displays part of its workspace. *See tile vertically and cascade.*

tile vertically To resize and arrange the windows on the desktop *side by side* so that each window displays part of its workspace. *See tile horizontally and cascade.*

title bar The horizontal bar at the top of a window that holds the window's name.

toolbar A row of buttons that provide quick access to frequently used commands.

tree A representation of the hierarchy (structure) on a computer system (especially a horizontal representation).

TrueType fonts Scalable fonts that are shipped with Windows; Arial, Courier New, Lucida Console, Symbol, Times New Roman, and Wingdings.

U

unchanged file A file that has not been modified (edited) since it was last saved.

unpressed A 3-D effect in which a button (or other item) appears raised, indicating it is deselected (or inactive). *See pressed.*

user *See you.*

user name A name given to a Windows user. By using different user names and passwords for different people, each user's work can be kept secure.

User Profiles A feature that lets more than one person use the same computer and retain their own personal desktop colors, icons, and program groups. *See Appendix B.*

W

warm boot The process of restarting the computer by pressing
`Ctrl` + `Alt` + `Del`

window The rectangular work area for a task, folder, program, or document.

window title The name of a window, located just to the right of the Control menu button. The document name, if any, is listed first followed by the program name.

window, active *See active window.*
window, folder *See folder window.*

Windows Explorer *See Explorer.*

Wizard A feature found throughout Windows in which step-by-step instructions walk a user through unfamiliar procedures.

Word for Windows A sophisticated and commonly used word processing program made by Microsoft but not shipped with the Windows 95 program.

workspace The inner part of the window where the work in a program or document is carried out.

Y

you The operator (or user) of the computer system (its hardware and software).

INDEX

INDEX

INDEX